Selecting Women,
Electing Women

Magda Hinojosa

Selecting Women, Electing Women

Political Representation and Candidate Selection in Latin America

TEMPLE UNIVERSITY PRESS   PHILADELPHIA

TEMPLE UNIVERSITY PRESS
Philadelphia, Pennsylvania 19122
www.temple.edu/tempress

Library of Congress Cataloging-in-Publication Data
Hinojosa, Magda, 1975–
  Selecting women, electing women : political representation and candidate
selection in Latin America / Magda Hinojosa.
      p. cm.
  Includes bibliographical references and index.
  ISBN 978-1-4399-0847-1 (cloth : alk. paper) — ISBN 978-1-4399-0848-8
(pbk. : alk. paper) — ISBN 978-1-4399-0849-5 (e-book)
  1. Women—Political activity—Latin America. 2. Women political
candidates—Latin America. 3. Women and democracy—Latin
America. I. Title.
  HQ1236.5.L37H56 2012
  320.98082—dc23
                                                             2012008893

♾ The paper used in this publication meets the requirements of the
American National Standard for Information Sciences—Permanence
of Paper for Printed Library Materials, ANSI Z39.48-1992

Printed in the United States of America

2 4 6 8 9 7 5 3 1

Contents

Acknowledgments

This book would not have been possible without the generosity of the many women and men in Chile and Mexico who shared their stories with me. All of them taught me so much—from national political elites with decades of experience to newly minted municipal council members who had never faced an interviewer's questions.

The Fulbright-García Robles International Scholarship financed my fieldwork in Mexico for this project. Funding from the Fulbright International Scholarship, the Harvard Graduate Student Council Grant, the David Rockefeller Center for Latin American Studies at Harvard University Summer Field Research Grant, and a Texas State University Research Enhancement Program Grant allowed me to finance multiple research trips to Chile. The Ford Foundation Postdoctoral Fellowship was invaluable in moving this project forward.

In Santiago, I benefited from the institutional support provided by Harvard University's David Rockefeller Center for Regional Studies. I am especially indebted to Steve Reifenberg and Marcela Rentería for their support. I also enjoyed affiliation with the Universidad Católica del Maule in Talca, Chile. In Mexico, I was privileged to be associated with the Instituto Tecnológico Autónomo de México. I owe special thanks to Alejandro Poiré for so generously sharing with me his knowledge of Mexican politics. Jorge I. Domínguez, Susan Pharr, and Steven Levitsky at Harvard University provided invaluable feedback on the dissertation that informed this project.

I am grateful to Susan Franceschet, Jennifer Piscopo, Miki Caul Kittilson, Hillel Soifer, Carolyn Warner, Jorge I. Domínguez, Celeste Montoya, Victoria E. Rodríguez, and Ana Romo for their comments on parts of this work. I am indebted to the anonymous reviewers for helping to make this a much better book. Alex Holzman, my editor at Temple University Press, also deserves thanks for his encouragement and work on this project. Jeffrey Popowski and Jean Crissien merit special recognition for their terrific work as research assistants.

My dear friends Sarah Kozma, Ana Romo, Hillel Soifer, Andrew Karch, and Amy Risley have been with me every step of the way. I am also grateful to Mala Htun and Kenneth Greene for their generous encouragement over the years. My colleagues at Arizona State University are a wonderful bunch. They are a source of constant inspiration and support.

My parents have always believed in me and encouraged my intellectual pursuits. My son, Roman, now a toddler, deserves my gratitude for introducing me to the literary works of Sandra Boynton. Countless readings of *Hippos Go Berserk* (along with bath times, first words, and all the rest) have put work into perspective. I am most grateful to my husband, Daniel Cuaron. His constant quiet support sustains me; his love makes everything better.

1

Electing Women

Female Political Representation in Latin America

> Parties have no interest in having more women: to have
> more women would mean losing men.
>
> —María Antonieta Saa, Chilean legislator (quoted in Nikki Craske,
> *Women and Politics in Latin America*)

In March 2006, Michelle Bachelet was sworn in as president of Chile. The following year neighboring Argentina also elected a woman to the presidency: Cristina Fernández de Kirchner, who took office in December 2007. These women seemed to have little in common. Bachelet had never held elected office prior to beginning her presidential term. When Fernández ran for the presidency, however, she was an experienced politician—first having been elected to the legislature of her home province of Santa Cruz—and then occupying a seat in the Chamber of Deputies from 1997 to 2001 before serving three terms in the Senate. Bachelet was a single mother of three and an avowed agnostic. Fernández was not simply a married woman with children, but was married to the president. She transitioned from being First Lady of Argentina to being president. Bachelet became president of what many refer to as the most conservative country in Latin America. Argentina, on the other hand, recently legalized gay marriage and may well be the most liberal country in the region. Since the passage of the world's first gender quota law in 1991, Argentina has welcomed ever-increasing numbers of women into politics.

The political biographies of Michelle Bachelet and Cristina Fernández may be quite different, but these women's paths to presidential power are fundamentally similar: the stories of these two women are stories of candidate selection.

Among Chileans, the victory of the candidate of the Concertación, the governing coalition, was a foregone conclusion. Polls conducted repeatedly between 2003 and 2005 indicated as much. Survey data revealed that the candidates of the right (Joaquín Lavín and Sebastián Piñera) would be defeated by any of the favorites for the Concertación's nomination. The question was, *Who would be the candidate of the ruling coalition?* How did Bachelet become the candidate of a coalition that had governed Chile for two decades? What pushed the incumbent president to make his preference for Bachelet clear long before the election, even saying in 2004 that "the greatest indication of change would be to have the first female president in the country"? (quoted in Franceschet 2006: 16).

Bachelet's medical background as a pediatrician and her commitment to the Socialist Party earned her a seat on President Ricardo Lagos's cabinet as Minister of Health in 2000. Two years after accepting that post, she became Minister of Defense. President Lagos handpicked Bachelet as his preferred successor, a decision that the Socialist Party, and the other two parties of the coalition's left wing, ultimately adhered to. A scheduled primary between Bachelet and the candidate of the Christian Democratic Party for the Concertación's nomination was canceled by her opponent,[1] who recognized Bachelet's greater popularity.

In the first round of the election, Bachelet received 45.9 percent of the vote. The two candidates of the right together earned a majority of the vote—Piñera received 25.4 percent of the vote and Lavín won 23.2 percent. In the runoff election that followed, Bachelet received 53 percent of the vote. Her opponent received 46.5 percent of the vote. The vote totals had been accurately prognosticated for months: the candidate of the ruling coalition would win the 2005 elections.

The election of Fernández was indisputable from the moment that her candidacy was announced. Fernández was attempting to succeed her husband, Néstor Kirchner, in the presidential office and had been hand-chosen by him to run for the presidency. Because Argentine law bars presidents from immediately succeeding themselves in office more than once but allows them to serve an indefinite number of nonconsecutive terms, Argentines speculated that Fernández and her husband had plans to alternate power between themselves to avoid these term limits.

The lack of competition in the election was undeniable: "Fernández will switch places with Kirchner without having competed in a primary for the nomination, debated the other presidential candidates or even campaigned much for votes. That's Peronism for you: Kirchner designated his wife as successor and a clientelistic machinery turned the election into a coronation" (Pérez-Stable 2007). Ultimately, a divided opposition and the immense popularity of the sitting president resulted in an easy win for Fernández, who won the election with 44.9 percent of the vote. Her nearest rival, Elisa Carrió, obtained 22.9 percent of the vote. The third-place finisher received 16.9 percent of the vote.

The stories of Michelle Bachelet and Cristina Fernández illustrate the importance of candidate selection. The elections that these two women faced had been decided months before voters headed to the polls. The candidate of Chile's ruling coalition would triumph in 2005. President Kirchner's enormous popularity would assure his party's candidate an easy win. The real stories here are about the candidate-selection and candidate-nomination procedures that allowed these women's names to get on the ballot. In this book, I present the argument that candidate selection is instrumental to understanding women's representation in politics and the variation that we see in women's candidacies across political parties in the region. I categorize candidate-selection procedures on two dimensions (exclusivity and centralization), propose a theoretical framework that allows us to understand the effects of exclusivity and centralization on women's representation, and demonstrate that candidate-selection processes that are more exclusive and centralized prove beneficial to women, while those that are more open impede women's access to candidacies. Why do the most "democratic" selection procedures not produce the most representative results? Why is it that exclusive-centralized selection, which is characterized by one or two party elites at the national level making decisions, can lead to increases in female candidacies? This book demonstrates that exclusive and centralized procedures can prove beneficial to female candidacies because they allow women to circumvent both self-nomination and power networks. Those processes that are less centralized and less exclusive magnify the obstacles to women's candidacies. Although candidate-selection processes that are inclusive and decentralized are considered more "democratic," these procedures have the unanticipated and unintended effect of suppressing female candidacies.

I study the effects of these processes on women's municipal-level representation. Graph 1.1 demonstrates that women are poorly represented in local-level politics but that there are significant differences across countries. Analyzing women's representation in municipal politics is important because local office can serve as a stepping-stone to more important political positions. Because these seats are "often less competitive, require less costly campaigns, and are less likely to require relocation away from familial demands," they should be more accessible to women (Vengroff, Nyiri, and Fugiero 2003: 163).[2]

Furthermore, traditional ideas of women's proper roles, which allow women to enter politics as "as an extension of their family role to the arena

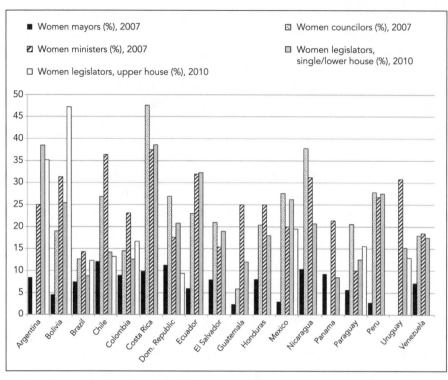

Graph 1.1   Women's Political Representation in Latin America

Source: Data on suffrage: Beatriz Llanos and Kristen Sample, *30 años de democracia ¿En la cresta de la ola? Participación política de la mujer en América Latina* (Miraflores, Peru: International IDEA, 2009), 25. Data on women ministers: ibid., 19. Data on women's representation in legislatures: compiled from http://www.ipu.org/wmn-e/classif.htm (accessed June 28, 2010). Data on the Dominican Republic: compiled from http://www.ipu.org/wmn-e/classif.htm (accessed October 15, 2010). Data on Colombia: compiled from http://www.congresovisible.org/congresistas/ (accessed October 15, 2010; data for Colombia were unavailable from the Inter-Parliamentary Union between June and October 2010).

of public affairs," may place local office within women's reach (Chaney 1979: 20). It is also important to study women's representation at the local level because a lack of female officeholders at this level could decrease women's political interest, activism, and sense of political efficacy (see, for example, Atkeson 2003; Brill 1995; High-Pippert and Comer 1998).

Although this chapter begins with two success stories, women in the region remain inadequately represented at all levels of politics. The fact that Bachelet and Fernández—along with Violeta Chamorro (Nicaragua, 1990–1997), Mireya Moscoso (Panama, 1999–2004), Laura Chinchilla (Costa

Rica, elected 2010), and Dilma Rousseff (Brazil, elected 2010)—have been elected to their nations' highest and most visible office should not obscure the unequal gender balance in politics. Slightly more than half of all Latin American citizens are female, but women occupy only one of every seven seats in legislatures and only about 1 of every 20 mayoral posts in the region. Graph 1.1 details the inequalities that continue to exist for a variety of elected and appointed positions by presenting the most recent data available on women's representation in local- and national-level politics. The data here make clear that tremendous variation can exist not only across countries (for example, Argentine and Brazilian women's representation in the lower house) but also across political offices within countries (for example, women's representation as mayors versus as ministers in Peru). The data in Graph 1.2 put women's current representation in national legislatures in historical context by providing figures on women's legislative representation for 1970, 1980, 1990, 2000, as well as data for 2010. Here we can see striking changes in women's legislative representation in many countries, especially since 2000.

Explaining Women's Underrepresentation in Politics

Much empirical work in the field of women and politics is aimed at studying differences across countries (like those shown in Graphs 1.1 and 1.2), or even across politico-geographic regions, at the expense of research that might explain variations that exist across political parties.[3] However, differences across political parties within countries are more significant than the differences that exist across countries; for data on in-country differences across all major political parties in Latin America, see Appendix A.[4] For example, in Nicaragua, the Frente Sandinista de Liberación Nacional (FSLN) holds 38 seats in the National Assembly; 14 of these are occupied by women. The next-largest political party has 25 deputies, but only 2 of these deputies are women. While 37 percent of the legislators in the FSLN are women, only 8 percent of representatives from the Partido Liberal Constitucionalista are female. In Peru, which uses a national gender quota, differences across political parties are still substantial. The Fujimorista Party has more female representation than other parties (42 percent); only one of the seven deputies from the much smaller Unión por el Perú party is a woman. Understanding women's political representation requires examination of the party level, since it is here that significant variation exists.[5]

The primary reasons for women's underrepresentation that have been offered examine socioeconomic variables, cultural factors, and institutional

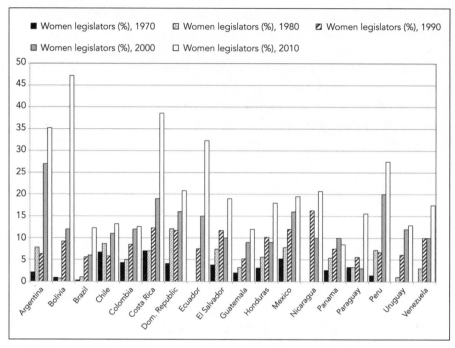

**Graph 1.2   Women's Representation in Latin American Legislatures,
1970–2010**

Source: Data on women's representation in legislatures for 2010: compiled from http://www.
ipu.org/wmn-e/classif.htm (accessed June 28, 2010; later accessed to include data missing
for Colombia and the Dominican Republic). Data for 2000: also available from the Inter-
Parliamentary Union website, http://www.ipu.org/wmn-e/arc/classif151200.htm. Data for
1970, 1980, and 1990: compiled from the Inter-Parliamentary Union publication *Women in
Parliaments, 1945–1990*, http://www.ipu.org/PDF/publications/women45-95_en.pdf.

Note: Because many of the countries were not continuously democratic between 1970 and
2010, a country's legislature may have been suspended during the year for which data are
provided; therefore, data in each of these columns represent the election of that year or the
closest previous election. The 1980 data for Nicaragua reflect the composition of the Council
of State, whose members were appointed.

variables. I first turn to these reasons and describe their limitations in accounting for the cross-national variation in women's representation. Then I
point out how these explanations are wholly unsatisfactory for a party-level
analysis. Finally, I discuss potential explanations that can be used to specifically examine differences in women's representation across political parties.

The first set of reasons focuses on socioeconomic factors, using variables
such as literacy rates, educational levels, and economic development to explain cross-national variation in women's representation. Norris and Ingle-

hart present a compelling narrative that details how modernization leads to increases in women's representation:

> Modernization creates systematic, predictable changes in gender roles, observable in two phases. First, industrialization brings women into the paid workforce and dramatically reduces fertility rates. During this stage, women make substantial gains in educational opportunities and literacy. Women are enfranchised and begin to participate in representative government, but they still have far less power than men. The second, postindustrial phase brings a shift toward greater gender equality, as women move into higher-status economic roles and gain greater political influence within elected and appointed bodies. Over half the world has not yet begun this process, however, and even the most advanced industrial societies are still undergoing it. (2001: 129)

The chain of events that they describe, however, assumes that women's educational and professional gains, and the corresponding changes in their roles within the family unit, will automatically result in greater representation in politics. This has simply not been the case, as Norris and Inglehart acknowledge (but see Reynolds 1999).[6] If this were the case, then we would expect to see that those Latin American countries with higher scores on modernization variables would also have greater participation by women in politics. We would not anticipate the substantial differences that exist between Argentina and Uruguay, since these two countries have some of the highest gross domestic products (GDPs) per capita in the region (World Bank 2011). We would expect Guatemala and Bolivia to be doing much worse than Brazil and Chile, but this is not true either. A simple correlation coefficient demonstrates that there is almost no relationship between GDP per capita and women's representation in national legislatures (-0.106). There is even less of a correlation between scores on the human development index and women's representation in national legislatures (correlation coefficient of −0.045). These types of socioeconomic explanations have insufficient explanatory power.

The second set of reasons uses cultural variables to explain women's presence in politics by looking at societal attitudes about women's proper roles. Given the difficulties of systematically measuring a concept as nebulous as culture, religion is often used as a proxy for culture, and religion has been found to correlate with women's representation in politics (Kenworthy and Malami 1999; Reynolds 1999; Tripp and Kang 2008). The traditional dominance of the Catholic Church in Latin America, however, makes this an unsatisfying explanation for the variation that we have seen in the region. Nonetheless, the rise of Protestantism and the growth of evangelical Christian movements in Latin America during the last three decades now provides some cross-national variation in the percentage of adherents to Catholicism. This does little to further our understanding of women's disproportional access to politics: there is little relationship between the percentage of Catholics in a country and the percentage of women in national legislatures (correlation coefficient of 0.18).

Others have used survey data to measure traditional attitudes in order to gauge culture's effects on women's political representation (see, for example, Norris and Inglehart 2001; Inglehart and Norris 2003). Such surveys tend to ask individuals whether women should participate in politics, whether they would vote for a woman for office, or whether men are better suited for politics. Cultural explanations cannot account for the variation in women's representation in Latin America, as demonstrated by polls conducted by Latinobarómetro. For example, Latinobarómetro asked respondents whether they agreed with the following statement: "Men are better political leaders than women." Only 14 percent of Mexicans agreed or strongly agreed with this statement, as did 17 percent of Uruguayans; 50 percent of Dominicans agreed or strongly agreed with this statement, and 35 percent of Nicaraguans and 32 percent of Colombians agreed. However, the differences in representation rates as shown in Graph 1.1 fail to correspond to these percentages (Llanos and Sample 2009).

Surveys like this are problematic in no small part because respondents may wish to appear more egalitarian than they really are; cognizance of a "politically correct" or socially desirable answer may vary across and within countries. One survey, conducted by Gallup in 2000, avoided this potential pitfall by instead asking whether the respondents thought their country was likely to elect a woman president in the near future. The poll was commissioned by the Inter-American Development Bank and carried out in Brazil, Colombia, Mexico, and El Salvador. About three-quarters of those interviewed thought that their country would elect a woman president in the next 20 years. Argentines were much less optimistic: only 47 percent believed that they would elect a woman president over the next two decades (Inter-American Development Bank 2000). Argentines, of course, elected a woman president in 2007, indicating that citizens may have a skewed assessment of their country's culture and an inadequate grasp of their co-nationals' willingness to support female politicians. Culture, regardless of how it is measured, fails to account for the substantial variation that we see in women's abilities to enter politics in Latin America.

A third group of reasons analyzes political institutions to understand women's representation in politics: proportional representation systems are more advantageous to women than first past the post systems; greater district magnitude leads to a greater proportion of women in office; women are more successful in multimember rather than single-member districts; incumbency prevents women from getting into office, because incumbents usually win and incumbents are usually male;[7] and gender quotas increase women's representation (Duverger 1955; Rule 1981; Andersen and Thorson 1984; Norris 1985; Norris 1987; Rule 1987; Darcy, Welch, and Clark 1994; Matland and Taylor 1997; Duerst-Lahti 1998; Matland 1998; Htun and Jones 1999; Norris and Inglehart 2000; Caul 2001; Saint-Germain and Chavez Metoyer 2008). These institutional explanations have proven useful in understanding women's political underrepresentation but cannot account fully for the variation that exists. For example, women are more poorly represented in the Brazilian lower house of congress than in the equivalent Mexican institution despite the fact that the Brazilian legislature is elected via proportional representation and the Mexican chamber uses a mixed system that incorporates single-member district plurality to elect two-fifths of representatives. Furthermore, these institutional approaches are often incapable of explaining change across time. To illustrate, the percentage of women in the Nicaraguan National Assembly has doubled in the past 10 years despite consistency in electoral rules and a failure to adopt a national gender quota law.

Socioeconomic, cultural, and institutional approaches have limited explanatory power. They cannot explain the type of variation that we see across countries within Latin America. Furthermore, these explanations are less useful for an analysis of party-level variation. While significant variation in socioeconomic indicators exists within countries, especially as we compare urban and rural areas, this difference is unlikely to affect a party-level analysis. Unless most political parties are regional parties, socioeconomic variables will not prove useful in explaining women's levels of political representation. Similarly, culture varies within countries, but political parties are not apt to reflect this unless they are predominantly oriented as regional parties. Institutional explanations are often inapplicable to party-level analyses, because electoral systems and rules are held constant—for example, open-list proportional representation is used regardless of which Brazilian political party is under examination. The same is true of district magnitude and the use of term limits.

Two approaches to studying women's representation are potentially fruitful for a party-level analysis: gender quotas and ideology. One institutional explanation that has recently gained scholarly interest is the use of gender quotas. These quotas can be applied nationally or by individual political parties. In the former case, when gender quotas are a matter of law, they are less likely to explain party-level differences in women's representation (though this is a matter of enforcement mechanisms and party incentives).[8] Gender quotas are a means of altering candidate-selection procedures by compelling parties to select a certain number or percentage of women candidates and at times dictating the spots that women must occupy on candidate lists. Political parties, even prior to the initial use of national gender quotas, had regularly used gender quotas. Gender quotas, which are an important element of candidate selection, are discussed in greater detail in Chapter 8.[9]

Ideological explanations assume that parties of the left, because of their emphasis on egalitarianism, are more likely to place women into office than parties of the right, which have more conservative ideas about women's public and private roles (Duverger 1955; Rule 1987; Matland and Studlar 1996; Caul 1999; Craske 1999). Furthermore, historic links between women's movements and parties of the left would also lead us to believe that these parties are more likely to have female representation (Kittilson 2006: 45). Kittilson argues that having a leftist party facilitates the adoption of mechanisms that can lead to increases in women's representation. In the Latin American cases, we see that placement on the left–right spectrum does not go as far toward explaining variation across political parties as we might expect. For example, women in Chile's conservative Unión Demócrata Independiente (UDI) party are much better represented in local-level politics than women from the parties of the left and center, including those parties that have gender quotas in place (Hinojosa 2009). Alicia Barrera, Secretary General for the leftist Partido por la Democracia of Chile, has stated, "Progressive parties have marginal female representation, because the men have a monopoly on the power" (Praamsma 2005). Saint-Germain and Chavez Metoyer's analysis of the Central American countries found that only the Sandinista Party (FSLN) in Nicaragua was a clear-cut case of a leftist party increasing women's representation (Saint-Germain and Chavez Metoyer 2008: 89–90). In Ecuador, while over 40 percent of female council members were members of right-wing parties, just over 10 percent represented parties of the left; similarly, in Brazil, nearly one-third of mayors were members of parties of the right, while less than 10 percent belonged to left-wing parties (Del Campo 2005). The data in Appendix A confirm that parties of the left do not consistently have higher levels of women's representation than parties of the right. Htun (2005) pointed out that while it appeared that leftist parties did place women into office in the 1990s, this was no longer true by 2005. A rigorous statistical analysis of parties from 18 Latin American countries confirmed this, revealing that ideology did not have a significant effect on women elected or on women nominated to legislative positions (Roza 2010a: 169). Moreover, this type of ideological analysis may be best suited to strong party systems and less useful when applied to a number of the Latin American countries.

This section of the chapter has demonstrated the limited ability of the most commonly used explanations of variations in women's representation in politics. Many of these justifications are simply ill suited to explain the more significant variation that we see: the variation that exists across political parties. The institutional explanation (gender quotas) that is useful to understanding party-level variation, one that alters the candidate-selection procedures that political parties use, is discussed in greater detail in later chapters. Ideological explanations, the most commonly used to describe the type of variation that we are concerned with here, are shown to be less useful in understanding women's representation than the study of candidate selection. The following section presents an argument for the importance of focusing party-level analyses on candidate recruitment, selection, and nomination procedures.

Why Study Candidate Selection?

> It's in the selection procedures for candidacies that women are getting left behind.
>
> —High-ranking PRI official (Interview, February 13, 2003)

> The parties are the main filter [and reason] for why women do not assume greater responsibilities in public decisions.
>
> —ADRIANA DELPIANO, Chilean politician (quoted in Susan Franceschet, *Women and Politics in Chile*)

We have long recognized that the process used to select candidates "determines the quality of the deputies elected, of the resultant parliament, often of the members of the government and, to some extent, of a country's politics" (Gallagher 1988: 1). Only recently have we begun to uncover the consequences of candidate-selection procedures for women's political representation. Recruitment and selection processes are malleable, as the overwhelming adoption of primaries in countries across the Latin American region (Poiré 2002; Carey and Polga-Hecimovich 2004) has demonstrated, making the study of these processes an especially promising area for research. Candidate selection is especially important in Latin America given that parties have a monopoly over candidacies in a significant number of countries.[10]

Because of the pivotal role that political parties can play in correcting the current gender imbalance—they not only present candidates for office but also, once in government, guide the political agenda and propose nominees for political appointments—they have been called the "missing variable" in research on women in politics (Baer 1993). The candidate recruitment and nomination procedures that parties use are particularly important since researchers have found that the lack of female officeholders is a consequence of a lack of female candidates (Burrell 1992; Darcy, Welch, and Clark 1994; Seltzer, Newman, and Leighton 1997; Hinojosa 2005; Sanbonmatsu 2006a). As the two quotes that introduce this section indicate, female politicians recognize that candidate recruitment and selection serve as a notable impediment to women's political representation.

Pippa Norris and Joni Lovenduski's study of political recruitment in Great Britain forged a new path for scholars of women and politics (1995); academic attention turned to using candidate recruitment and selection to explain the scarcity of female candidates in different national contexts (Niven 1998; Caul 2001; Tremblay and Pelletier 2001; Fox and Oxley 2003; Lawless 2003; Fox and Lawless 2004; Kittilson 2006; Niven 2006). Research on the effects of candidate selection on women's representation has largely focused on national-level office, with the exceptions of Sanbonmatsu's (2006a, 2006b) and Niven's (2006) work on the United States and Hinojosa's (2009) study of Chile.

While important work has recently analyzed candidate selection in Latin America (Smith 1979; Camp 1995; Martz 2000; Crisp 2001; De Luca, Jones, and Tula 2001; Taylor-Robinson 2001; Navia 2004; Wuhs 2008; as well as Siavelis and Morgenstern's 2008 edited volume and various works by Joy Langston and Kathleen Bruhn), only a handful of academics have examined the effects of candidate recruitment and selection procedures on women's political representation in the region (Baldez 2004a, 2004b; Escobar-Lemmon and Taylor-Robinson 2004; Heath, Schwindt-Bayer, and Taylor-Robinson 2005; Hinojosa 2005; Escobar-Lemmon and Taylor-Robinson 2008; Roza 2010a, 2010b).

This book makes an important contribution to this emerging literature. The informal nature of political recruitment in the region may explain the dearth of scholarship on candidate-selection procedures up until recently; studies of candidate selection tend to focus on rules as they are set forth in official party documents, but the "weakness of this approach is that formal rules may have little bearing on informal practices" (Norris and Lovenduski 1995: 9). Because of this disconnect between "what really happens in parties and what the rules indicate should be happening in parties," the constant rule changes that take place in the region, and the difficulty in obtaining reliable data from political parties (Freidenberg 2003: 11), understanding candidate-selection processes "requires a substantial amount of research as well as country-specific and party-specific expertise" (Field and Siavelis 2008: 623).[11]

Studies in advanced industrialized countries indicate that discrimination by political party elites (in the form of failing to recruit women candidates, having them run in unwinnable seats, and refusing to support their candidacies) has been substantially reduced (Darcy, Welch, and Clark 1994; Burrell 1998; Carroll 2001). In searching for a candidate, however, elites may inadvertently seek qualities or professional backgrounds that are more likely to belong to men than to women (Norris and Lovenduski 1995; Peterson and Runyan 1999; Tremblay and Pelletier 2001) and may place women candidates in more difficult districts or steer them away from running in districts where their party is strong (Studlar and McAllister 1991; Niven 2006) or from seeking better political positions (Lublin and Brewer 2003). Some have argued that elites may be reluctant to nominate women because they believe that women candidates will cost their party votes (Norris and Lovenduski 1995; Sanbonmatsu 2006a). Academics have analyzed characteristics of candidate-selection procedures to determine which types of processes are advantageous to women.[12]

Methodology

This book seeks to understand women's disproportional representation in politics within the Latin American region by examining the candidate-selection processes that political parties use. As I have shown previously, more attention needs to focus on variations in women's political representation across parties within countries rather than on cross-national analysis. In my examination of candidate-selection procedures, my unit of analysis is at the party level; the unit of analysis, though, is not each political party (for example, the Partido Revolucionario Institucional [PRI] in Mexico), but rather the party in each of the municipalities that I studied because a single political party may employ a variety of recruitment and nomination procedures. In other words the PRI is not one case, but four (i.e., the PRI in Amanalco, Pueblo Viejo, Tianguistenco, and Mérida); my number of cases, then, is a function of studying four municipalities in two countries and studying three to six parties in each of those eight municipalities. The total number of cases under study, then, is 36.[13]

Analyzing two national settings provides a way to dispel concerns that my findings can be applied to only a single country. Thus, my analysis provides both cross-country and within-country (both cross-party and within-party) comparisons. The research for the main empirical chapters draws heavily from eight months of fieldwork in Chile and seven months of fieldwork in Mexico performed over the course of 2001 to 2004. The majority of interviews, which are listed in Appendix B, were conducted between July 2002 and July 2003. I chose Chile and Mexico for in-depth analysis because they maximize variation in terms of the party system (Chile has a multiparty system often channeled through two coalitions while Mexico now effectively has a three-party system), party stability (at the time of my research Chile had a stable system, whereas Mexico had recently undergone a historic transition away from authoritarianism), and state structure. The use of a federal case (Mexico) and a unitary one (Chile) added substantially to my analysis.[14] Variation in state structure was significant because federalism allowed increased administrative autonomy within parties, whereas in a unitary system like Chile, candidate selection tended to be governed at the national level. Although sub-national party offices exist in both cases—municipal offices in both countries, state-level organizations in Mexico, and provincial and regional offices in Chile—the administrative autonomy seen in the federal government was replicated within political parties. Substantial differences existed among the party organizations in the municipalities studied in Mexico.[15]

Because my intent was to study the effects of selection processes on female candidacies, it was important to choose cases in which women had actually been selected as candidates. To ensure that I chose municipalities where women had been candidates, I selected cases in which women were mayors.[16] Because women who run for office win in numbers comparable to those of men, it was reasonable to choose cases on the basis of the presence of female mayors. At first glance, such a methodological strategy may appear to be an instance of choosing cases on the dependent variable; however, my approach avoided that misstep. Because each party in each municipality was a separate case, I also obtained cases in which women were not mayoral candidates or elected mayors. For instance, in Amanalco, I studied the PRI (which chose a female mayoral candidate) and two cases in which the candidate that emerged was not a woman (the Partido Acción Nacional [PAN] and the Partido de la Revolución Democrática [PRD]). Another advantage of this research strategy is that I control for variation within each municipality on a number of variables that could potentially have explanatory power (for example, education levels or culture).

In each of the two countries, I chose three municipalities that had sitting female mayors. The very limited number of female mayors in both countries

TABLE 1.1. GENDER AND PARTY COMPOSITION OF CASES

Municipality	Gender of Mayor	Party of Mayor	Council Members	Female Council Members	Political Parties in Council
La Serena, Chile	F	RN	17	3	2 RN, 2 PDC, 1 PPD, 1 PRSD, 1 PS
Maule, Chile	F	PDC	5	0	1 RN, 1 PDC, 1 PS, 1 PRSD, 1 PPD
Peñaflor, Chile	M	PDC	5	0	2 PDC, 1 UDI, 1 RN, 1 PS
Talagante, Chile	F	UDI	5	2	2 UDI, 1 PPD, 1 PDC, 1 RN
Amanalco, Mexico	F	PRI	10	1	6 PRI, 2 PAN, 1 PRD, 1 PCD
Mérida, Mexico	F	PAN	17	6	9 PAN, 8 PRI
Pueblo Viejo, Mexico	F	PRD	5	1	3 PRD, 1 PRI, 1 PAN
Tianguistenco, Mexico	M	PRI	10	1	6 PRI, 2 PAN, 2 PRD

PAN, Partido Acción Nacional; PCD, Partido de Centro Democrático; PDC, Partido Demócrata Cristiano; PPD, Partido por la Democracia; PRI, Partido Revolucionario Institucional; PRSD, Partido Radical Social Demócrata; PS, Partido Socialista; RN, Renovación Nacional; UDI, Unión Demócrata Independiente.

dramatically decreased case study options. Of 341 Chilean municipalities, only 40 had female mayors; of 2,443 Mexican municipalities, only 81 were being governed by women. From within this set of possible cases, I selected six cases, chosen to maximize variation in municipal size and political party dominance. I also then chose a fourth municipality in each of the two countries that featured the much more common situation: a male mayor. Case study details are provided in Table 1.1.

Selecting cases that varied in municipal population[17] was important to gauge any possible effects that size might have on the candidate-selection procedures, since I had hypothesized that smaller settings might allow gate-keepers to personally know qualified female candidates.[18] I therefore chose to study small, medium, and large municipalities in each of the two countries (the fourth shadow case, with a male mayor, was a medium-sized municipality).[19] Because I wanted to study a variety of candidate-selection procedures, I tried to maximize variation in the political parties included in my study.[20] Random selection of municipalities with female mayors would have resulted in the overrepresentation of municipalities with PRI mayors in Mexico and

TABLE 1.2. MUNICIPAL CHARACTERISTICS OF CASE STUDIES

Municipality	Location	Capital City (Provincial/State)	Population
La Serena, Chile	Fourth region	La Serena	144,767
Maule, Chile	Seventh region	Talca	15,840
Peñaflor, Chile	Metropolitan region	Talagante	58,772
Talagante, Chile	Metropolitan region	Talagante	58,909
Amanalco, Mexico	Mexico state	Toluca	21,095
Mérida, Mexico	Yucatán state	Mérida	705,055
Pueblo Viejo, Mexico	Veracruz state	Xalapa	50,329
Tianguistenco, Mexico	Mexico state	Toluca	58,831

UDI mayors in Chile.[21] I chose female mayors representing the UDI, Renovación Nacional (RN), and Partido Demócrata Cristiano (PDC) in Chile, and in Mexico I chose female mayors representing each of the three major political parties. Because I was interested in the process of becoming a candidate and it might be more difficult for people to recall how they became candidates when more time had elapsed since their initial candidacies, I would have liked to limit my analysis to municipalities where the mayor was in his or her first term. However, I found this impossible in Chile[22] because the vast majority of female mayors who fit this criterion were UDI members from small municipalities, which precluded variation in either party or municipal size. I had hypothesized that there might be some cultural differences across regions that could affect women's experience with the candidate-selection process, and this led me to consider selecting municipalities from diverse regions.[23] Unfortunately, the very small number of female mayors in the two countries, coupled with my need for variation in terms of parties represented and municipal size, made it impossible to obtain as much geographical variation as I desired, as can be seen in Table 1.2.[24]

I gathered information on candidate-selection procedures from all major parties[25] in these two countries through party documents such as party constitutions and from available secondary sources. In addition to archival work designed to unearth further information on official candidate-selection processes, I conducted over 130 interviews with local-, regional-, and national-level party officials, local-level politicians (predominantly mayors and council members), and academics and political consultants. Within the eight municipalities, I interviewed representatives of all parties that were represented in either the current municipal council or the council of the previous administration. These interviews were semistructured and were intended to (1) assess the backgrounds of local officeholders, including information on initiation into their political parties, party offices held, previous candidacies, and family, educational, and career profiles; (2) reveal the processes that were used for recruiting and nominating candidates; (3) determine whether elites desired particular characteristics of candidates; and (4) assess the existence of discrimination toward female candidates and imputed discrimination on the part of decision makers.

Interviewing approximately 15 to 30 individuals representing the relevant political parties in each municipality allowed me to triangulate interview responses. Data triangulation, in which data are collected from several different sources, was integral to my research as it allowed me to validate the veracity of the data that I obtained from my respondents. Trotter and Schensul have noted that the "most effective way to ensure reliability and validity of ethnographic data is to obtain comparable, confirmatory data from multiple sources" (1998: 719). Though my research design was positional-approach oriented (interviews with individuals who held formal positions, such as mayor or local party president), interviewees provided me with reputational data (in response to queries about other politically important individuals who might affect candidate selection), which led to further interviews. As Putnam has stated, "Positional analysis tends to overemphasize spurious influence and to underemphasize indirect influence" (1976). By obtaining reputational data from respondents, I extended my research beyond those who held formal power in the municipalities under study.

The case study research that I detail in greater length in the chapters that cover each of the four types of candidate selection is supplemented with a larger N analysis of all Chilean municipal candidacies in the 2000 elections.[26] The results of that analysis are provided in Chapter 6. In addition, anecdotal evidence is introduced throughout the empirical chapters to illustrate (rather than test) my argument. This evidence has been gathered from countries across Latin America and includes candidate selection for municipal-level office, as well as positions at regional and national levels. For example, the discussion of exclusive-centralized selection in Chapter 6 is supplemented with a brief description of the candidate-selection practices used by Peruvian president Alberto Fujimori.

The need for scholars of women and politics to study the party level is undeniable. It is here that we see significant variation that simply cannot be explained without examining candidate-selection procedures. In this book, I present an argument concerning the effects of different mechanisms of selection on women's abilities to become candidates and then use data primarily from Chile and Mexico to demonstrate these effects.

Overview of the Book

This introductory chapter sets the stage for an analysis of women's representation in Latin America by presenting data on the disproportional presence of women in elected office. It also addresses the problems with the most widely used variables to explain this underrepresentation and argues for studying the role that candidate selection plays in determining how women fare politically.

Chapter 2 focuses on the question, *What is keeping women out of politics?* I argue that the percentage of female representatives cannot be explained by examining either the supply of potential female candidates or the demand by the population for women candidates. I demonstrate that women's underrepresentation in politics is not a result of a lack of qualified women to run for office (supply problem). If women who do run for office are unable to win seats because voters are unwilling to cast their ballots for them, then the problem is one of demand, but that is not the case either. Using data from across Latin America on women's educational levels, labor force participation rates, and professional paths, as well as cross-national data on marriage and childbirth, I prove that a large supply of potential female candidates exists. By analyzing survey data on women's interest in politics and their historical record of political participation, I determine that there is also a supply of women who are interested in entering politics. Polling and electoral data from select Latin American countries indicate that no demand problem exists: men and women are overwhelmingly willing to vote for female candidates. The bottleneck to women's political representation results from neither a lack of female candidates nor discrimination in the voting booth.

Chapter 3 provides a theoretical framework for understanding where the bottleneck really is. The chapter examines the role of candidate-selection processes in limiting the participation of women; the theoretical framework focuses on two dimensions—exclusivity and centralization—to develop a typology of selection processes and explain their gendered effects. I present the central argument of this book: candidate-selection processes that are more centralized and exclusive (i.e., those processes that take place at the national level and in which decisions are made by a very small group) can lead to increases in female candidacies because they allow women to circumvent both self-nomination and power networks, while those processes that are less centralized and less exclusive will increase obstacles to women's candidacies. While either centralization or exclusivity will have positive effects on female candidacies, the combination of decentralized decision making and more inclusive procedures is argued to have especially negative results.

Chapter 4 analyzes the paradox of primaries. The global consensus that primaries are the most "democratic" process for choosing party nominees has led to their wholesale adoption, from Argentina to Uruguay. The effects of these primaries on women's representation have been largely understudied, despite the fact that the causes and consequences of the switch to primaries have received substantial scholarly attention. Women do win primaries, but Chapter 4 presents qualitative and quantitative data to support the claim that inclusive-decentralized selection results in fewer female candidacies and provides a detailed accounting of the reasons why primaries in particular are problematic for women. The chapter uses case studies from the Chilean parties of the center-left coalition and Mexico's PRI and PRD to demonstrate that inclusive-decentralized selection processes are disadvantageous to women's representation.

Chapter 5 establishes that inclusive-centralized and exclusive-decentralized candidate-selection procedures have both advantages and disadvantages for female candidacies. While the inclusivity of the process keeps women out, the centralized selection is beneficial to female candidacies. Drawing extensively from data collected on Mexico's PAN and supplemented by data from other Latin American parties, I show that inclusive processes negatively affect female candidates. The lack of recruitment by party personnel in an inclusive-decentralized system forces candidates to self-nominate. Using case studies, I show that when women nominees do emerge from these exclusive-decentralized systems, they are likely to be part of traditional monopolies of power. By avoiding one obstacle to women's representation, each of these two candidate-selection procedures yields mixed results.

Chapter 6 demonstrates that selection processes that are exclusive and centralized can prove advantageous to female candidates. I draw from municipal case studies from Chile's UDI and Mexico's PRI, as well as other cases from across Latin America, to illustrate that exclusive-centralized candidate selection processes can prove beneficial to women's candidacies. However, these practices, which we can group under the name of *dedazos*—the term regularly applied to the practice of handpicking candidates in Mexico—are falling out of favor. Using the cases of Juan Perón during his second and third administrations, Peru during the authoritarian period of the 1990s, and others, I argue that candidate selection in authoritarian periods and in situations of party-system collapse can produce an increase in women politicians because of reliance on exclusive-centralized selection processes. Chapter 6 also notes that the process of appointment has unexplored parallels to exclusive-centralized selection. By analyzing women's inclusion in appointed positions, I establish that, like exclusive-centralized selection, appointment systems lead to greater female representation.

Chapter 7 explores a form of candidate selection that hits closer to home. Hereditary rule is most likely the oldest means of candidate selection, but its importance in producing both male and female politicians has been largely undertheorized in the modern study of candidate selection. Women in Latin America have often risen to power in their roles as—and perhaps because they are—family members of political men. These women are a varied bunch: from the mayor of the small town of Pueblo Viejo in Mexico (who while campaigning for the seat that her husband had previously occupied often heard, "Just don't be like that husband of yours") to Susana Higuchi of Peru (who attempted to challenge her own husband for the presidency). The chapter uses the framework developed in Chapter 3 to explain the candidacies of widows, daughters, and wives and analyzes recent legislative efforts from across Latin America to prevent family members of incumbents from running for office.

Chapter 8 studies the use of gender quotas. Quotas have altered candidate-selection procedures across Latin America. Not all countries in the region have legislated quotas, but even in those countries without national quotas, many parties have adopted quotas. The chapter analyzes the complex interaction between quota rules and candidate selection and explores the effects of the former on the latter. Quotas have the potential to dramatically increase women's representation, but in order for quotas to have this effect we must understand how quotas and candidate-selection processes interact.

Chapter 9 concludes the book by summarizing the counterintuitive findings of this text—that it is not the candidate-selection procedures that are normally considered more "democratic" that increase women's representation but rather those that are closed off to most and are being made at the national level—and details the substantial empirical implications of these findings. I then address ways in which parties, civil society, and states can mitigate the effects of gendered candidate-selection procedures. These recommendations are meant to be compatible with a broad range of selection procedures, thus allowing parties to retain favored practices while still counteracting obstacles to female representation.

2

Why Selection Matters

Explaining Women's Representation in Politics

> Women face more discrimination within their marriages
> than in politics.
>
> —PRI councilwoman, Interview, May 16, 2003

> More than a few times people said to me, "I'm going to
> vote for you because you're a woman." They just don't have
> as much faith in male politicians anymore. People have the
> idea that male legislators are corrupt.
>
> —PRI mayor, Interview, March 25, 2003

Women's political underrepresentation results from bottlenecks at different points in the process of becoming an officeholder. There are four stages in this process, as Figure 2.1 illustrates.[1] Stage 1 marks the move from being a part of the general population to becoming an eligible (anyone who is legally allowed to run for office). Stage 2 demonstrates the transition from eligible to aspirant (individuals who have an interest in running for political office). Stage 3 marks the move from aspirant to candidate (someone who has entered the race). Participants in primary elections are referred to as pre-candidates and become candidates only after they have officially become the candidates of their parties. Stage 4 shows the transition from being a candidate to being voted into office and becoming an officeholder. Within the recruitment process, political elites are capable of motivating eligibles to become aspirants and of allowing aspirants to become candidates. The four stages in the process of becoming an officeholder are represented by small arrows in Figure 2.1.

Figure 2.2 catalogs the possible explanations for women's underrepresentation that this chapter discusses at length. These explanations are character-

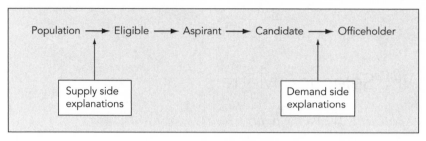

Figure 2.1   The Process of Becoming an Officeholder

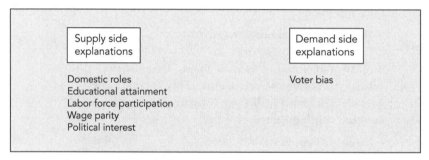

Figure 2.2   Possible Explanations for Women's Underrepresentation

ized as either supply side or demand side. This chapter first turns to supply side explanations and then analyzes whether demand side explanations are fruitful for understanding women's political underrepresentation.

Supply Problems: Are There Enough "Qualified" Women to Enter Politics?

Although political elites may regularly explain away the lack of women in political office by arguing that there are not enough "qualified" women,[2] there is an ever-growing pool of Latin American women qualified to enter politics. By analyzing the changes that have taken place in women's traditional roles as wives and mothers, as well as their increased educational, professional, and earning opportunities (i.e., the first four entries under supply side explanations in Figure 2.2), we can see that women's extreme underrepresentation in politics cannot be explained by problems of supply. The following sections briefly examine the changes that have taken place in Latin American women's lives over the last decades and have thus created opportunities for women to participate in politics. These structural factors that are discussed in turn "should influence political outcomes for women" (Paxton, Hughes, and Green 2006: 903).[3]

Changes in Women's Domestic Roles

Women's roles as wives and mothers have seen dramatic changes in the last few decades. Marrying later and postponing childbearing have freed up women to pursue educational endeavors, enter the labor force, and participate politically.

Across the region, women are delaying marriage. The average age of marriage is now 22.6 for Latin American women, with a median age of 22.7 (25.8 for men, median of 25.8), and although women in all countries are marrying later than they were just a few decades ago, variation exists within the region. For example, in Brazil, women married at age 23 in 1970 and 30 years later this figure barely budged to 23.1; during the same time period, Costa Rica saw sizeable change. Women in some countries are marrying later than in others. In Argentina, Chile, Costa Rica, and Peru, women are marrying after age 24, while in Guatemala and Nicaragua women enter into wedlock before turning 21 (UN DESA 2008).

Women are also postponing childbearing and having fewer children. This drop in maternity levels has allowed women to pursue careers. Data from Mexico indicate that women with greater levels of education are more likely to delay having children. By 1987, among women in that country between the ages of 25 and 49, those without formal education gave birth to their first child at 19.2 years of age, while those women with at minimum a junior high school education had their first child on average at age 24.1 (Valdés and Gomáriz 1995: 45). Fertility rates have dropped substantially since the 1950s, when women in the region bore 5.9 children on average (see Valdés and Gomáriz 1995 for earlier data and UNESCO 2009 for recent data). The average number of births per woman in the region is now down to 2.5 (the median is also 2.5). Bolivia, with an average of 3.5 births per woman, and Guatemala (4.2) push the regional fertility rate up (UNESCO 2009).

Increases in Educational Attainment

In much of Latin America today, women have achieved educational parity with men. These significant changes in women's educational achievements have far-reaching implications:

"Education is not the panacea for all development problems, but the impact of improved educational attainment is significant. . . . It changes expectations about what life has to offer" (Craske 1999: 42). The increases in women's educational attainment open the doors to not only a wealth of occupational endeavors but also participation in formal politics. Although political parties may not "require" diplomas or college degrees of their candidates, examining the résumés of current officeholders makes it evident that Latin American parties are considerably more likely to select individuals with advanced degrees (Hinojosa 2005; Saint-Germain and Chavez Metoyer 2008; Franceschet and Piscopo, 2012; see also earlier works by Camp).

The most minimal indicator of educational attainment is literacy. UNESCO data indicate that literacy has increased substantially over the last half century throughout Latin America. Literacy rates are above 90 percent in most countries of the region, and progress continues to be made; for example, literacy for Guatemalan women aged 15 to 24 climbed from 69.7 percent in 1995 to 73.8 percent in 2003 (Valdés, Muñoz, and Donoso 2005: 35). There are few gender differences in literacy. Only Bolivia, Guatemala, and Peru see sizeable gender disparities—about 10 percentage points in these cases (UNESCO 2009). Excluding these three cases, there is a 1 percentage point difference in literacy between men and women in the region.

Examining school enrollment rates provides another indicator of women's educational gains. Girls have not only caught up to boys; they have surpassed them in almost all countries of the region. Recent data indicate that gender disparities in primary school enrollment have been overwhelmingly eliminated, as Graph 2.1 makes clear. Only in Guatemala are girls lagging behind boys, and even there the difference between primary school enrollment rates is only 4 percentage points. Secondary school enrollment data, found in Graph 2.1, demonstrate that girls are more likely to be enrolled than boys (with Guatemala once again the sole exception). In countries like Argentina and Brazil, girls are considerably more likely to attend secondary schools (UNESCO 2009). The schoolgirls of today are creating a large pool of qualified political candidates for the years to come.

Understanding whether supply problems actually explain women's political underrepresentation requires that we examine men's and women's university enrollment and graduation rates (Hinojosa 2005, however, notes that university degrees are not an informal requirement for local-level officeholders in Chile and Mexico). By the 1970s, women across Latin America had made substantial inroads into universities and comprised a whopping 48 percent of university students by the mid-1990s (Valdés and Gomáriz 1995: 108). Mexican women were 36 percent of university students by 1970, were 42 percent of university students by 1980, and had reached parity by the end of the 1990s (Valdés and Gomáriz 1995: 108). Similarly in Chile, women

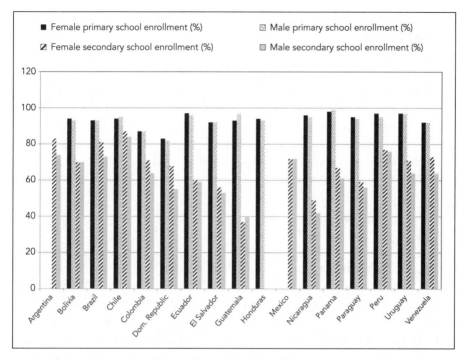

**Graph 2.1   Primary and Secondary School Enrollment Rates
in Latin America**

Source: Data on primary and secondary school enrollment rates: compiled from the UNESCO
Institute for Statistics database, 2010 Education for All Global Monitoring, http://unesdoc.
unesco.org/images/0018/001866/186606E.pdf.

Note: Data for male and female primary school enrollment for Argentina and Mexico and
secondary school enrollment for Honduras are unavailable.

were 42 percent of university students in 1980 (SERNAM 2001) and quickly
outpaced men in university enrollments.

Gender-disaggregated enrollment data for individual universities in the
region are rare. Such data would allow us to determine whether women are
matriculating at institutions of higher learning that are known to provide
networking opportunities. For example, Camp has identified the National
Autonomous University of Mexico as a nexus of recruitment into political
careers (Camp 1979, 1995, 2002). By 2000, women were approximately 55
percent of students at the National Autonomous University of Mexico (Sandoval 2000). Gender-disaggregated data of degrees awarded by universities
would also provide us with information useful in evaluating whether women
are entering professions that regularly serve as conduits to politics. In the

case of Chile, 44 percent of law degrees in 1998 were awarded to female students (SERNAM 2001).[4]

Women's access to higher education is important when examining entry into national politics. Research from the 1990s analyzed the backgrounds of Central American women politicians; 93 percent of the women in the Costa Rican legislature had college degrees, as did 80 percent of Guatemalans, 60 percent of Salvadorans, 50 percent of Nicaraguans, and 33 percent of Hondurans (Saint-Germain and Chavez Metoyer 2008). More recent data confirm the importance of college degrees: 88 percent of Argentine female legislators held college degrees (Franceschet and Piscopo 2012).

Increases in Women's Participation in the Labor Force

Latin American women are more likely now than they have ever been to work outside the home. Women's participation in the labor forced increased dramatically during the previous century, tripling from 1960 to 1990 (Valdés and Gomáriz 1995: 63). Women's presence in the labor force allows us to see whether women's severe underrepresentation in politics is a result of a supply problem.

Women have made tremendous gains in this area, although it is clear that women are not yet participating at similar rates to men (with women trailing men on average by 28 percentage points). Graph 2.2 provides recent data on women's and men's inclusion in the paid labor force. Examining women's labor force participation rates, however, does little to illuminate whether women are participating in those professions that are known conduits to political careers. The pipeline argument—"that as more and more women come to occupy the careers that are most likely to lead to political candidacies, more and more women will run for office" (Pearson and Lawless 2006: 6)—requires that we examine women's presence in select careers.[5] Obtaining this type of data for Latin American countries is onerous; while data on college degrees are useful, knowing the percentage of law degrees does not tell us what proportion of students have chosen to continue in that profession.[6]

The data on women's participation in the labor force certainly demonstrate that there is a ready supply of women who could enter politics and that women's lower rates of labor force activity cannot account for their much lower rates of political representation. Furthermore, the data presented here might actually underestimate women's true representation in the workforce. Craske notes that those countries with large rural sectors tend to have lower rates of women in the workforce, but this finding may be because "wom-

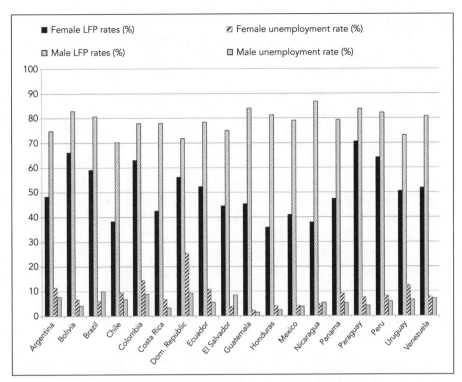

Graph 2.2   Labor Force Participation (LFP) and Unemployment Rates in Latin America

Source: Labor force participation and unemployment rates data: from International Labour Office, Key Indicators of the Labour Market (KILM), 6th ed., table 1 (data are from 2008). Data are also available online at http://kilm.ilo.org/KILMnetBeta/default2.asp.

Note: Data are from the most recent year available for each country.

en's work is invisible due to narrow definitions of work" (1999: 49). Women's participation varies during the course of their lives. Women are most likely to participate in the workforce between the ages of 25 and 49 (Craske 1999: 49), an age range that corresponds closely to women's reproductive years. Data can also be used to illuminate inequalities that women face in the workforce, which could have effects on women's abilities to enter politics. For example, despite the fact that nearly half of Argentine women are employed, only 7 percent of corporate board positions are held by women (Maxfield 2005: 18).

However, it is important to note that participation in the paid labor force is not a requirement for office holding, although many women who have obtained political positions not only have been employed but also have followed certain career paths. Women have entered politics without having worked outside the home; especially when women define themselves and are defined by others as *supermadres*—"tending the needs of her big family in the larger *casa* of the municipality or even the nation" (Chaney 1979: 21)—they may not require experience in the workforce to be viable candidates. Examining women's participation in the paid labor force is useful because it signals women's ability to participate in work outside the home and to take their talents to the public sphere. Argentine academic María del Carmen Feijoó has argued that participation in the labor force is key to political development because it offers the opportunity to build "networks with co-workers," and this "helps form the basis for the development of political identities" (quoted in Craske 1999: 90). Women's educational attainment in recent years has almost certainly been translated into increased participation in the labor force, explaining the huge surge in paid labor for women in the last two decades. The continued educational achievements of women are likely to positively affect women's future workforce participation.

Changes in Wage Parity

While it is certainly no secret that money matters in politics, little work has been done to unearth the role that money plays in keeping women in the region from entering the political arena. The literature from the United States demonstrates that women are less likely than men to spend their resources to start or further their political careers, meaning that women may be less disposed to run for office if it means they have to go through added expenses, such as primaries (Burns, Schlozman, and Verba 2001). Anecdotal evidence from Latin America indicates that the same is true there. Those women who have succeeded politically have often noted the role that personal finances have played. For example, as one deputy explains: "I have not had many obstacles, personally, but I am an exception and not representative of most women. . . . I had an economic situation that permitted me to have the basic necessities for a political career" (quoted in Schwindt-Bayer 2006: 3). Del Campo notes that "A large proportion of women, even greater than in the case of male deputies, come from a high social class" and finds that 58 percent of deputies from the region claim to come from the upper or upper-middle classes (2005: 1705). Simply put, financing elections keeps women out of office: as Chilean politician María Antonieta Saa stated, "Men will take risks, they will sell the family house . . . but a woman is not going to put her family at risk" (quoted in Franceschet 2005: 89).

Income inequality continues to be a serious concern for women, despite the fact that the wage gap narrowed substantially during the 1980s and 1990s in all Latin American countries except Chile, Mexico, and Venezuela (UNIFEM 2001). Graph 2.2 illustrates that women are still more likely to be unemployed than men; female unemployment averages 8.3 percent in the region, while male unemployment is 5.7 percent. On average in the region, women's incomes are half of men's, with earned income ratios ranging from a high of 0.71 in Colombia to a low of 0.34 in Honduras and Nicaragua. A different indicator that examines the ratio of average female income compared to average male income reveals that on average in the region women are earning 69.2 cents for every peso earned by a man (Valdés, Muñoz, and Donoso 2005: 31).

Throughout Latin America, the wage gap decreases as educational levels rise. In other words, the wage gap is smaller for those with a fifth-grade education than for those with a first-grade education. However, once we examine the most highly educated across Latin America—those with post–high school educations—the wage gap actually increases; women with college degrees earn a smaller proportion of a similarly educated man's salary than women with less education. For example, in Argentina, women with 10 to 12 years of schooling earn 80.9 cents for every peso earned by a man with the same number of years of education. However, women with more than 13 years of education earn 69.3 cents for every peso that a similarly educated man pockets (United Nations 2004). This is particularly troubling as we assess the impact of money on women's political representation, since more educated women are more likely to enter politics.

Unequal wages can explain some of the political underrepresentation of women that we see. Wage parity would almost certainly increase the supply of women for public office. This wage gap that exists is all the more alarming considering women's more limited access to campaign financing; as one female deputy stated, "There is one obstacle that all women have: this is economic. As women, we are more timid when it comes to soliciting money and resources to participate in a political fight" (quoted in Schwindt-Bayer 2006: 2–3). We certainly know that men's and women's campaign resources are not equal (Htun and Jones 2002). The inability to finance an election can prevent a woman (or a man) from being seen as "qualified" for office; in Chapter 4, as we turn our focus to primary campaigns, we examine the financial pressures that women face as pre-candidates. Although unequal wages may explain why some women have not entered politics, wage disparity cannot fully explain women's underrepresentation in politics. Women face much greater inequities in their representation in political office than they do in their paychecks.

Gauging Political Interest

A final element of measuring the supply of qualified women is establishing that there is a pool of women who are politically interested and willing to hold office—that is, we must measure political interest in order to assess supply side explanations as seen in Figure 2.2. As Niven states, "Women could lack interest in politics and political office" (2006: 474), and that would certainly explain their absence from politics. There is, however, substantial evidence to indicate that Latin American women are interested in politics and would be willing to serve in public office. We can assess women's interest by examining survey data and analyzing women's political participation.

The World Values Survey recently polled Argentines, Brazilians, Chileans, Mexicans, Peruvians, and Venezuelans about their attitudes toward politics and their involvement in party politics. No consistent patterns emerge from the data; women and men do not differ substantially in their attitudes toward politics or in their participation within their parties. For example, while women in Brazil were more likely than men to say that politics was very important to their lives (16.1 percent versus 13.1 percent), the opposite was true in Peru (8.6 percent versus 14 percent). Women were on average slightly less likely than men to say they were active in their parties (3.6 percent versus 5.3 percent), but men were more likely than women to say that they were inactive in their parties (7.2 percent versus 6.5 percent). Early polling data from Mexico suggested that differences in political interest between men and women did exist. In 1959, 22 percent of men said that they were very interested in political campaigns, but only 11 percent of women said the same thing. By 1991, however, these gender differences had disappeared (25 percent versus 24 percent) (Domínguez and McCann 1998: 32). Men's and women's similar attitudes toward politics and their interest in following politics are evidence that women's absence from elected office is not a function of political disinterest.

Looking at voting rates provides further indication that women are politically interested.[7] Although limited cross-national data from Latin America on women's political participation exist, the available evidence indicates that women are about half of eligible voters and make up a similar percentage of actual voters. The only Latin American country that appears to break with this general pattern is Guatemala, where women are 57 percent of eligible voters but only 38 percent of actual voters. Data on voter turnout by gender are available for only two of the countries in the region. In Chile, 88.4 percent of women who are registered to vote turn out on election day, while 85.7 percent of men do. Similarly, in Ecuador, women are slightly more likely to turn out to vote: 72.1 percent versus 70.3 percent (International IDEA 2009).

Women are not only as likely as or more likely than men to turn out to vote; they are also less likely than men to spoil their votes, according to Chilean data. In 2000, 91.9 percent of women's votes were valid, while 89.4 percent of men's ballots were valid (SERNAM 2001). Data from Mexico indicate that women's commitment to voting extends to their presence as voting booth volunteers; 54.9 percent of such volunteers in the midterm elections of 1997 were women (UNIFEM/CONMUJER 2000). Also, women were almost half of voting booth presidents and secretaries: 47.6 percent and 48.7 percent, respectively (UNIFEM/CONMUJER 2000).

Data collected in 2009 for GEPPAL revealed that 51 percent of party members are women, but only 16 percent of executive national committee members are women (Roza 2010a).[8] Data from Panama from 2007 confirm this: women are poorly represented in leadership positions in their parties. For example, in the Panamanian Partido Revolucionario Democrático (PRD), women hold only 27 percent of the 2,063 party posts despite the fact that women are 51 percent of PRD members. Considerable variation in women's presence in party leadership positions exists. According to Del Campo, women's presence in parties' national directives reaches lows of 3 percent and highs of 50 percent (2005: 1706); Roza, on the other hand, found that lows for female membership on national executive committees were at 13 percent (Chile and Panama), while the high was 42 percent in Bolivia (2010a: 112). These highs are often the result of internal gender quotas. Women's representation as party presidents in the 92 largest political parties in the region was only 11 percent (Roza 2010a: 115). Women's limited participation in decision-making positions within parties could be read as evidence of a lack of political interest, but it can also be interpreted as further indication that parties are a substantial obstacle to women's fuller political involvement. Especially when coupled with figures that reveal that women register to vote, turn out to cast their ballots, join parties, and help supervise elections, the latter explanation appears more promising.

Women's collective action efforts in the region are further proof of their interest in the political world. Women's demands for suffrage were often the first large-scale political effort in which women in the region participated. (As Table 2.1 notes, women gained suffrage in 1929 in Ecuador, but not until 1961 in Paraguay.) But women's participation in political activity has

TABLE 2.1. WOMEN'S PARTICIPATION IN POLITICS

Country	Year of Suffrage	Percentage of National Electorate	Percentage in Top Party Posts	Percentage on Party Executive Boards
Argentina	1947	51.0	16.7	29.5
Bolivia	1952	49.9	40.0	—
Brazil	1932	51.8	16.0	—
Chile	1949	52.4	12.7	20.1
Colombia	1957	51.0	33.7	27.0
Costa Rica	1949	50.0	40.9	43.9
Dominican Republic	1942	50.4	14.4	14.0
Ecuador	1929	50.5	16.8	20.0
El Salvador	1939	54.1	25.0	15.8
Guatemala	1945	45.8	15.5	18.2
Honduras	1955	50.6	37.9	34.6
Mexico	1953	51.9	22.9	30.6
Nicaragua	1955	54.0	20.0	24.3
Panama	1945	58.3	13.1	18.8
Paraguay	1961	52.5	15.5	18.9
Peru	1955	49.7	31.0	25.5
Uruguay	1932	52.4	18.5	12.5
Venezuela	1947	50.0	21.2	—

Source: For the percentage of the national electorate and the percentage of women on party executive boards, see Beatriz Llanos and Kristen Sample, *30 años de democracia ¿En la cresta de la ola? Participación política de la mujer en América Latina* (Miraflores, Peru: International IDEA, 2009). For the percentage of women in top party posts, see "Politics and Parties: Without Equality, Far from Parity," International IDEA, 2009, available at http://www.idea.int/gender/without_equality.cfm. The data in that article are based on a sample of 84 parties and political movements with sampling for major parties in each country (see the Gender and Political Parties in Latin America [GEPPAL] database, available at http://www.iadb.org/research/geppal/).

since escalated, demonstrating their political interest. Women in the region have played an important role in social movements.[9] For example,[10] conservative women in Chile were active in protesting the Allende government and in calling for a military coup: even before Allende took office, 3,000 women gathered to incite the military to take action against the incoming president (Baldez 2002: 59). During dictatorships, "women were among the first to protest against the mass imprisonments and disappearances; organizations based on women relatives of the disappeared formed the backbone of human rights groups" (Jaquette 1989: 4). In Argentina, Chile, and other countries of the region, women's "illegal" political activities during times of dictatorship aroused less suspicion than men's because women were presumed to be nonpolitical. In Chile, women denounced human rights abuses and formed collective organizations to deal with the economic crisis created as a result of Pinochet's neo-liberal economic policies. In Argentina, during the Dirty War, women joined together to publicly protest human rights abuses, formed networks to find their loved ones, and covertly continued their political work; the most well known of these women's groups is the Madres de Plaza de Mayo. In countries like El Salvador and Nicaragua, women were extraordinarily active in guerrilla movements. In El Salvador, nearly one-third of the revolutionaries from the Frente Farabundo Martí para la Liberación Nacional (FMLN) were women (Silber and Viterna 2009). Women in the Andean countries have been active participants in indigenous movements over the last four decades.

Demand Factors: Are Voters Preventing Women from Getting into Office?

Is women's underrepresentation in politics due to a demand problem? In other words, do voters exhibit bias against women? We can assess this issue by examining survey data as well as the electoral record. The available evidence indicates that there is very little voter discrimination against women candidates. Survey results demonstrate that while some voters are unwilling to cast their ballots for women, the vast majority are willing to do so. Further, polling data also reveal that some voters actually prefer to vote for women. The best evidence of willingness to vote for women is electoral data, and this confirms survey data: voters support women. While some bias certainly continues to exist, demand side explanations cannot account for women's underrepresentation in politics.

Survey Data

We can measure voter bias against female candidates by asking voters whether they would cast their ballots for women if given the opportunity.[11] Overwhelmingly, the data collected have asked voters whether they would vote for women for the presidency rather than whether they would vote for women for municipal council, congress, or some other elected post. Despite the fact that most polls ask about the nation's highest office, voters nonetheless appear willing to vote for women. We would expect that voters would demonstrate more bias against women seeking higher-level office—that is, that they would be more willing to vote for a woman for the town council but less likely to vote for a woman for the presidency. The willingness of respondents to cast their ballots for female presidential candidates should indicate an even greater likelihood to vote for women for other political positions.

Results from the Latin American Women Leadership Study, a poll conducted by Gallup for the Inter-American Dialogue in five Latin American countries, demonstrate that voters are overwhelmingly willing to cast their ballots for women candidates (WLCA 2001). Respondents were asked, "If your party nominated a generally well-qualified person for president (of the country) who happened to be a white woman, would you vote for that person?" More than 9 in every 10 respondents said that they would. The pollsters then asked, "Now thinking of a local election such as mayor, if your party nominated a generally well-qualified person for mayor who happened to be a white woman, would you vote for that person?" Respondents were slightly more likely to vote for a woman for mayor; 94 percent answered that they would, while 93 percent had said that they would vote for a woman for president.[12]

More recent polls have asked respondents about their willingness to vote for women for presidential office in the context of women pursuing the presidency or in other situations that have increased the question's salience.[13] Peruvians in two major cities were asked in 2010 whether they would vote for a woman president. While 89.4 percent said that they would, this percentage had dropped from a high of 95 percent in 2009. The decline may have occurred because respondents associated this question with Keiko Fujimori, daughter of the former dictator who was running for president at the time. Even so, only 8.6 percent of the population said that they would not vote for a woman for president. There was a small gender difference, with 87.4 percent of men saying they would vote for a woman for president but 91.4 percent of women saying the same. There were also differences by age, with 90.1 percent of those under the age of 27 answering that they would vote for a woman and only 83.2 percent of those over 48 answering affirmatively. Peruvians have previously had the opportunity to vote for a woman for the presidency, but no woman has yet won the nation's highest post (Grupo de Opinión Pública de la Universidad de Lima 2010). In 2007, Panamanians were asked whether they would vote for a woman running for president of the country; 66 percent said that they would. Because Panamanians have already had a woman president (Mireya Moscoso 1999–2004), they would probably be more likely to take this question seriously (UNDP 2007). Furthermore, a Uruguayan poll in 2008 asked whether parties should include women in their presidential formulas: 74.4 percent (67.2 percent of men and 80.6 percent of women participating in the poll) thought that parties should do this, while only 3.9 percent disagreed (International IDEA and Department of Political Science of the University of the Republic 2008). At the time, two other countries in the southern cone had women presidents, making this question particularly pertinent.

Another means of uncovering voter bias is to look at polling data that ask respondents whether women should participate in politics, since we can presume that those saying that women do not belong in politics would be unlikely to cast their ballots for women. Furthermore, those respondents who indicate that women should participate politically only under certain circumstances may also be unwilling to vote for women when presented with the opportunity to do so. Polls that ask whether voters believe that women are inequitably represented in politics also serve to highlight discrimination on the part of voters.

Latin Americans are now more likely to believe that women belong in the public sphere. The Latin American Public Opinion Project (LAPOP) asked about women's participation in politics. About 1 in 20 respondents in the Dominican Republic, El Salvador, Nicaragua, and Panama thought that women should not participate in politics. A minority of respondents felt that women should participate in politics only when their home and family obligations allow them to (from a low of 4 percent in Nicaragua to a high of 18.8 percent in the Dominican Republic). The LAPOP polls revealed that the vast majority (84 percent on average) of respondents felt that women should participate in politics "just the same as men" (with 75 percent of respondents in the Dominican Republic and 91 percent of Nicaraguans believing that women should participate equally) (Latin American Public Opinion Project 2008). In a 2007 poll of Panamanians, 79 percent disagreed with the statement "Politics is more for men than for women" (UNDP 2007).

Surveys also indicate that voters believe that women are underrepresented in politics. A survey conducted in 2008 by Uruguay's Universidad de la República, with the assistance of International IDEA, found strong support for women's political participation. Nearly 60 percent of the population believed that women should be better represented in congress, and only 3.4 percent of those polled thought that there should be fewer congresswomen. The poll demonstrated clear gender differences: while 55.9 percent of men thought there should be more women in congress, 73.4 percent of women felt this way. Similarly, greater proportions of men thought that the number of women in congress was adequate (16.9 percent versus 14.3 percent) and that whether a congress member was male or female was irrelevant (23.7 percent versus 8.2 percent). Both men and women with the highest levels of education and from the highest socioeconomic classes were most likely to believe that women needed to be better represented (International IDEA and Department of Political Science of the University of the Republic 2008).

Polling data found that a majority of Chileans believed that women were underrepresented in politics and only 9 percent thought that women were overrepresented politically (Palacios and Martínez 2006: 15).

We can also gauge discrimination against female candidates by examining polling data that seek to measure whether respondents believe that men are better political leaders than women. We would assume that those voters who believe that men are better political leaders are less disposed to vote for women. A demand problem would exist if a significant proportion of voters felt that women are inadequate leaders, since we would expect that opinion would result in voters casting ballots against female candidates. More bias is evident when we examine the results of these types of survey questions. The phrasing of the questions posed by the Latin American Women Leadership Study is, however, more useful. Those questions asked respondents what they would do if their own party nominated a well-qualified woman for office. Respondents may believe that men are generally better leaders but may be unwilling to cross party lines to avoid voting for a woman. Respondents who agree that men are better leaders may also be less likely to exhibit bias against a woman who is described as well qualified.

LAPOP asked respondents whether they agreed, very much agreed, disagreed, or very much disagreed with the statement "Men are better political leaders." The results of this survey are presented in Graph 2.3. Bolivians were most likely to disagree with this statement, with 77.2 percent of them responding with either "disagree" or "very much disagree." Dominicans were much more likely than other Latin Americans to agree with this statement.

In 2004, Latinobarómetro asked respondents in all of the Latin American countries whether they agreed or disagreed with the statement "Men are better political leaders than women." While the LAPOP surveys from 2008 did not include Argentina, Chile, and Venezuela, results from the Latinobarómetro poll indicate that only 24 percent of Argentines, 26 percent of Chileans, and 35 percent of Venezuelans agreed or strongly agreed that men are better political leaders than women (Llanos and Sample 2009).

The available polling data indicate that there is little voter bias against female candidates. Furthermore, there may be a subset of the population that would prefer to vote for women.[14] One Mexican mayor recounted that while on the campaign trail she learned that some people wanted to vote for female candidates: "More than a few times people said to me, 'I'm going to vote for you because you're a woman.' They just don't have as much faith in male politicians anymore. People have the idea that male legislators are corrupt" (Interview, March 25, 2003). Stereotypes about women may make them appear to be more promising candidates in the eyes of some voters. Polls that

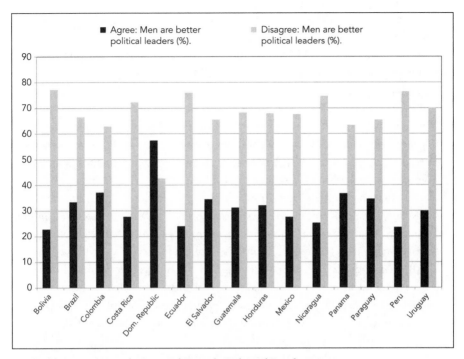

Graph 2.3   Attitudes toward Female Political Leaders

Source: Compiled from Latin American Public Opinion Project (LAPOP), the
AmericasBarometer 2008, available at www.LapopSurveys.org (accessed July 2010).

ask respondents whether women are better at governing than men and those
that ask whether respondents have more confidence in women than in men
can be used to detect a pro-woman bias in the electorate.

When asked if they thought their country would be governed better or
worse if more women were in political office, 55 percent of Mexicans re-
sponded that it would be governed better. Only 10 percent of men and 6
percent of women said that the country would be governed worse if more
women were in office (WLCA 2001). Also in 2001, Chilean women overwhelmingly felt that women were as good as or better than men in public
office. A survey by Grupo Iniciativa Mujer found that 90 percent of women
believed this (Moya 2001).

LAPOP asked respondents in four countries, "At voting time, in whom
are you more confident?" Only in the Dominican Republic were respondents
most likely to answer that they were more confident in men. In El Salvador,
Nicaragua, and Panama, respondents were most likely to say that their confidence in a candidate at voting time would be the same regardless of whether

the candidate was male or female (Latin American Public Opinion Project 2008).

The results of the LAPOP poll indicate that a sizeable proportion of the voting population might prefer female candidates. Stereotypes about women may play a significant role in this greater confidence in female candidates and may ultimately result in a preference for women over men. Earlier polling data by the Latin American Women Leadership Study, which attempted to gauge attitudes about women's abilities to govern, revealed that 66 percent of respondents in five Latin American countries agreed with the statement "Women are more honest than men" (WLCA 2001).

Furthermore, voters are also aware of the obstacles that female candidates face. One poll conducted by the University of Lima revealed that only 56 percent of respondents thought that women and men had equal opportunities in politics (Grupo de Opinión Pública de la Universidad de Lima 2010). Respondents were more likely to believe that women were not entering politics because of machismo (45.8 percent) and a lack of respect for women (21 percent) rather than because of their household obligations (10.5 percent) (Grupo de Opinión Pública de la Universidad de Lima 2010). The fact that nearly half of respondents reported that women and men did not have equal opportunities is also promising for female candidates. Voters who understand the unequal conditions facing men and women in politics may be more willing to vote for women.

Electoral Data

A second means of gauging whether there is a demand problem is to examine electoral data. While voters indicate that they are willing to vote for women, only electoral data can demonstrate whether in practice they are as willing to vote for women candidates as they say they are. When women appear on the ballot, do voters vote for them?

Analyzing election results is undoubtedly problematic. Are voters, for example, expressing gender solidarity by voting for Michelle Bachelet or simply voting for the candidate who is most closely aligned with them? Does the incumbency advantage explain why a female candidate did not win her election, or were the voters of São Paulo expressing their doubts about women's abilities to lead? The lack of high-quality, gender-disaggregated electoral data for Latin America makes teasing out the effects of incumbency, party, financing, and district demographics difficult.

When analyzing only the highest offices, we see that voters do appear willing to vote for women. Most recently, Dilma Rousseff was elected president of Brazil and Laura Chinchilla was elected president of Costa Rica. Rousseff obtained 46.9 percent of the vote in the first round of voting; 14 percentage points separated her from the second-place finisher. Three weeks later in the second round, Rousseff emerged victorious. In Costa Rica, the candidate of the National Liberation Party won her election with 46.78 percent of the vote. The second-place finisher received only 25.15 percent of the vote. Argentines overwhelmingly voted for women for the office of president in 2007. Cristina Fernández de Kirchner won the election with 44.92 percent of the vote. Her closest challenger was also a woman, Elisa Carrió of the Civic Coalition, who received 22.95 percent of the vote. In 2005, Chilean voters had the opportunity to vote for a woman. Michelle Bachelet obtained 45.96 percent of the vote in the first round of the presidential elections (see Morales Quiroga 2008 for an interesting analysis). The second-place finisher obtained 25.41 percent of the vote. These two went on to a second round, in which Bachelet beat Sebastián Piñera with 53.50 percent of the vote to 46.50 percent. Panamanians also elected a woman president. In Panama, Mireya Moscoso won her election with 44.81 percent of the vote, beating Martín Torrijos by 7 percentage points. More than half of Nicaraguans (54 percent) cast their ballots for Violeta Chamorro in 1990. While there have, of course, been women in countries across Latin America who have lost their presidential elections, the fact that women have been elected to the presidency in Brazil, Costa Rica, and other countries indicates that voters are willing to cast their ballots for female presidential candidates.[15]

A recent analysis of legislative elections in the region found that "men perform better than women at the ballot box but the difference, on average, is not considerably large" (Roza 2010a: 127). The ratio of women elected to female candidates was 0.76, while the ratio of men elected to male candidates was 1.1. However, cross-national differences were found; in Chile, female candidates were more likely than male candidates to get elected, but Paraguay and Uruguay showed substantial gender differences. It is important to understand that this analysis was incomplete because it excluded data from smaller parties (data were collected from 79 parties in total) and because these ratios were calculated using only complete data on candidacies and elected officials.[16] While 16 percent of female candidates were elected to the legislature, 22 percent of their male counterparts won office (Roza 2010a: 185).

Data from Chile indicate that that no voter bias exists for national elections. Ríos and Villar found that while 49.5 percent of male candidates to parliament won their elections, 51.3 percent of female candidates were elected (2006). Their findings were later confirmed by Roza (2010a). Recent work on Chilean municipal elections indicates that bias is more likely to exist for executive positions (mayor) than for legislative ones (municipal council member). There was a 0.1 percentage point difference in men's and women's election rates for the 2004 municipal council elections. For the 2008 council elections, when only major party candidates were examined, differences were minor: 32.7 percent of women won their elections compared to 34.6 percent of men. Differences were greater for executive positions, with 19.9 percent of female candidates gaining office in 2008 compared to 29.7 percent of male candidates. Even when only candidates from major parties were analyzed, there still appears to be a bias against female candidates: 32.3 percent of women from these parties won office, as did 40.7 percent of men. This study determined that there was enormous variation in women's electability across the major parties (Hinojosa and Franceschet, forthcoming). However, Hinojosa and Franceschet did not control for incumbency advantage and did not examine the effects of district demographics.

The prohibition on immediate re-election for all elected positions in Mexico makes the Mexican case ideal for testing whether bias exists against women candidates (because no incumbency advantage exists). Data from the 2003 mayoral elections in the state of Mexico found no evidence of bias against women; in fact, women had an advantage and won 44.4 percent of their seats compared to 29.9 percent for male candidates (Hinojosa 2005). Research on municipal elections in Brazil also showed that female candidates were as competitive as male candidates (Setzler 2006, as cited in Roza 2010a: 7).

Academic work presents mixed results on the question of gender solidarity; while Macauley indicates that women receive more of their votes from other women, Molina argues that women are not voting for women (Macauley 1993; Molina 2000). Valenzuela argues that women candidates of parties of the right receive more female votes than male votes, while female candidates of the left obtain greater support from men (Valenzuela 1998). The best data available on the issue of gender solidarity come from Chile, since Chile maintains separate voting places for men and women. The different findings of academics on this topic most likely point to (1) changes over time, (2) differences, as Valenzuela notes, in gender solidarity based on ideology, and (3) the salience of gender to particular elections or candidates.

The research to date indicates that limited bias against female candidates does continue to exist. The data that we have reveal that (1) political party is a powerful predictor of a candidate's ability to win election, (2) the incumbency advantage can exaggerate differences in men's and women's abilities to gain office, and (3) bias against female candidates is waning and has disap-

peared altogether for some elections. Analyses of election results that control
for party, incumbency, and in particular district demographics would shed
even more light on the continued existence of discrimination toward women
candidates. Regardless, the data from Latin America that we do have speak
volumes: the bias that does exist simply cannot explain the extraordinary
underrepresentation of women for all elected positions across the region.

The commonly held view that the lack of women in office is a result of
voter bias has pernicious consequences. First, this belief discourages political
elites from recruiting women for political office. Second, women themselves
are less likely to run for office if they believe that they have little chance of
winning. Third, voters may decide not to vote for a female candidate because
they believe that other voters are unwilling to cast their ballots for women;
rather than "waste" their votes on female candidates, voters may instead opt
for men, whom they believe to be a safer choice.

Conclusion

Women must first become eligibles, then aspirants, and finally candidates
before they can become officeholders. As this chapter demonstrates, the supply of women candidates is large and growing quickly. Data on marriage,
fertility rates, education, and employment indicate that finding female eligibles is not problematic in the Latin American countries. In addition, the
information presented on women's involvement in politics allows us to dis-
cern women's interest in political office holding. The demand for women
candidates reflects what happens in voting booths: are voters biased against
women candidates? Recent polling and electoral data show that voter prejudice cannot account for women's underrepresentation.[17] The two most
often-repeated explanations for women's underrepresentation in politics (that
there are not enough women qualified for office and that voters are unwilling
to cast their ballots for women) cannot explain the deficit of female politicians. The bottleneck in the process of turning a member of the general population into an officeholder, then, is the responsibility of parties, which filter
out aspirants and nominate candidates.

3

How Selection Matters

A Theoretical Framework

> It's all partly our fault. We're the best at supporting our
> party and our [male] candidates during the campaigns,
> doing everything from marching to making enchila-
> das; but then when our candidate wins, we go back
> home—instead of demanding a position within the new
> administration or some political compensation for all our
> hard work.
>
> —BLANCA ÁLVAREZ, prominent member of the Mexican political
> party PAN (quoted in Victoria E. Rodríguez, *Women in Contemporary
> Mexican Politics*)

The discussion of the four stages on the path to office holding in Chapter 2 focuses on the first and last stages. The chapter's analysis of the
first stage debunks supply explanations that blame women's underrepresentation on a lack of "qualified" women to run for office. The data
presented on marriage, fertility, education, employment, and women's political participation from across Latin America indicate that the supply of
women candidates is large and growing quickly. The examination of the
final stage on the path to office holding provides the opportunity to assess
whether women's absence from politics results from voter bias (i.e., whether
it is a demand problem). Polling and electoral data indicate that a minor
amount of prejudice against women continues to exist in the region but that
it alone cannot explain the sizeable deficit of female politicians.

This chapter, then, focuses on the bottlenecks that occur in the second
and third stages, as eligibles become aspirants and later as aspirants transform into candidates, as illustrated in Figure 3.1. These two stages depend
heavily on parties, whose candidate recruitment and selection procedures

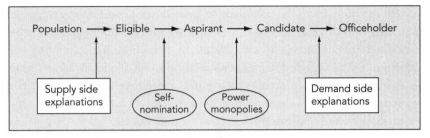

Figure 3.1   The Process of Becoming an Officeholder

routinely filter out potential aspirants and turn aspirants into bona fide candidates. Candidate recruitment refers to the process by which parties attract potential candidates. Candidate selection refers to the "predominantly *extralegal* process by which a political party decides which of the persons legally eligible to hold an elective public office will be designated on the ballot and in election communications as its recommended and supported candidate or list of candidates" (Ranney 1981: 75). These two processes are "so entangled that it is seldom possible to determine where recruitment ends and selection begins" (Siavelis and Morgenstern 2008: 8). If women are losing little ground in the first and final stages on the path to office holding, then there is compelling reason to examine what happens in the "private process" (Field and Siavelis 2008: 623) that makes up the second and third stages.

Candidate recruitment and selection procedures vary along two dimensions. While the first dimension gauges the exclusivity of the selection process (Ranney 1981; Rahat and Hazan 2001), the second dimension assesses the degree of centralization of these selection activities (Ranney 1981; Norris and Lovenduski 1995).[1] The exclusivity dimension describes how open or admissible the selection process is on the basis of the size of the selectorate (i.e., the people who make candidate-selection decisions). Decision making is considered exclusive when the selectorate is small and inclusive when the selectorate is large.[2] For example, if a single party leader handpicks candidates, then those selection procedures are exclusive.[3] Primary elections, on the other hand, are considered inclusive. Even primaries, though, can be more inclusive (open primaries in which any citizen regardless of party affiliation can vote) or less so (closed primaries that require party affiliation and previous attendance at meetings). The centralization dimension assesses where real power lies by determining where decisions are being made, either locally or at the national level. Centralized systems are characterized by decision making that takes place at the highest levels, while in more decentralized systems, those same decisions are made locally.

By categorizing candidate-selection procedures in this way, we can see potential impediments for women as they transition from eligibles to aspirants and from aspirants to candidates. In particular, understanding the degree of exclusivity and centralization of selection processes allows us to examine the effects of obstacles to women's representation in politics. The most significant problems that keep women from becoming aspirants and candidates are self-nomination and power monopolies.

The Problem of Self-Nomination

What does making enchiladas have to do with women's representation in politics? As Blanca Álvarez, a prominent member of Mexico's Partido Acción Nacional (PAN), divulges in the quote that opens this chapter, women do real political work—they organize rallies, they go door to door with their candidates, and they cook for campaign events—but they fail to demand a reward for their labor.

As a male member of Mexico's leftist Partido de la Revolución Democrática (PRD) noted, "Although women do all the structural work . . . they get left behind and they don't put themselves forward as candidates" (quoted in Huerta García and Magar Meurs 2006: 268). This reluctance to request political compensation illustrates one of the most significant problems that women face on the path to elected office. Men are more likely than women to require that their work for a candidate or for a party be recognized with a future candidacy or an appointed post (Multiple interviews). Women's socialization has not led them to expect payback for their hard work and to solicit political compensation. These skills are necessary, however, to self-nomination.

Self-nomination refers to the act of throwing one's own hat into the political ring, and it includes not only the nomination process but also the recruitment process that precedes it. This serves as a contrast to what can be termed external nomination: recruitment and nomination by party individuals, political elites, informal groups, or others. Self-nomination is important in creating aspirants as well as candidates. For women, the need to self-nominate proves disadvantageous.

Understanding why women are unwilling to run for office is difficult "given that many of the decisions and actions that lead an individual to enter an electoral contest are neither public nor fully documented" (Fox and Oxley 2003: 847). Studies in the United States find that women are more likely than men to believe themselves "unqualified and incapable" of running for office (Duerst-Lahti 1998: 25; Fox and Lawless 2004).[4] Fox (1997) has also argued that because of their fear that they will not seem sufficiently "credible," women may be more reluctant to pursue office or they may strive for only positions that are seen as appropriate for women. Research has also demonstrated that women are more likely than men to base their decision to run on self-assessments (Fox and Lawless 2004: 275). Aspirants for political office choose to run in part by evaluating their chances of winning (Stone and Maisel 2003: 1); women's beliefs that they are not as competitive will undoubtedly keep them from pursuing office. Women, then, may be less likely than men to even consider pursuing political careers, even when controlling for such factors as educational levels and occupation (Mellman, Lazarus, Lake, Inc. 1994; Lawless 2003; Fox and Lawless 2004). As one Republican leader in the Ohio legislature learned, "Women are a harder sell because they are more realistic about what their chances are and what you are going to do for them. They ask tougher questions. They are less likely to be risk takers because they have less confidence in themselves" (quoted in Mellman, Lazarus, Lake, Inc. 1994: 103; Moncrief, Squire, and Jewell 2001). A similar sentiment was voiced by Sandra Herrera Flores, a former director of the Political Promotion of Women agency of the Mexican PAN party, who stated that a primary obstacle to women's representation "is that they don't recognize their own abilities to be leaders" (quoted in Huerta García and Magar Meurs 2006: 256).

Recruitment is important for both men and women; studies have demonstrated that being asked to run for office is critical (Rosenstone and Hansen 1993; Verba, Schlozman, and Brady 1995; Mueller 2002; Lawless and Fox 2005).[5] Neither men nor women were likely to consider running if they had not been asked to do so, but if encouraged or requested to do so, men and women were likely to at least consider it (Lawless and Fox 2005; Hinojosa 2009). Lawless and Fox found that those eligibles who received some external push were twice as likely to consider running for office; in other words, eligibles are much more likely to become aspirants if they are encouraged to run or simply asked to do so. Gary Moncrief, Peverill Squire, and Malcolm Jewell found that the largest group of politicians "had been mulling over the notion of running, but had not yet decided what to do, when someone else encouraged them to run" (2001: 39). They call this group the *encouraged* but distinguish these from the *persuaded*, who had not considered running for office until someone encouraged them, and from the *self-starters*, who required no such encouragement. Women are less likely to belong to this group of *self-starters*: "Studies have shown that women are much more likely to run for the state legislature after having been recruited to run; meanwhile, men are more likely to run because they are 'self-starters'—arriving at the decision to become a candidate without external encouragement. Women are much less likely than men to report that the main reason they ran for office was that it was something they always wanted to do" (Sanbonmatsu 2006b: 203–204).

Women's reluctance to self-nominate may be due to lower levels of political ambition. Numerous studies of political ambition in the United States have determined that women are less ambitious than men (Constantini and Craig 1977; Farah and Sapiro 1980; Jennings and Farah 1981; Constantini and Davis Bell 1984; Bledsoe and Herring 1990; Constantini 1990; Carroll 1994; Fox 1997). Women in most societies have traditionally been socialized "into passive and nonpublic roles which provided an internalized deterrence against pursuing public office" (Clark, Clark, and Chou 1993: 494). Fowlkes argues:

> If women socialized into the traditional feminine gender role even considered running for office, they likely perceived a run to include not only the same costs and benefits faced by ambitious men, but also an additional one defined in that early socialization process and reinforced through the adult years. This additional cost would be largely psychological: overcoming perceived opposition to and even expected punishment for adding the role of political officeholder to the traditional feminine gender role. Theoretically, such additional costs would deter many, but not all women from running. (1984: 6)

According to some scholars, those women who do end up pursuing public office experienced some form of counter-socialization.[6] Experiences in both childhood and adulthood, such as having a mother active in politics or a husband who supports women's participation in politics, as well as coming from a high socioeconomic background and being cognizant of reasons why women should be involved in politics, were all theorized to play a role in this counter-socialization. The traditional socialization that steered women away from the public sphere and concentrated their efforts in the private sphere may be changing. For example, Cal Clark, Janet Clark, and Bih-er Chou (1993: 506) found that there was a generational effect when it came to ambition, even when controlling for a number of other important factors. Furthermore, Putnam points out that political interest and ambition can be awakened by both education and membership in the upper classes, and that these factors have the effect of "fostering political skills and self-confidence. To some extent, therefore, the law of increasing disproportion results from self-selection" (Putnam 1976: 40). Despite evidence from the United States that women today are more likely to have their ambition "awakened," women nonetheless lag behind men in notable ways. Lawless and Fox (2005) have confirmed that even the women we expect to be most likely to run for office do not think of themselves as qualified to run and are less likely to become candidates.

How we choose to measure political ambition may affect whether we determine that women are indeed less ambitious than men. For example, Clark, Clark, and Chou (1993) measured ambition by asking female politicians whether they planned to (1) run again for their current office or (2) pursue a different political office. However, Moncrief, Squire, and Jewell categorize ambition in three separate ways. Those with *discrete ambition* serve for short periods before returning to their normal lives. Those with *static ambition* tend to serve in the same position for many years, while those with *progressive ambition* work their way up to higher political office (Moncrief, Squire, and Jewell 2001: 23). Moncrief, Squire, and Jewell describe those with *discrete ambition* as citizen-legislators.[7] The ways in which we measure ambition may unwittingly reflect not women's interest in politics or their desire to continue as political representatives, but rather (1) the realities of women's responsibilities within their families and (2) whether women are less likely than men to express ambition, since ambition is perceived as a masculine trait.

Women's lower levels of ambition are not indicative of a lack of political interest or knowledge. Political interest may have less to do with who chooses to run for office than previously considered. Lawless and Fox (2005) found that despite the fact that men were less interested than women in local politics (31 percent to 41 percent), they were more likely than their female counterparts to have considered running for office (59 percent to 43 percent). Elder has presented data that call into question the importance of political knowledge in explaining the lack of women running for office; her study of high school students indicates that while there is no knowledge gap between these boys and girls, there is a significant difference in ambition: while less than 12 percent of girls said they would consider running for office, slightly more than 28 percent of boys said they would (2004: 38).

For women, then, self-nomination is a significant obstacle to office holding, since they are more likely than men to believe they are unqualified to pursue office, more likely to make decisions based on their own self-assessment, and less likely to be recruited. Women's unwillingness to self-nominate only increases the importance of external nomination, but women are "significantly less likely than men to receive a political source's encouragement to run for office" (Fox and Lawless 2004: 275), despite the fact that this encouragement appears to be more important to women (see, for example, Erickson 1993). Lawless and Fox's study of women in the United States discovered that 43 percent of men, but only 32 percent of women in their sample, were encouraged or recruited to run for office (2005). The lack of external nomination that women receive is likely to "solidify women's self-perceptions" that they are not qualified for public office (Fox and Lawless 2004). Candidate recruitment and selection processes are especially problematic in light of women's unwillingness to self-nominate.

The Problem of Power Monopolies

Power monopolies are small, informal groups of people connected by kinship, social, or business associations, which concentrate power. In Latin America, these networks can often be traced to the nineteenth century, when "many notable families formed networks through which they and their allies extended their power into government—of town, city, region, or nation—and became the ultimate arbiters of its direction" (Balmori, Voss, and Wertman 1984: 6).[8] Entrance into these monopolies is typically guarded and requires sponsorship. Women were historically excluded from these types of associations and continue to be less likely to belong to them.

These networks go by different names.[9] In the United States, these groups are often called old boy networks. The same term is applied in England, where those informal organizations are based on attendance at one of the top public schools. The equivalent term in Chile is a *club de Tobi*,[10] a reference to an old American cartoon whose central character, a little girl, was excluded from participating in her friend's club. The term *traditional elite* has been used by Hagopian to describe "closed circles of power holders that dominate a range of state institutions and political processes, and that concentrate political as well as economic power within a limited number of families" (Hagopian 1996: 68), although she uses the term to refer strictly to conservative forces within society.[11] In the case of early-twentieth-century Russia, one scholar described these power monopolies as "informal cliques held together by personal ties that eventually became centered around organizationally powerful party secretaries acting as patrons" (Rigby 1981 as quoted in Easter 2000: 28). In Mexico, the term *camarilla* has been used to refer to personal cliques, "small, informal groups whose most successful member advances the careers of his own circle, whose advancement depends on the leader's own professional mobility. Camarillas are often built on mentor-disciple relationships, but they tend to be exclusive to public life" (Camp 2002: 28). These power monopolies regularly play a role in candidate recruitment and selection.

These monopolies prove disadvantageous to women because (1) elites are likely to belong to these monopolies and to use these groups as a recruitment pool, and since women are less likely to be a part of these groups, women are less likely to end up as candidates when these networks have power, and

(2) women are less likely than men to benefit from the political mobilization and financing that these groups provide, again because they are less likely to belong to these informal organizations. These power monopolies are invaluable for political mobilizing and campaign financing. An individual's network connections are a form of social capital (Bourdieu 1986). A lack of access to these monopolies can keep women from becoming aspirants and candidates—perhaps knowing or believing that they lack the resources necessary for a campaign—and even keep them from winning seats, if they do end up running for office. Sanbonmatsu (2006b) notes that social networks in the United States remain gender-segregated; as she explains, "The upshot of these differences in social networks is that men tend to know other men. . . . [T]he leaders who recruit candidates tend to look to whom they know—people they do business with, people they play golf with, and so on" (Sanbonmatsu 2006b: 201–202). Research has found that women politicians in the United States have less contact with other political leaders than their male counterparts (Moore and White 2000). Little research has examined networks in Latin American politics.[12]

Scholars have long hypothesized about the role that networking plays in women's political underrepresentation. Gehlen's study of the U.S. Congress found that male congressional members thought women incapable of being elected to important party positions because women did not have the "informal relationships" that such leaders require (Gehlen 1969: 39–40). Moore and White (2000) confirmed that women did indeed lack these contacts. Women are unlikely to belong to networks that wield power. Studies done on the United States have noted that women are more likely than men to be a part of networks that include family members and neighbors (Marsden 1987; Moore 1990; Stoloff, Glanville, and Bienenstock 1999). Furthermore, networks populated by large numbers of women are likely to be ineffectual. Research on U.S. racial and ethnic minorities participating in the paid labor force indicates that "using personal contacts can be disadvantageous for minorities if the personal contact used is a fellow minority" (Stoloff, Glanville, and Bienenstock 1999: 94). Jennifer Stoloff, Jennifer Glanville, and Elisa Bienenstock argue that the role of gender may be similar and urge diversity in women's networks for the following reasons:

> First, gender diversity could represent access to a larger social world of contact than a gender-segregated network. Second, men have stronger and deeper connections to the labor market than women. Men occupy more powerful positions within the workforce than women, and may represent a resource for women when present in their social

networks. When a woman works in a male-dominated occupation, a male alter may be particularly helpful. (1999: 94–95)

The effect of these networks, then, is political homogeneity. Not only do party leaders prefer candidates who are similar to them (Niven 1998), but these leaders are also likely to recruit from a pool of people whom they are already familiar with (i.e., they are more likely to draw from within their own networks). Furthermore, candidates backed by power monopolies have tremendous resources, making them formidable opponents.

Explaining the Effects of Candidate-Selection Processes

Self-nomination and power monopolies keep women from aspiring to office and limit female candidacies, effectively curbing women's entry into politics. However, the selection processes that a party uses determine how acutely the problems of self-nomination and power monopolies will be felt, as Figure 3.2 illustrates.

The more exclusive selection processes diminish the importance of self-nomination and therefore its effects on female candidacies. When decisions are being made exclusively, a very small number of people are involved in candidate selection; typically, party leaders handpick candidates, thereby circumventing self-nomination. Conversely, with inclusive selection processes, women's reluctance to propose their own candidacies will have unfortunate effects for overall levels of female representation.

The centralization of decision making also has significant effects. Castles (1981: 25) argues that women are more likely to emerge as candidates when selection is in the hands of national rather than local elites; similarly, other scholars have noted that centralization of candidate selection is more conducive to promoting women's political participation (Beckwith 1989; Norris and Lovenduski 1995) or that national leaders are more concerned with women's underrepresentation (Schmidt 2006). Leijenaar argues that this is because regional party leaders are likely to place their own preferred (and often male) candidates and because national leaders are "more concerned about female-male balance than are the local or regional branches" (1993: 222). Matland and Studlar share the same concern that the local level fails to carry out the wishes of a national elite concerned with gender equity (1996: 709). I argue that centralized candidate selection has these effects because it dilutes the importance of local power monopolies. When centralized decision making takes place, as happens in both exclusive-centralized and

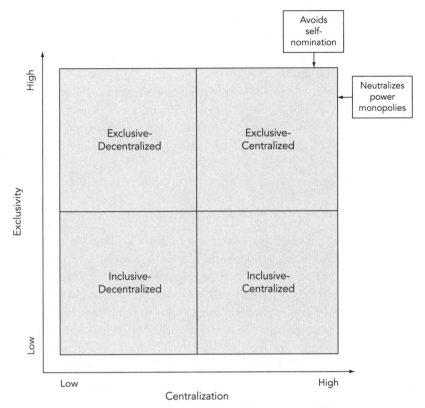

Figure 3.2   Candidate Selection and Obstacles to Women's Representation

inclusive-centralized selection methods, decisions are typically made beyond the reach of these local power monopolies. Decentralized candidate selection allows power monopolies greater say in decision making.

The exclusivity and centralization dimensions operate at different points in the process of transforming eligibles into aspirants and aspirants into candidates. Self-nomination comes into play in the second stage of Figure 3.1, as eligibles become aspirants. The power of networks is evident in the third stage, as aspirants become candidates.

Classifying parties on the basis of the dimensions of exclusivity and centralization yields four types of candidate selection: exclusive-decentralized, exclusive-centralized, inclusive-decentralized, and inclusive-centralized, as seen in Figure 3.2. When candidate selection is both exclusive and centralized, as shown in the upper-right square of Figure 3.2, then potential officeholders skip the second and third stages of selection: eligibles become candidates. By avoiding the obstacles to female candidacies posed by self-nomination and power monopolies, parties using exclusive-centralized selection can increase their percentages of female candidates and ultimately officeholders. The candidate-selection methods that parties use have significant consequences for women's representation.

In the section that follows, I explain how the theoretical framework outlined previously can be useful in prognosticating the effects of particular selection procedures on female representation, and I elaborate on the observable implications of each of the four selection types.

The Four Types

Inclusive-Centralized Candidate Selection

Inclusive-centralized candidate selection incorporates a potentially large selectorate. Decision making is done at the regional or national level rather than locally. In this type of system, a meeting might be called that would be open to all members. Members would be allowed to put forth nominees. A candidate would then be chosen through either voting or some form of discussion leading to general consensus. The decision reached by the party membership would still require approval from a higher level, perhaps the state party office or the national office. This higher level is aware of the decisions that are taken at lower levels and can choose to intervene by either proposing its own preferred candidate during the initial meeting or by replacing the candidate chosen by the party membership with a candidate of its own choosing.

Inclusive-centralized candidate selection can disadvantage women as they attempt to become officeholders. Because this process is inclusive, eligibles have to become aspirants: they must make the decision to pursue office and promote their own pre-candidacies by announcing their intentions to seek the post, encouraging other party members to participate in decision making, and obtaining recognition and support from party members and elites operating at the national level. The requirement for self-nomination leads to fewer female nominees, despite the fact that the more centralized decision making would prove useful; since those at the highest echelons of power must approve final decisions, the importance of local power monopolies is thereby decreased.

Inclusive-Decentralized Candidate Selection

When inclusive-decentralized selection methods are used, the selectorate can be quite large.[13] Decision making takes place at the local level. Primaries are one type of inclusive-decentralized selection, though not the only form of such decision making. This type of selection might involve a time period in which members may register themselves as pre-candidates, followed by a campaign period in which they try to gain support by disseminating information about themselves and their platforms. A primary election follows, which may be open to party members, party members and independents, or perhaps all voters in the district. Voting and vote counting proceed in an official manner. In many cases, results are sent to the national party office, and while the national office may technically have the power to override these results, such a scenario would occur only under extraordinary circumstances.

Although inclusive-decentralized selection is often perceived as the most "democratic" system for selecting candidates,[14] this process might be most disadvantageous to women. Because women are less likely to believe that they would make strong candidates and more likely to rely on external encouragement to launch a campaign, in a situation such as this where they must self-nominate, women's potential candidacies are undermined. Decentralized decision making places greater power in the hands of power monopolies, which are less likely to support women's campaigns. The use of these types of selection systems, then, proves doubly problematic to women, who must contend with both self-nomination and traditional networks.

Exclusive-Decentralized Candidate Selection

Exclusive-decentralized candidate selection is characterized by a limited selectorate and decision making that occurs locally rather than at the national level. In the case of a municipal election, exclusive-decentralized selection might take the form of an outgoing mayor handpicking his successor. Alternatively, in the case of a parliamentary election, two or three local elites, such as the regional party president or elected officials from that area, might tap an individual for office. In this type of selection, personal connections—and hence local power networks—are important. Camp writes of the value of these personal connections:

> Both recruitment and advancement are guided by the same unwritten rules. Networks of friends evolve into small informal groups. Within a political environment, these groups perform socializing functions, reinforcing certain values and political behavior, as well as recruitment functions, typically selecting individuals who comport with their values, who will enhance their group's capabilities, and from whom the group can obtain influence. (1995: 13)

The lack of self-nomination would prove useful to women, but the emphasis on local monopolies would undermine women's potential candidacies.

Exclusive-decentralized candidate selection is disadvantageous to women because of the need for support from these networks.

Exclusive-Centralized Candidate Selection

Exclusive-centralized candidate selection involves decisions that are made by a very small group, or possibly a single individual, at the national level. Exclusive-centralized selection might involve the national office fielding representatives to identify potential candidates. Once possible candidates have been identified, the selectorate would choose among these. In the case of a municipal-level election, a senator from a particular region might be asked to find candidates. He might notice the work of a certain individual in one of the towns that he represents and ask her to run for office. This decision might be rubber-stamped at a local party meeting. In choosing a parliamentary candidate, the party president might ask the outgoing officeholder to find a suitable replacement. She might come up with a list of four individuals, who would be vetted by the party president. The party president would then introduce the new candidate at a party event.

Candidate selection that is exclusive-centralized can benefit women. Because decision making takes place at the national level, it is disconnected from local monopolies, allowing the selectorate to make decisions based on electoral concerns and expected outcomes. The selectorate is effectively disconnected from these local networks, allowing not only women but also other traditional outsiders a chance to enter politics. Women are also advantaged by exclusive-centralized selection because they do not need to self-nominate. Eliminating these twin obstacles to women's advancement should result in increased female candidacies. However, this will be the case only if the selectorate is not actively discriminating against women and is not intentionally endeavoring to keep women out of politics. Removing the obstacles posed by self-nomination and power networks will prove advantageous for women even if parties and party elites are not attempting to increase women's representation in politics.

The classification of a party's selection processes is not static. Candidate selection can vary both spatially and temporally (leading scholars to describe selection processes in Colombia as "persistently impermanent party procedures") (Taylor, Botero Jaramillo, and Crisp 2008: 287). A party can employ a variety of selection procedures simultaneously: for example, using exclusive-centralized selection for senatorial candidates but inclusive-decentralized methods to choose mayoral candidates. A party could use exclusive-

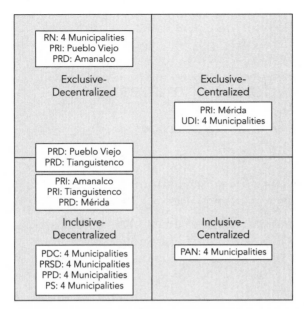

Figure 3.3   Candidate Selection in Four Municipalities

PAN, Partido Acción Nacional; PDC, Partido Demócrata Cristiano; PPD, Partido por la Democracia; PRD, Partido de la Revolución Democrática; PRI, Partido Revolucionario Institucional; PRSD, Partido Radical Social Demócrata; PS, Partido Socialista; RN, Renovación Nacional; UDI, Unión Demócrata Independiente.

centralized selection in 2006 but adopt primaries for the 2010 elections. Similarly, candidate selection itself is malleable, and reforms can be adopted that would mitigate the effects of self-nomination and power networks, thereby eliminating substantial obstacles to female candidacies, an issue that is discussed in greater length in Chapter 9.

Having established that the problem lies in the processes of candidate recruitment and selection, we move to an analysis of these issues in practice in the chapters that follow. Chapters 4 to 6 present further data on each of the four types in countries from across Latin America to demonstrate how parties whose practices avoid self-nomination and power networks increase women's representation, while those employing methods that do nothing to avoid these problems have failed to field more female candidacies. Figure 3.3 provides a look at the selection procedures used across each of the cases, which the three chapters that follow discuss.

4

The Paradox of Primaries

Inclusive-Decentralized Selection

> Because we've had so many [primary] elections, we haven't
> had time to get any work done.
>
> —PRI municipal party president (Interview, May 26, 2003)

olitical primaries have been adopted en masse in recent years (see Field
and Siavelis 2008 for examples from across the globe and Alcántara
Sáez 2002 for information about Latin America) in response to the
consensus that primaries are a means of increasing "openness and internal
party democracy, and therefore normatively preferable to traditional, less inclusive methods of candidate selection" (Carey and Polga-Hecimovich 2004:
1).[1] Inclusive selection is seen as preferable because democratization results
from "widening participation in the process, i.e., when the selectorate that
is adopted following a reform of the candidate selection method is more inclusive than the previous one" (Rahat and Hazan 2001: 309). There is also
an "implicit assumption that selection made at the local level is more democratic, as the decision is decentralized to those who will be represented by
the candidate, and that the more persons eligible to participate in the selection process the better" (Cross 2008: 598).[2] In other words, the belief is
that if more people participate in decision making, then the process is more
democratic. Scholars have noted that "success in a primary might also validate the democratic credentials of a candidate that would likely have been
awarded his party's nomination under any procedure" (Carey and Polga-
Hecimovich 2006: 534). It is perhaps not surprising, then, that parties in
Argentina, Brazil, Chile, Colombia, Costa Rica, the Dominican Republic,
El Salvador, Guatemala, Honduras, Mexico, Nicaragua, Panama, Paraguay,
Uruguay, and Venezuela have all experimented with primaries, since, "For
many analysts, primary elections are the only reform available to parties if

they really want to democratize" (Lara Rivera 2006: 16, as cited in Baldez 2007: 70).[3]

Theorists may wish to debate just how democratic primaries are relative to other forms of candidate selection, but it is important to recognize that we cannot be certain about how democratic so-called primaries really are in practice. This chapter presumes that the electoral contests convoked by parties are in fact true primaries, while Chapter 5 discusses some candidate-selection methods that were cloaked as primaries but did not function as such.[4]

The most common explanation for the switch to primaries is that parties wish to appeal to voters by increasing voter involvement and decreasing the fraud often found in convention systems (Hopkin 2001; Ware 2002).[5] Primaries can be a means of invigorating a party that is facing electoral difficulties by giving it a new democratic face (Katz and Mair 1995; Hopkin 2001), which is particularly important in Latin America because of declining citizen support. Primaries can also alter the internal balance of power within a party and can be a powerful means of introducing change to a political party (Hopkin 2001). Scholars have also argued that parties find primaries attractive because these are likely to produce more electable candidates (Serra 2011).[6]

Work on Argentina demonstrates that incumbents' ability to run for re-election and the status of the party nationally explain the use of primaries for selecting congressional candidates (De Luca, Jones, and Tula 2002). Poiré presents a different story based on the Mexican case: party leaders will open up candidate selection in an effort to keep strong potential candidates in the party and, in this way, improve the party's chances of winning election (Poiré 2002). Poiré argues that strong aspirants will defect if passed over for candidacies; because primaries allow them to *compete* for the nomination, they are less likely to take their talents to other parties. Similarly, Bruhn argues that party leaders are forced into using primaries "to resolve conflicts of ambition" (2010: 43). As Galderisi and Ezra explain:

> While enhancing the attractiveness of a major-party nomination, a democratic primary system also removed a major justification for partisan infidelity. Losses would henceforth be democratically decided defeats; nominations could no longer be viewed as the machinations of backroom politicians, at least not visibly. Vanquished opponents, subsequently, could not as easily justify a decision to embark on an independent or minor-party run for office as they once could. (2001: 14–15)

In a similar vein, others have argued that political elites may want primaries—even if they do not expect their preferred candidate to win—because primaries provide a very public assessment of the strength of their group, which can be useful later when dividing political spoils (Kemahlioglu, Weitz-Shapiro, and Hirano 2009: 343).

Primaries can prove desirable to parties because they increase accountability between politicians and rank-and-file party members and allow members to participate more actively in their parties (Hopkin 2001). Some have argued that the use of primaries not only means that candidates will hew more closely to the party line, thereby "anchoring the parties more tightly in their respective ideological spaces," but may also create greater responsiveness to emerging issues (Hopkin 2001: 346).

Because primaries advantage those with personal political resources, they may actually "reduce the ability of party leaders to make demands upon their politicians, and make the attainment of cohesion a complicated feat" (Poiré 2002). Primaries also increase the costs associated with campaigning; some scholars have hypothesized that officeholders will become more dependent on "the sectors that contributed to their campaign financing" if primaries are used (Gallo 2006: 30). Furthermore, primaries may benefit those with the most money to spend rather than the most electorally viable candidates (Hernández Valle 2008: 489). While Colomer (2002) finds no electoral advantage for those candidates chosen via primaries and Bruhn finds that primaries (or, more generally, what she terms "internal elections") do not lead to more successful candidates (Bruhn 2010), Carey and Polga-Hecimovich (2004) do find evidence that candidates chosen via primary enjoy an electoral bonus.[7]

Primaries come with an additional set of disadvantages for parties. Some scholars argue that primaries, by usurping one of the essential functions from parties, can "lead to political parties effectively disappearing as cohesive organizations" (Hopkin 2001: 347).[8] Furthermore, primaries may exacerbate divides within parties. While the expectation is that party members will unite behind the winning candidate after the primary, in practice, party members may be either so disappointed with the results or so incensed by the actions or words of the pre-candidate that they will either abstain from voting or cross party lines (Ezra 2001; Huneeus 2008). Bruhn found that Mexican party leaders tried to assess "the risk of divisions as a result of holding an internal election against the risk of party divisions as a result of not holding one" when deciding whether to use primaries. She writes, "When the question was asked how the party chooses whether or not to hold a primary in a given district, the conversation rarely turned to the need to select better candidates or to reach out to new social groups. Instead, party leaders usually referred to the demand for internal elections" (Bruhn 2010: 42).

Furthermore, primaries can strain the organizational and financial capacity of a party. In Peru, parties are supposed to choose presidential and vice presidential candidates, as well as candidates for the presidential, vice presidential, and council member positions for the regional level and all mayoral and municipal council candidates, via primary. Filling 14,369 candidacies using primaries proved onerous (Tuesta Soldevilla 2008: 847). Bruhn compellingly argues that the primaries of the Partido de la Revolución Democrática (PRD) were too burdensome for the organizationally weak party (2010: 45–46), and she further explains that parties in Mexico are more likely to use primaries in safe districts because that is where they "are better funded and better organized" (2010: 42). Primaries may be far too expensive for smaller parties (Carey and Polga-Hecimovich 2006).

The literature on primaries forecasts mixed effects for politicians who engage in primaries. Primaries may be beneficial to winning candidates because they increase media coverage, legitimate a candidate, and "can provide an inexperienced candidate with an opportunity to fine-tune his or her skills before facing the general election opponent" (Ezra 2001: 49). But primaries also have the potential to create substantial negative publicity early in the campaign season and deplete nominees' campaign funds months before the general elections (Ezra 2001: 49).

The exclusivity of primaries—and hence a party's position on the exclusivity continuum—is dependent on whether they are open or closed. While open primaries allow all citizens who are registered voters a vote in the primary, closed primaries allow only party members or sympathizers to cast a ballot. Open primaries can lead to crossover voting, which occurs when a person votes in the primary of a party to whom he or she does not belong (sincerely or strategically). When a voter participates in a primary for a party that he does not affiliate with because he wishes to vote for the candidate that he hopes to cast his ballot for in the general election, he is engaging in sincere crossover voting. If a voter with no intention of voting for a party in the general election nonetheless participates in that party's primary and casts her ballot for a candidate she believes will be the weaker candidate in the general election, then her crossover voting is strategic (Kanthak and Morton 2001). Party members and candidates are often worried about strategic voting in primaries. Both open- and closed-list primaries have been used in Latin America. The Unión Cívica Radical (UCR) in Argentina, the Frente Sandinista de Liberación Nacional (FSLN) in Nicaragua, and the Partido Revolucionario Institucional (PRI) in Mexico have all used open primaries at some point to choose their presidential candidates (see Freidenberg 2003). Meanwhile, such diverse parties as the Partido Colorado in Paraguay, the Partido Justicialista in Argentina, the PRD in Mexico, and the Partido Conservador in Colombia have all utilized closed primaries for choosing presidential candidates.

The ill effects of primaries may partly explain why they are sometimes not applied and also why "it is not uncommon for parties to go back and forth between primaries" and other selection procedures (Serra 2011: 22).[9] Alcántara Sáez warns that "strictly speaking" when primary results are ignored, then a real primary election has not taken place. The results of primary elections are sometimes disregarded, as in Nicaragua when the FSLN leadership chose Juan Manuel Caldera as its vice presidential candidate rather than the winner of the open primary (Alcántara Sáez 2002: 27–28). Primaries are sometimes used for only a short period of time and then abandoned (and sometimes re-adopted); for example, the Unión Civica Radical (UCR) in Argentina held primaries to choose a presidential candidate in 1989, 1995, and 2003, but not for the 1999 elections. After years of experimenting with primaries, the PRI did not use primaries to choose its candidates for the 2006 legislative elections; the other two major parties in Mexico witnessed serious declines in the use of primaries: the Partido Acción Nacional (PAN) saw a 40 percent decrease in the use of internal elections, and the PRD's use of primaries decreased by more than half (Bruhn 2010: 45). The use of primaries for selecting some candidates is legally mandated in several countries of the region, including Bolivia, Paraguay, Uruguay, and Venezuela, but even then parties often fail to use primaries (Gallo 2006; Brewer-Carías 2008: 1009).

The Paradox of Primaries

The paradox of primaries is that while they may be more "democratic," they pose a significant obstacle to women's participation. It is essential to study any gender bias that occurs because of the use of primaries in part because primaries may decide the election; when a district is regularly won by the same party or a municipality has traditionally been ruled by one coalition, the primary election becomes more important than the general election. As primaries become more commonplace in the region, it becomes critical that we understand their gendered effects.

Work by Baldez indicates that primaries in Mexico do disadvantage women candidates (2004b). Based heavily on the finding that women and men are equally likely to win primary elections, much of the current research that has been done on the United States now argues that primaries do not disadvantage women. However, Pearson and Lawless point out that primary election results are not the only way to assess whether primaries are disadvantageous to women. It is also necessary to examine whether men and women enter primaries in equal numbers and the level of competition that male and female incumbents and challengers attract. After taking these elements into account, Pearson and Lawless conclude that women face larger hurdles in primary elections than men. They explain:

> Only the most qualified women may be willing to take on such a battle, winnowing women from the field before the contest begins. It is, therefore, not surprising that the women who emerge from primaries to compete in general elections are more likely to have electoral experience and raise more money than their male counterparts (Pearson and McGhee): to make it through the primary process, women must be stronger candidates, or at least candidates who are willing to endure greater challenges than their male counterparts face. (2006: 21)

Pearson and Lawless state that "the candidate-centered primary process may be to women's detriment" because women are "less likely than men to be part of the political establishment, as well as less likely than men to receive encouragement and support, however limited, from party officials, elected leaders, and political activists" (2006: 2).

Primaries are problematic for women because they require potential candidates to self-nominate and increase the influence of local monopolies of power. Self-nomination is obligatory for primaries; at minimum, to become a pre-candidate, an aspirant would need to formally register her interest, though often she would need to make her intentions known long before this. Women's reluctance to self-nominate will keep them from office holding.

Furthermore, primaries increase the power of local monopolies. The clientelistic practices that continue in Latin America give local monopolies incredible influence over candidacies. As Helmke and Levitsky point out, "In a context of pervasive clientelism, where primary participation is limited largely to those who are induced to vote by local brokers, such elections are won not by ideological candidates but by those with the largest political machine" (2004: 726). That situation is still a reality of municipal politics in both Chile and Mexico. While, in principle, primaries are won by the most talented political contender, in practice, primaries are won by the pre-candidate who is able to muster the most people to show up on the day of the election. During her study of primaries in Mexico, Bruhn heard from a former PRD secretary that "the candidate who wins the primary is frequently either the richest candidate or the local cacique, not necessarily the best or the most electable" (quoted in Bruhn 2010: 27).

In addition to providing individuals who will cast ballots in primary elections, local monopolies can provide financing for primaries. Participation in primaries routinely requires that aspirants use their own funds, since there are no party contributions for these elections. General elections can attract campaign contributions, as can well-heeled primary elections for national-level office. As my interviewees in Chile and Mexico indicated, the financing for primaries comes either from the aspirant's own savings or from local networks.

Financial considerations need to be taken into account in devising selection rules and recruitment and nomination policies.[10] First, as Chapter 2 indicates, nowhere in Latin America are women's wages on par with men's; furthermore, the wage gap actually widens for women who pursue higher education. Second, women are more likely to be unemployed and underemployed, since many companies will downsize a woman rather than a man, who is presumed to be the family breadwinner. Third, because Latin American women are less likely to control the finances in their families, they may be less willing to spend money that they consider to belong to their families on their own political careers. The literature from the United States demonstrates that women are less likely than men to spend their resources to start or further their political careers, meaning that women may be less disposed to run for office if it means they have to go through added expenses, such as primaries (Burns, Schlozman, and Verba 2001).[11] Fourth, women are also less likely to have the types of business connections that result in campaign financing because they are less apt to be in the professions most conducive to these types of connections.[12] Additionally, the early negative publicity that primaries produce can be particularly damaging to women, who are less likely to have early funding and for whom this early negative publicity can result in a subsequent inability to raise funds (WEDO 2007). Because gender is more salient in primaries than in general elections, this early negative publicity may focus on the candidate's gender and play on stereotypes. Finally, even women who do belong to local power monopolies that could provide campaign funding may be less willing than men to ask for contributions and consequently may receive less money for their campaigns. Women may therefore abstain from participating in primaries because of the financial costs.

There is another paradox to primaries: although they employ a gender-equitable selectorate—generally half of voters in primaries are women—primaries produce gender-inequitable results.[13] Gender discrimination is more likely to exist in primaries than in general elections. In primary elections, voters may use gender stereotypes to differentiate among candidates since party identification is constant (Matland and King 2002; McDermott 1998).

The following section uses data from my fieldwork to illustrate how inclusive-decentralized candidate selection works in practice and the effects that this type of selection has on women's political representation. I discuss each of the four parties of the Concertación—the Chilean center-left coalition that maintained itself in power from the end of the Pinochet dictatorship until 2010—as well as three different cases from Mexico. The first two cases are examples of candidate selection from the PRI, while the last describes the candidate-selection procedures of the PRD in the city of Mérida.

The Partido Socialista in Chile

The Socialist Party re-emerged after being stamped out by the Pinochet dictatorship. The Partido Socialista (PS) has softened ideologically since the return to democracy and now has a "catch-all, electoralist orientation" (Roberts 1998). It nonetheless maintains a strongly pro-feminist agenda and is concerned with women's political underrepresentation. However, the party has never had a female president. Isabel Allende served as vice president of the PS in 1990 and as acting president in 1993. The PS established a vice presidency for women's issues, which exists at the national, regional, and municipal levels. In many municipalities, however, this vice presidency went unfilled or, in some cases, was filled by a man (Multiple interviews). Women's presence in appointed positions has grown dramatically in recent years, under the two Socialist administrations of Ricardo Lagos (2000–2006) and Michelle Bachelet (2006–2010). Women's share of ministries rose from 3 of 19 ministries in 1999 to 5 of 16 ministries under the Lagos administration, and was briefly at parity under Bachelet. The percentage of subsecretaries also increased dramatically between 1999 and 2000—from 16 percent to 32 percent. More of the 95 ambassadorships went to women in 2000: 7.5 percent compared to 4.3 percent in 1999. Women were 7.7 percent of intendants (there are a total of 13 intendancies, one for each of the 13 regions) in 1999 and 23.1 percent in 2001, reflecting President Lagos's commitment to increasing women's representation. The percentage of governors (an appointed position) similarly increased from 10 percent in 1999 to 30 percent in 2001 (SERNAM 2001). As of 2005, the party had 10 deputies and five senators, but only one of these was a woman: Isabel Allende, daughter of the former president. As of 1996, the PS's membership was nearly 42 percent female, but the gender makeup of its leadership continued to be guided by quota goals (Muñoz D'Albora and Wojciechowski Levine 1996). By 1989, the PS already had a 20 percent quota for women in place for internal elections. In 1996, the party voted to increase the quota rule to 30 percent in the internal party elections of 1997 and to 40 percent in the internal elections of 1999 and 2001. These percentages were to be used as goals when nominating candidates.

Members of leftist parties were willing to acknowledge their parties' shortcomings. Socialists noted that work still needed to be done in order to arrive at gender equity and mentioned the party's desires to increase women's participation and representation in the party. As one woman explained, "It's easy to discriminate against women. Men can simply say, 'There are no capable women' or 'Women don't want to be candidates.' It's much easier to drop a female candidate than a male candidate. They will find a way to do it. They'll find some way, even if it's not part of the formal process" (Interview, August 6, 2002). Other women also complained that the party was not supportive; as one PS politician who had served as an intendant announced, "My party did not accept me as a national candidate, even though my region recognized that I was the natural choice" (Interview, August 12, 2002). Others argued that the party inherently disadvantaged women because "women don't have economic support" (Interview, August 6, 2002). One important PS woman politician stated, "When women are equal, then they'll have equal posts to men" (Interview, September 9, 2002), indicating that women's inequitable representation in candidacies and in elected positions was evidence of their unequal treatment within the party.

The PS has employed varying processes to choose candidates for national elections. Since the return to democracy, the PS has used both closed primaries and appointment by the party's central committee to designate candidates, though "the process has been primarily characterized by the strong influence of the local party organization in selecting candidates" (Navia 2004: 15). The same decentralized procedures are in effect when choosing municipal candidates; those processes are explained in the following section.

Candidate Selection for Municipal Office

The PS uses inclusive-decentralized selection.[14] Party members nominate potential candidates. The list of possible names is voted on at a party meeting by all members in attendance. A PS councilman in the medium-sized city of Peñaflor explained that there were about 250 party members in the municipality and that, at most, 30 percent of these would participate in internal voting (Interview, October 24, 2002). Active members of the party find it problematic that inactive party members nonetheless retain the right to vote. As this chapter later clarifies, primary elections do sometimes see high voting rates, which indicate that inactive members (or possibly nonparty members in the case of open primaries) are voting when mobilized to do so.

The inclusive-decentralized system that the PS was using also led to a clear failure to increase women's representation in municipal candidacies. Only 17 percent of candidacies in the 2000 elections went to women. This is roughly equivalent to the percentage of women on the party's national directorate, indicating that the party has been unable to meet its own goals for women's representation at multiple levels. Although the party has a commitment to increasing women's representation and affirmative action statements, it managed to place fewer women into candidacies than either of the parties of the right. An ideological commitment to increasing women's representation within the party is obviously not enough, and the party's stated gender goals for external elections (in lieu of gender quotas) have not translated into an increase in female candidacies. Only 1 of the 40 female mayors in the country was a PS member, and less than 15 percent of the party's municipal officeholders were women.

Self-nomination is critical to candidacy in the PS. Interviewees remarked that women were less willing to come forward as candidates—a female governor maintained that she knew of only a couple of women in the Concertación who were willing to run for mayor: "No one believes that she can be mayor; perhaps [she can be a] councilwoman. They ask themselves, 'How can I compete?'" (Interview, September 9, 2002). Informal selection further disadvantaged women aspirants. Individuals who want to be candidates can circumvent the formal process for selection and approach the regional level directly instead of going through the municipal party office. But most women do not do this "because it's not the way it's supposed to be done" (Interview, August 6, 2002). These informal approaches place an even greater emphasis on self-nomination and self-promotion.

The Partido por la Democracia in Chile

The Partido por la Democracia (PPD) was formed in 1987 by previous members of the Socialist Party in an effort to bring about the end of the dictatorship through participation in the 1988 plebiscite. Members of the PS initially held dual membership with the PPD, but in 1992 the parties decided to have their members choose between them (Valenzuela and Scully 1997). Because the party was started for "instrumental reasons," it is often accused (as even the party's Declaration of Principles notes) of lacking ideology, but the party is social democratic. One municipal party president of the PPD said that the party had no ideology (Interview, September 30, 2002), and a councilman who had joined to voice his opposition to then president Pinochet learned that he was a PPD member only when they called him up to attend a meeting (Interview, November 6, 2002).

The party's social democratic values are reflected in its statement on women found in its Declaration of Principles:

> The PPD rejects the discrimination that women currently face in our society, and is committed to promoting equal rights for men and women. The PPD wants to end gender discrimination . . . allowing women to be free of limits in the work force and in their personal lives, and at the same time allowing men to participate more in domestic work and in childcare. With discrimination against women, society also suffers because it fails to take advantage of the energy, talent, and imagination of women that society needs for its own development. The full incorporation of women would represent a change of immense proportions that would enrich society in all of its fields.[15]

The PPD had a female vice president in 1988 and its first female president (Carolina Tohá) in 2009. The party first began applying an internal 20 percent quota in 1989. By 1998, there was a push to increase the quota percentage and to extend the quota to external elections. The quota was raised to 40 percent and applied to external elections despite the fear that there would be an insufficient number of female candidates (Moltedo 1998). The party did not encounter a problem in finding candidates. By 2005, the PPD had 20 deputies in office, but only 4 of these were women. None of its three senators was a woman. Only one of the female mayors in the country was a member of the PPD. In 1996, slightly more than 44 percent of the PPD membership was female (Muñoz D'Albora and Wojciechowski Levine 1996). One national party higher-up explained that the PPD's lack of women mayors was caused by its focus on getting women into higher office (Interview, September 10, 2002). Another national PPD operative attributed fewer women to the fact that there is an open-list proportional system for elections and not a closed-list system since "it's not the party's decision" (Interview, September 10, 2002). The assumption on the part of this PPD representative was that women's underrepresentation was a result of voter bias, but as Chapter 2 demonstrates, demand side factors have little explanatory power. These comments indicate that party women believe that the PPD is committed to increasing women's representation.

The PPD's selection processes for national elections have varied over the last 15 years. At times, the regional councils have formally made suggestions to the national directorate (which has final authority), but there have also been cases of closed primaries being used to select candidates (Navia 2004). Navia notes that, "unlike other Concertación parties, the PPD leadership takes an active role in recruiting potential candidates and securing good districts for them" (2004: 16). The party does not appear as proactive at the local level. The PPD's candidate-selection processes for municipal elections are explained in the following section.

Candidate Selection for Municipal Office

Even people working at the PPD party offices in Santiago found the candidate-selection processes for the municipal elections confusing because "all the elections have been different" (Interview, August 2, 2002). Despite the changes that have taken place, the selection procedures of the party continue to be inclusive-decentralized. The size of the selectorate is determined by the number of members who choose to attend the closed primary. Although the national party can technically veto decisions or put in someone it wants without consulting the local party office, that would be quite unusual and it is certainly the norm that the decision taken at the municipality is respected.

This inclusive-decentralized selection disadvantaged women. One failed PPD pre-candidate for the municipal council of Talagante said, "If you have money, they'll leave you a spot" (Interview, September 13, 2002). She found the selection process unfair and "undemocratic" and said of the party, "They don't even stop to think about the harm they are doing the party." The women who had been willing to vote for her in the general election would now be voting for other parties, she explained. Her support came predominantly from women because she had worked at two government-run women's organizations in the community. A local PPD president stated that primaries were about money. She said that although there were about 800 party members in her medium-sized city, only about 100 of them vote in party elections; she added that people will vote for someone "because they give them a cup of coffee and a slice of cake" (Interview, September 30, 2002). In Maule, a town of approximately 15,000, about 35 people voted in the closed primary (Interview, November 6, 2002). Though candidate selection may be inclusive, many questioned how fair the process really was. One woman termed the process undemocratic because of the nearly 40,000 registered voters in her city, there were only about 200 PPD members. Only 47 of them voted in the internal election, which she lost by five votes (Interview, September 13, 2002). The selection process had so turned her off that she said she considered running as the candidate of a different party.

The PPD's inclusive-decentralized candidate selection prevented the party from meeting its own expectations. Despite its pro-feminist ideology and its use of 40 percent quotas for external elections, only 18.6 percent of candidates in the 2000 municipal elections were women. In comparison, by 1998, nearly 30 percent of the party's directorate was female. Because of its use of primaries, the party failed to meet its own quota. The party's inability to develop a method of candidate selection that would respect the party's gender quotas calls into question its commitment to women's representation.

The Partido Radical Social Demócrata in Chile

The Partido Radical Social Demócrata (PRSD) has waned considerably; the Partido Demócrata Cristiano (PDC) displaced the Radical Party in importance in the early 1960s, and the PRSD has been unable to increase its representation and is currently the smallest party of the coalition. In 2005, the PRSD had no female representatives in Congress (the party was represented by six male deputies). Only 1 of the 40 female members in the country was a PRSD member. The PRSD has never been headed by a woman. The party's National Feminine Organization was considering disbanding (Interview, August 2, 2002). The party is situated to the right of both the PPD and the PS. It does not use gender quotas for internal or external elections. Though the party makes mention of ending discrimination in its statutes, it does not specifically refer to discrimination against women:

> A party that believes in equality of opportunities and the eradication of all forms of discrimination, and which defends the right to hold individual beliefs. . . . A party that believes that the family is the essential nucleus of society and that it should work to strengthen and develop the family through its values which permit individual growth and collective human growth.[16]

The PRSD's status as the smallest party within the Concertación has affected the party's candidate selection for the legislature; as Navia explains, it simultaneously seeks to obtain some electoral representation and get enough votes to maintain its legal status as a party (2004). The party's declining electoral viability has also affected its candidate-selection processes for local elections.

Candidate Selection for Municipal Office

The PRSD is making candidate-selection decisions in an inclusive-decentralized manner. Municipalities with more than 15 members have assemblies. If an assembly exists, then the assembly votes to choose its candidates. All members may nominate themselves or others for candidacy. If no assembly exists, then the local party officers make the candidate decision. The Regional Tribunal approves candidacies after a background check. The decision goes to the national level in only extraordinary instances.

There was some confusion about the exact process for choosing candidates. One PRSD local vice president explained that there were no rules for how candidates should be chosen, though he did say that the process was slowly becoming more transparent (Interview, November 26, 2002). Of the PRSD, he said, "It needs a dose of internal democracy." Although the PRSD claimed to use internal elections to choose candidates, in one city there was no election because there was only one contender; that sole contender, who was the local party president, commented, "Maybe they knew that I would win" (Interview, November 19, 2002). This situation more likely indicates the pervasiveness of boss rule. Though less formal internal elections were used in his party to select candidates, a PRSD council member stated that it was good that his party did not have primaries "because that way you don't have to fight with anyone" (Interview, October 31, 2002).

The PRSD's inclusive-decentralized candidate selection has posed significant obstacles to women. Though it has neither a strong commitment to increasing women's representation nor any gender quotas in place, the party nonetheless had a slightly greater proportion of women municipal candidates in 2000 (14.7 percent) than women on its national directorate (13.3 percent). The PRSD had the lowest proportion of women candidates of any of the other major parties.

Unlike parties employing exclusive candidate-selection procedures, the PRSD does not seek out candidates for office. One local PRSD president observed that as opposed to the Unión Demócrata Independiente (UDI) and the Communist Party "that go out looking for people," his party "waits for people to come to the party" (Interview, November 1, 2002). The emphasis on self-nomination proves detrimental to women's candidacies.

The Partido Demócrata Cristiano in Chile

The Christian Democratic Party was founded in 1957 and established itself as the centrist force in politics in the 1960s. As the country transitioned to democracy at the end of the 1980s, the party chose to join the Concertación, which included its former political enemies, because of its opposition to the Pinochet dictatorship. The party has noticeably weakened since the return to democracy; although at the time of the transition the PDC was the country's largest party, the PDC has been losing its relative strength. Its position of dominance within the Concertación was clearly established early on because the first two presidents elected after the dictatorship were Christian Democrats (Agüero 2003).[17]

As a result of its more conservative nature, the PDC, unlike other Concertación parties, is internally divided on the issue of quotas. The PDC uses a 20 percent quota rule for its internal party posts. The percentage of female provincial presidents increased from 4.5 percent to 11.9 percent following the adoption of this quota in 1998. The percentage of female municipal party presidents, however, increased only from 11.5 percent to 11.9 percent. The percentage of female National Meeting delegates climbed substantially following the implementation of a quota, from 14 percent to 33.5 percent (Moltedo 1998). The division that exists over quotas was evident in one PDC councilwoman's statements: "The PDC doesn't make it easy for women." Women are "ill-prepared politically" but "women's electoral chances are the same as men's with respect to the voters" (Interview, September 9, 2002). This councilwoman was saying that voters were not keeping women out of office, but rather that the process of candidate selection was impeding women from entering politics.

As of 2005, the PDC had 22 deputies and 12 senators. Two of its 22 deputies were women, as was 1 of its 12 senators. The PDC also has the most women mayors of the Concertación parties. In 1996, 39.3 percent of PDC members were women (Muñoz D'Albora and Wojciechowski Levine 1996). Almost 20 percent of the party's directorate was female by 1998. Carmen Frei Ruíz-Tagle was vice president of the PDC in 1999, and more recently (2006–2008), Soledad Alvear served as the party's president.

Women acknowledged ongoing discrimination within the party. One female local party president proclaimed, "Prejudice against women has changed in the party, though there is always discrimination against women" (Interview, December 2, 2002). Though a national PDC party official said that in her role in the Front for Women, she often hears from women that problems with male leaders are keeping them from becoming candidates (Interview,

October 7, 2002), men in the PDC unequivocally stated that in the PDC "there is no form of discrimination" and blamed women's limited representation either on the difficulty of having a "triple workday"—their jobs and careers, work inside the home, and work in the parties—(Interview, September 23, 2002) or on women themselves, for being, in their view, unwilling to support the candidacies of other women (Interview, October 10, 2002). One PDC local vice president said that women have the same chances of being elected as men, but "things get complicated at the internal level." But "it's all the same to the voters" (Interview, September 13, 2002). The electoral record in Talagante certainly seemed to confirm her suspicions since, in the 2000 elections, women had received more than two-thirds of all votes cast. Talagante had elected a woman mayor and two female councilors (of a total of five).

Over the years the PDC has sought to open up its national candidate-selection processes. While the party used closed primaries in 1993 and 1997, in 2001 open primaries were used in those districts in which the incumbent was not seeking re-election. Navia explains, "Overall, the PDC has fostered a process in which militants have a greater influence in selecting the candidates for the party. However, as several interviewees suggested, the PDC has suffered from unilaterally promoting more democratic participation in the candidate selection mechanism" (2004: 14). As former party president and deputy Gutenberg Martínez noted, "When closed primaries (or open primaries with very low levels of participation) are held, a small organized faction of the PDC militants can elect a local party leader, who lacks the skills and appeal beyond party militants to win enough support to clinch a seat" (quoted in Navia 2004: 14). The party has been moving toward more inclusive selection. It has also opened up its candidate-selection processes for municipal councils, with similar results. Those selection mechanisms are described in the next section.

Candidate Selection for Municipal Office

Fresia Faúndez became mayor of the small town of Maule after she successfully competed in a primary for her party's nomination. Faúndez had long been active in local politics. After the end of the dictatorship, Faúndez, then still just a teenager, worked alongside her husband to re-establish the PDC in their hometown. Their work was recognized by the party; while still in their early twenties, he became party president and she became the party secretary. When he ran for mayor, few people expected that he would win because of his youth, but at age 27 he became the youngest mayor in the country. Faúndez's husband was killed in a car crash while driving home from a conference in

Peru. At the funeral, there was talk of her taking on the role of interim mayor. Though ultimately one of the council members took on the position of interim mayor as mandated by law, she was nonetheless consulted by her coalition about this decision. A year later, Faúndez decided to run for the position that her husband had occupied, but first she needed to compete in a primary.

The influence of local power monopolies was certainly evident in the party's primary elections. Candidates or party bosses who favored a particular candidate would send out hordes of people to the primaries. In one city, where the PDC used primaries to choose its municipal candidates for 2000, a provincial party president argued that "it wasn't good because the results weren't representative of the reality." This provincial party president noted, though, that one local candidate received 350 votes in the primary and 4,090 in the general election, while another party candidate received 340 votes in the primary and 851 in the election. These figures clearly demonstrate that the ability to obtain votes in a primary is not an accurate measure of a candidate's ability to gain general election votes. While we might expect that primary results will not mirror general election results—for example, many would argue that those party members who participate in primaries are more partisan and less representative of the median voter—we would expect that an individual would receive more votes in the general election than he or she did in the primary election. The provincial party president pointed out that in a nearby city, one person (not, incidentally, the mayor's favorite) received over 1,000 votes in the primary but only 322 votes in the general election (Interview, November 28, 2002); as the interviewee revealed, the mayor had clearly played a role in increasing the candidate's vote share in the primary. In one medium-sized Chilean city, the party expected that at most 800 people would vote in the primary, but instead 1,200 showed up to vote (Interview, December 12, 2002). The primary in Peñaflor, a city of approximately 60,000, drew over 1,200 voters, even though the municipality has only 360 PDC members (Interview, October 24, 2002). By cajoling locals into participating in primaries, power monopolies can warp the results of primary elections. The use of primaries was heavily criticized by numerous interviewees; one PDC deputy said, "I doubt their efficiency" (Interview, September 16, 2002). A national party official for the PDC remarked that having members participate in a primary is a "more democratic system" but also mentioned that only about 1 percent of the population within a typical municipality were likely to be party members (Interview, August 2, 2002).

Some disliked primaries because of the financial imposition. One successful PDC candidate for the council said she disagreed with the primaries because "the one with the most money gets the most votes" (Interview, December 2, 2002). The fact that "money means winning" could prove particularly difficult for women, who are less likely to have the finances to fund campaigns for both a primary and a general election campaign (Interview, December 3, 2002). Furthermore, even parties that provide their candidates with some campaign funding for the election do not fund primary campaigns. Pre-candidates either pay for these primary costs out of their own pockets or remain dependent on members of the local party establishment to cover their campaign costs (Multiple interviews).

The PDC was employing inclusive-decentralized selection procedures. The party used primaries in the 2000 elections in some municipalities, in which members of the municipality and independents could vote. The national party made the decision about where it would hold primaries on the basis of electoral results from the 1996 municipal elections. In municipalities that did not hold primaries, candidate selection was made by regional councils on the basis of local selection. This latter form of selection was also inclusive and decentralized. The PDC requires that its candidates be party members, have the signatures of 10 other members, and undergo a background check in order to become pre-candidates. The PDC found that primaries caused deep internal divisions that ultimately cost the party votes in the general election. As a former PDC candidate to the Chamber of Deputies said, "Primaries end up hurting the party because then people don't cooperate with that side in the end" (Interview, November 12, 2002). Having primaries in which both members and independents voted also proved difficult for the PDC, since so-called independents attempted to foul elections by voting for the least attractive candidate (Multiple interviews). The use of open primaries also increased the power of local monopolies.

Only 16.6 percent of the PDC's candidates in the 2000 municipal elections were female. The party has less of an ideological commitment to increasing women's representation than other coalition parties. The use of primaries in particular had disastrous consequences for women's representation, but the party came close to reaching the goals outlined by its gender quotas. Faúndez avoided the obstacles of inclusive-decentralized selection because of her status as a political widow. Faúndez, who relished the opportunity to prove herself in a primary, won the general election with more votes than her deceased husband had obtained in his first mayoral election. She then went on to win re-election in 2004 with more than 40 percent of the vote. Chapter 7 discusses how her situation as a political widow allowed her to avoid common impediments that women face.

The Partido Revolucionario Institucional in Mexico

The Mexican political system was defined by the PRI for most of the twentieth century. The PRI formed in 1929 and built its success on its strategic corporatist inclusion of peasants, bureaucrats, and the working classes, but it used nondemocratic practices when necessary to maintain its political domination. The PAN provided steady opposition to the PRI since the 1940s, while the Partido de la Revolución Democrática (PRD), an amalgamation of PRI splinter groups and small leftist parties from a variety of ideological backgrounds (both are discussed in Chapter 5), began actively fighting PRI hegemony in 1989. The Mexican transition to democracy was extraordinarily slow but was "finalized" with the presidential victory of the PAN's Vicente Fox in 2000.

The PRI's commitment to women's rights is part of its socially liberal program. However, the party's Declaration of Principles sets out its statement concerning women as its 24th point; in contrast, the leftist PRD puts its statement on women near the top of its list of principles. This statement delineates the party's commitment to gender equity and a desire for equality of opportunities, and it specifically mentions the commitment that men must make to these goals. The PRI has maintained a women's section, currently known as the Organismo Nacional de Mujeres Priístas (ONMPRI), throughout its history. The party has also had three female presidents. The first, María de los Ángeles Moreno, presided over the party from 1994 to1995; the second, Dulce María Sauri, served from 1999 to 2002; the third, Beatriz Paredes, was elected in 2007. The percentage of women among PRI deputies has been relatively stagnant over the last decade. Women were 14 percent of PRI deputies in 1994, 18.4 percent in 1997, 15.9 percent in 2002, 17.9 percent in 2005, and 21 percent by 2010. Women have fared considerably better in the Senate, where their representation increased from 14.7 percent in 1994 to 26.6 percent in 2005 (SISESIM 2004). Women's representation in candidacies and in national-level office remains much lower than expected, considering that in 1996 the party passed a 30 percent quota law, which was raised to 50 percent in 2001. The internal party quota was also applied to women's representation in the national directorate of the party, which has remained low. This quota was revised in 2005, mandating that half of all candidacies for the national executive committee and municipal committees would be reserved for party women.

The PRI's method for candidate selection became an entrenched authoritarian element. Since the party was assured electoral victories—as a result of both electoral popularity and the party's willingness to engage in electoral fraud—until at least the late 1980s, these processes wholly determined who the representatives would be. The party's presidential candidates (who would become the country's presidents) were selected by the outgoing president; after he appointed his successor, the party officially ratified the candidate, who then ran in the general election. The president directly chose the candidates for state governors, and these state governors chose the mayoral candidates for the municipalities in their states (Rodríguez 1997), whom they could remove if they wished. Governors sometimes solicited the advice of the Congress member from the local district before choosing mayoral candidates. This system became known as the *dedazo*, from the Spanish word for "finger;" essentially, candidate selection consisted of a powerful person "pointing out" who the next candidate would be.

The reliance on *dedazos* for selecting candidates increased party discipline at all levels, since officeholders were in office not because of the votes of their constituents but because of decisions made by elites. Furthermore, the ban on immediate re-election made politicians continually dependent on party leaders, since officeholders knew that their terms would soon end and they would need to obtain a new post (Dresser 2003; Langston 2003). The move to open primaries changed this dynamic. In addition to decreasing loyalty to national elites, open primaries have made state-level party organizations much more significant since "open primaries are won in large part with the work of the territorial organization in the state" (Langston 2003: 301).

Candidate-selection procedures became an important issue for the party, as it sought not only to change its reputation but also to maintain electoral support during the 1980s and 1990s. In 1990, the PRI ushered in reforms stipulating that mayoral candidates needed either to be originally from their municipality and have spent the previous year living there or to have been a resident of the municipality for at least three years (Valdés 2001). In 1996, the PRI changed its internal rules so that all gubernatorial and presidential candidates were required to have served in elected office and to have been members of the party for at least 10 years (Eisenstadt 2002: 20). By 1998, the PRI was predominantly using primaries to choose gubernatorial candidates. In preparation for the 2000 elections, the PRI chose its presidential candidate via primary for the first time. The PRI now relies on various candidate-selection processes.

The PRI's adoption of primaries can be attributed to a desire to move away from its authoritarian image and to keep its politicians from defecting to other parties (Poiré 2002). Lawson notes that although the PRI has switched to using open primaries to select its presidential and gubernatorial candidates, party leaders are chosen through less transparent means.

Specifically, the president and political bosses continue to play an important role in selection (Lawson 2000: 281). Dresser (2003) argues that the PRI will continue to use primaries to select its candidates. The dissatisfaction caused by open primaries, however, may force the party to either switch to closed primaries—which would require stricter record keeping[18]—or move toward a convention-type system. In some states, however, party conventions are still used to choose gubernatorial candidates. The reliance on national-level elites had begun to wane once parties other than the PRI had a chance at winning elections; in particular, the creation of the PRD presented PRI politicians with the option of defecting when their own party refused to nominate them (Langston 2001).

Candidate Selection for Municipal Office: "From One Extreme to the Other"

The PRI has experimented with a broad array of selection methods for choosing its municipal candidates, especially in the last decade. The move from a *dedazo* to primaries in one city caused one local leader to comment, "Everything's done by election now—we went from one extreme to the other" (Interview, May 26, 2003). He then complained that "because we've had so many [primary] elections we haven't had time to get any work done" (Interview, May 26, 2003). Local politicians have been less than pleased with primary elections, which they viewed as excessively time-consuming and costly (Multiple interviews). Since municipalities became politically more competitive, candidate selection for local office has become more problematic: infighting "between PRI factions over local candidate nomination, either between local caciques or between the dictates of the center and a local cacique, grew increasingly belligerent" (Eisenstadt 2004: 244). While this chapter describes those methods that are inclusive and decentralized in two towns in the state of Mexico, the PRI also used exclusive-decentralized[19] processes in Pueblo Viejo and used exclusive-centralized selection in Mérida. The case of Pueblo Viejo is discussed in Chapter 5. Chapter 6 turns to exclusive-centralized procedures and examines the case of Mérida.

The PRI's Inclusive-Decentralized Selection: Primaries in Amanalco, Mexico

In 2000, when she was in her early thirties, Mercedes Colín became mayor of the small rural town of Amanalco in the state of Mexico. Colín is the daughter of Rutilio Colín, who was municipal president from 1985 to 1987, and the granddaughter of José Colín, who was municipal president from 1944 through 1945. The mayoral candidacy was decided by primary. Inclusive-decentralized selection processes fail to either circumvent local power monopolies or avoid self-nomination. Neither was an issue for Colín: as the daughter and granddaughter of former mayors, she belonged to the local power groups in Amanalco. Her name was proposed to the party when it started searching for possible candidates (Multiple interviews). She was also encouraged to run for office by an important local union, for which she had worked in the past. This initial push to pursue office was further propelled by some of her former professors in the state capital. She had the personal resources to finance both the primary and the general election. As she approached the end of her term as mayor, Colín ran for and was elected to the state legislature in 2003. Her case is further discussed in Chapter 7.

The PRI used inclusive-decentralized selection in this small town. In Amanalco, the mayoral candidate was chosen in an open primary from among six possible pre-candidates. The local PRI offices had requested nominations from members, and three names had been offered up, including the name of the sitting local party president. Three more pre-candidates were added prior to the primary (Multiple interviews). Colín financed an extensive primary campaign lasting three months.

The mayoral candidate was not able to choose all of the candidates for town council. The municipal trustee slot was reserved as a "consolation prize" for the runner-up in the primary (Interview, March 25, 2003). One candidate to the council was guaranteed a spot on the list because his local PRI section had obtained the highest vote totals in the previous elections (Interview, March 17, 2003). Another council candidate obtained a spot on the list to prevent infighting in the PRI. He was the third-place finisher in the primary (Interview, March 19, 2003). Interviewees in Amanalco confirmed that council positions were not decided solely by the mayoral candidate and that those councilor candidacies had previously been divvied up in this manner.

The PRI's Inclusive-Decentralized Selection: Primaries in Tianguistenco, Mexico

In Tianguistenco, in the state of Mexico, the mayoral candidate was also chosen by a primary election. Choosing council candidates was even more formalized here. The second- and third-place finishers in the primary were offered the municipal trustee candidacy and one of the council slots. The rest of the council candidates were chosen by local party elites (Interview, June 23, 2003). First, pre-candidates needed to be elected within their own local PRI sections. One of the sections was guaranteed a candidacy by the governor because it had obtained high votes in the previous election (Multiple interviews). Following that, the pre-candidates participated in a convention, where they gave speeches on topics related to public administration. The local PRI officers decided who would get a candidacy on the basis of this oratorical competition (Interview, June 16, 2003).

The adoption of these new selection methods may decrease women's ability to become PRI candidates. At the national level, PRI women officials are well aware of the disadvantages that primaries pose to women. Women "participate in conditions of inequality" (Interview, February 13, 2003) and are disadvantaged because primaries "require a lot of money and these aren't women of means" (Interview, July 31, 2001). Mexican women seemed to recognize primaries' negative effects: "It was easier before when there were less formal processes for women to become mayors" (Interview, July 31, 2001).

The various processes of candidate selection that the PRI is currently utilizing make it difficult to tease out the effects of each process on women's abilities to become candidates.[20] The PRI is a case of mixed success. The party had proposed the highest percentages of women candidates and had the most women mayors in office; however, its ability to propose women's municipal candidacies has trailed its ability to put women on ballots for national-level offices or into its own party offices. While female mayors were overwhelmingly members of the PRI, this was largely a function of the PRI's long-standing hegemony; in other words, most female mayors were Priistas because most mayors were Priistas.

The Partido de la Revolución Democrática in Mexico

The PRD used inclusive-decentralized selection only in Mérida, opting to use exclusive-decentralized selection in the municipalities of Pueblo Viejo, Tianguistenco, and Amanalco. Chapter 5 not only provides information on the selection procedures used in those three cities but also describes in detail the PRD, the party's actions to promote women, and its selection methods for national candidacies.

The PRD's Inclusive-Decentralized Selection: Primaries in Mérida

The PRD was using inclusive-decentralized candidate selection in the large tourist city of Mérida located in the Yucatán peninsula. Aspirants proposed their own nominations or were nominated by others. All party members were given a vote in a closed primary. The pre-candidate who won a plurality of votes was given the nomination (Multiple interviews). The PRD has made only small inroads in the Yucatán, and its mayoral primary meant little since the state-level party organization decided that the party would form a coalition with the much stronger PAN. The PRD was able to place only one person onto the municipal council after the PAN's electoral victory. This council member indicated that the primary elections did make "getting to be a candidate more difficult" (Interview, May 29, 2003).

Inclusive-decentralized candidate selection can prove problematic for women. The practices of the PS, PRSD, PPD, and PDC, as well as those of the PRI in the cities of Amanalco and the PRD in Mérida, require self-nomination and increase the influence of local power monopolies. While some women (including the so-called *mujeres de*, which will be discussed in Chapter 7) are asked to run for office or actively recruited by locals, most are not. Inclusive-decentralized procedures almost always require that women propose their own candidacies. The unique circumstances surrounding the candidacy of Faúndez meant that local power monopolies were not a potential threat to her candidacy; rather, as a member of the local elite, Faúndez was well connected to these networks, providing her with an even greater advantage. The same was true of Colín. For most women, their traditional exclusion from these groups means that local power monopolies serve to undermine their potential candidacies and foil their political campaigns. Inclusive-decentralized selection methods are much less likely to produce female candidates. The parties of the Concertación trailed behind the parties of the right in their abilities to get women into local-level office. Candidates from parties using exclusive-centralized selection were 55 percent more likely to be women than candidates from one of the four parties of the Concertación.[21] It is not surprising that two of those women who did emerge from inclusive-decentralized selection had such exceptional circumstances.

In addition to being negatively affected by the use of inclusive-decentralized selection procedures, women in the parties of the Concertación were at times disadvantaged by the coalitional nature of selection. As Navia notes, "Often the preferences of political parties with respect to candidate selection are trumped in the interests of coalitional unity" (2008b: 92). While much decision making between the four parties of the Concertación takes place long before elections, at times new candidates—representing a different group within the coalition—are chosen at the last minute. Women's efforts to gain candidacies, then, are even more precarious when coalitional bargaining takes place.

5

Inclusive-Centralized and Exclusive-Decentralized Selection

> They went to my house to talk to me about running for the Renovación Nacional. The woman who went to talk to me was the secretary of a mayor [of a nearby town]. She's a councilor now too. She remembered me.
>
> —Council member explaining how he was selected as a candidate
> (Interview, September 27, 2002)

Despite the growing use of inclusive-decentralized selection procedures, in particular primaries, for choosing candidates, parties continue to routinely select candidates using processes that are inclusive-centralized or exclusive-decentralized. These two types of candidate-selection procedures are on opposite ends of Figure 3.2, meaning that they each allow women to avoid one of the two most significant obstacles that women face on their path to becoming officeholders. Inclusive-centralized selection typically neutralizes the effects of local power monopolies because decision making takes place at the regional or national level instead of locally. Exclusive-decentralized methods prevent women from self-nominating; instead, local selectors handpick these candidates. These two selection methods, then, tend to yield mixed results since either self-nomination or local power monopolies, but not both, are removed. This chapter examines the use of inclusive-centralized and exclusive-decentralized selection in turn.

Inclusive-Centralized Selection

Inclusive-centralized candidate selection refers to selection that is open to a large selectorate. Decision making takes place at the national level. Such inclusive-centralized selection usually takes the form of conventions, which according to Freidenberg are commonly used in Latin America. Conventions are used by the Partido Liberal Constitucionalista in Nicaragua, the Partido Acción Nacional (PAN) in Mexico, and the Renovación Nacional (RN) in Chile for national elections, as well as the Alianaza Republicana Nacionalista in El Salvador, and can take place locally or nationally. Freidenberg notes that conventions can be used "when party elite decisions, or the decisions of a single leader, need to be legitimized, or simply when parties want to increase members' participation" (2003: 28–29). Similarly, these party conventions "serve more to demonstrate unity and solidarity than internal debate" (Alcántara Sáez 2004: 12).

None of the Chilean parties used inclusive-centralized selection to choose candidates for municipal office, but the Mexican PAN did use this method. This form of selection, as discussed in Chapter 3, forces women to self-nominate but avoids the power of local networks.

The Partido Acción Nacional in Mexico

Although Mexican politics was long defined by the Partido Revolucionario Institucional (PRI), the PAN has provided steady (though unsuccessful) opposition to the PRI since its founding in 1939. The PAN was formed by a group of conservatives to oppose the "allegedly socialist and state-led policies introduced by President Cárdenas" and immediately began to field candidates for public office (Mizrahi 2003: 7).

The PAN is a much more socially conservative party than either the more centrist PRI or the leftist Partido de la Revolución Democrática (PRD). Its strong ties to Catholicism shape the party's stance on the role of women in society. The PAN's primary concern is with maintaining the sanctity of the family and preserving women's traditional roles. In its Declaration of Principles, the PAN states:

All forms of discrimination or inequality of opportunity for reasons of sex, age, physical ability, ethnicity, religion, conviction, economic condition, or any other, should be rejected, corrected, and sanctioned. The National Action Party clearly recognizes the practical consequences of the common dignity of men and women, and of their common character as agents and collaborators in the construction, animation, and direction of society. Gender equity signifies that men and women should be able to develop freely and responsibly. The discrimination that exists against women in the family, the workplace, politics, and in all other social spheres is unacceptable. Men and women must both recognize their own worth and be responsible to one another, sharing the tasks that concern them in the family and outside of it on a basis of equal rights and obligations. A just social policy should not intend to substitute the state for the family.[1]

Women's representation within the PAN has grown incrementally for national office. In 1994, women were only 8.5 percent of PAN deputies, but that increased to 12.4 percent in 1997, and to 34.4 percent by 2003 (Hinojosa 2008). Similarly, women's representation increased in the Senate: women constituted 7.7 percent of PAN senators in 1994, 9.4 percent in 1997, and 13 percent in 2005. The presence of women in the PAN's national directorate has been erratic, though the trend has been toward a significant increase. The PAN has no women's section but does have a secretariat devoted to women's issues called the Secretaria de Promoción Política de la Mujer.

Although the PAN's opposition to quotas prevented it from passing a strict quota law, by 1999 the party had decided to include both a man and a woman for each pair of candidates and alternates chosen (Baldez 2004a). The national quota law that was adopted in 2002 was overwhelmingly approved by Congress; the seven votes against it came from male PAN deputies (Baldez 2004a). The PAN also added the provision to the quota law that exempts candidacies chosen via primary from meeting the quota requirements.[2] The PAN has met and often exceeded the quota law requirements that were first put into place for the 2003 midterm elections. Although it is ideologically to the right of both the PRI and the PRD, the PAN has a greater percentage of women in office than either of those parties (21 percent of PRI deputies are women, as are 29 percent of PRD deputies and 34 percent of PAN deputies). Furthermore, female Panistas convinced the party to adopt a quota for municipal council candidates. The quota, which has been set at 40 percent, is intended to train women in the party for higher-level office; this training is an effort to produce more electable female candidates who can be fielded for higher-level office (Piscopo 2011).

Female Panistas were less likely than female members of the PRI or the PRD to mention discrimination (Multiple interviews). Ana Rosa Payán, then mayor of Mérida but a nationally recognized figure in the party, was an exception. She remarked that while she rarely experienced discrimination from the public, she had experienced "strong clashes" with other party elites and had seen discrimination directed at other women, because "in the PAN, as in the rest of the country, there's machismo" (Interview, June 4, 2003). A prominent Panista laid a portion of the blame for women's underrepresentation in politics on women themselves, who participate actively in political campaigns but never demand compensation for their efforts when their candidate wins (Rodríguez 2003: 224).

The PAN presented itself as an alternative model to the authoritarian practices of the PRI, and unsurprisingly the party "prided itself on the democratic character of its selection processes" (Wuhs 2008: 44). Although often considered "the only democratic party in Mexico because of its long tradition of internal primaries, or rules and regulations, of time-honed methods to elect and rotate its leadership" (Dresser 2003: 330), the PAN did not always adhere to its own internal rules for candidate selection. The PAN circumvented its rules for state and local elections in its earlier years because it could not muster up enough pre-candidates and so was forced to appoint some of its candidates (Mizrahi 2003: 59). Because of the PRI's monopoly on political power, PAN candidates for many years were seen as martyrs and "becoming the party's candidate was regarded as a sacrifice"—according to Piscopo, this meant that those women who entered the PAN in its early years were able to rise up in the ranks (Mizrahi 2003: 7; Piscopo 2011).

The PAN has not only had to learn how to be the party in government instead of the perpetual party of opposition; it has also had to handle the side effects of success, including an upsurge in membership. When the PAN became electorally viable in the late 1980s and the number of aspirants subsequently multiplied, candidate selection became much more problematic. Throughout the 1980s, the party started to experiment with different selection rules, in part because as the party grew, so did its conventions and these were becoming "increasingly unwieldy" (Wuhs 2006: 39). After the 2000 selection process that produced Vicente Fox as the PAN's candidate, the president of the party's National Executive Committee (CEN), Luis Felipe Bravo Mena, announced that the party needed to "modernize" its selection processes (Langston 2008: 156).

The PAN's selection methods have long been participatory affairs.[3] According to Mizrahi, the candidate-selection procedures that are in place are skewed to favor the party's "longtime members who feel they deserve the party's nomination" instead of the newer elements of the PAN (2003: 99). State-level conventions or closed primaries are used to choose candidates to the Chamber of Deputies and Senate, as well as gubernatorial candidates (Wuhs 2006; Langston 2008). The PAN moved from using a convention to select its presidential candidate to using a closed primary. While the party first used a primary in 2000, since Fox was the only pre-candidate in the primary, the election served only to ratify Fox's candidacy (Wuhs 2006: 39–40).

Historically, all PAN militants were eligible to participate as delegates to these conventions. However, participation in these conventions was limited partly because delegates needed to finance their own trips (Mizrahi 2003: 99). The apparent desire to decrease the size of these conventions led to changes in 2003 "requiring delegates to demonstrate municipal party support and gain the approval of municipal party committees" (Wuhs 2006: 40). Wuhs points out that this is likely to have the "effect of strengthening the presence of doctrinaire voices at the convention" and decreasing the openness of these conventions (2006: 40).

Candidate Selection for Municipal Office

Unlike the PRI and the PRD, the rule-bound PAN is consistent in its application of inclusive-centralized procedures. Membership and candidacy in the PAN are tightly regulated. The PAN has two categories of membership: adherents and active members. Adherents have no rights or obligations within the party but can participate in certain activities. To gain active membership, a person must first be an adherent for at least six months and fill out an application. Becoming an active member also requires attendance at a week-long workshop to learn about the party's history and its principles.

Candidates for mayoral positions are required to have been active members for three years. To become a candidate of the PAN, an aspirant must first be nominated at a municipal assembly or propose his or her own nomination. The municipal assembly then votes on candidacies. Because the local membership votes on candidates, this process can appear to be inclusive and decentralized; like the selection for national elections, local selection processes could be mischaracterized as primaries. However, the state or national level office plays an active role, making selection centralized. The state party office or the national organization steps in to choose a candidate when the municipal assembly cannot reach a consensus on a candidate. The case of Mérida highlights the role of the state or national office in decision making.

The PAN has a long history in the Yucatán and enjoyed striking success in the capital city of Mérida during the democratic transition, earning between 49 percent and 60 percent of the vote in elections between 1990 and 2001 and losing the mayoral seat only in 2009. Mérida is important not only because it is the capital city of the state but also because more than 4 of every 10 residents of the state live in the municipality. With a population of over 700,000, Mérida is one of the largest municipalities in the country and the largest urban center in southeastern Mexico. Ana Rosa Payán was elected mayor of Mérida in 2001, after having previously served as mayor from 1991 to 1993. In the 2001 elections that once again brought Payán to head the city government, the PAN obtained 53.7 percent of the vote, while the PRI garnered 42.8 percent and the PRD received less than 1 percent of the vote.

Payán's candidacy is emblematic of the inclusive-centralized selection procedures that the PAN used to choose mayoral candidates. The politically ambitious Payán, who served as senator from 1997 to 2000, had not sought the nomination in 2001. Instead, Luis Correa Mena, also a former mayor of Mérida (1994–1995), tried to become the party's candidate. Despite the fact that he was the only pre-candidate, party members voted against his nomination. Correa Mena had publicly renounced the PAN years earlier and was no longer a PAN member. According to Payán, after the active members of the party's local office voted against Correa Mena "there was no time left; we had to have a designation," so the leadership of the national office decided who the party's candidate would be (Interview, June 4, 2003). Others confirmed that Payán had been handpicked for the position, but agreed it was necessary given the circumstances. The decision, then, to run Ana Rosa Payán was made by the national party office. There was no municipal vote about her nomination.

The process for choosing the rest of the party slate, however, much resembles the processes traditionally used by the PRI, but nonetheless it retains some elements of inclusivity and decentralization. The process incorporates a much larger segment of the party membership than would typically take place within the PRI, and most decisions are maintained at the local level. After the mayoral candidate has been chosen, he or she must compile a list of council candidates. The state and national party offices maintain an important say in this process as well (Multiple interviews). While some candidates are chosen directly by the mayoral candidate, other candidacies are decided by state committees (Multiple interviews). For example, in Mérida, one of the council candidates was chosen by the state office, four were chosen by the municipal office, and the rest were handpicked by the mayoral candidate (Multiple interviews). One municipal council member said that the lack of municipal control over the final decision had an important positive effect. Payán had much influence in choosing the candidates who would run with her on the party's municipal slate and was able to professionalize the council by selecting well-qualified candidates (Multiple interviews). Yucatán is one of the states that elect both relative majority council members, who belong to the same party as the mayor, and proportional representation candidates, who reflect the vote share given to other parties. After a slate of council candidates has been drafted, there is a second vote by the active membership of the municipality. The nonsecret yea or nay votes on each of the candidates on the list determine whether these individuals will be fielded as council candidates. If anyone is rejected, a replacement is chosen by the state party committee. The relative majority council members were predominantly male.

Only two of the nine were women. The proportional representation council members were more diverse. One-half of the eight proportional representation seats (all of which represented the PRI, since the PRD had received less than 1 percent of the vote in these municipal elections)[4] belonged to women.

Despite the PAN's stance against quotas at the time, the party made efforts to increase the representation of women and young people. In Mérida, the local party president indicated that the party tried to designate at least one spot for women because "the PAN knows that there is still no gender equity" (Interview, May 21, 2003). Clearly, the PAN's effort to increase the representation of some traditionally underrepresented groups was an open secret that respondents were willing to talk about. A councilman in the same city specifically attributed his candidacy to his youth; the local party elites sought him out because they wanted a young person on the list (Interview, May 21, 2003).

The state and national PAN offices remain influential even after elections. In one state, the national PAN office decreed that unsuccessful mayoral candidates would replace one of the council candidates elected to proportional representation municipal council seats. This was done to increase the visibility of the mayoral candidates, maintain them in the public eye, and better position them for a future run (Multiple interviews).

The PAN's use of inclusive-centralized candidate-selection procedures most likely benefited Payán. These selection procedures diminished the importance of local power monopolies but did not eliminate self-nomination. The lessened influence of local power monopolies was important to the success of Payán since she is not originally from Mérida and does not have family members in politics. Although Payán herself told me that she moved to Mérida from the state of Campeche before her first birthday, the majority of the individuals I interviewed felt compelled to notify me that the mayor "was not a native" of the city (Multiple interviews; see, however, Barrera Bassols and Massolo 1998: 101). After she received her degree in accounting, her parents actively discouraged her from entering politics and instead asked her to take over the family business. The need for self-nomination would not deter Payán, although there was no need for self-nomination in the hurried circumstances described previously. Payán has been a member of the party for over 20 years, has held many elected positions (including state and national deputy) and party positions (including serving on the party's national executive committee), and is a nationally recognized figure. She is politically ambitious and admitted in 2003 that she wanted to run for the governorship of Yucatán in the following elections. Although she was a pre-candidate for the PAN nomination for the gubernatorial elections of 2007, Payán ultimately lost to Xavier Abreu Sierra. Payán then defected from the PAN after the party National Executive Committee refused to annul the primary results. She publicly denounced the selection process and accused the governor of Yucatán and other state party elites of illegally supporting her opponent's campaign.

While the PAN's inclusive-centralized candidate-selection procedures have allowed the party to circumvent the power of local power monopolies, the problem of self-nomination remained. Self-nomination most likely would not have deterred Payán, who was already a politician with national recognition and had previously served in that same mayoral position, but it would be detrimental to most women. The PAN has enjoyed more success than it would were it using an inclusive-decentralized system, and its new quota rules for municipal elections are sure to bring the PAN success, given that the party adheres to its own rules and regulations. The party, however, does continue to use rules that disadvantage women—for example, requiring attendance at a week-long conference in order to gain active membership, which is a substantial burden for women with household responsibilities.

Exclusive-Decentralized Selection

Exclusive-decentralized selection is limited to a very small number of selectors, typically only one or two, but selection is done at the municipal level. Exclusive selection means that women do not have to self-nominate, as leaders typically handpick candidates; however, the decentralized nature of this selection is likely to mean that power rests in the hands of elites who make up local power networks. Rahat and Hazan argue that "decentralization might mean only that control of candidate selection has passed from the national oligarchy to a local oligarchy. Only if decentralization encompasses a more inclusive selectorate can it be considered a democratizing process. In other words, decentralization can limit, maintain or expand the extent of intraparty democracy" (Rahat and Hazan 2001: 309). Camp argues that social networks continue to wield power whether under democratic or authoritarian regimes; he therefore warned that "democracy would not necessarily lead to the specific changes one might expect from electoral competition at the local level. In some locales, politics might become less rather than more competitive" (Camp 2010: 23).

Exclusive-decentralized selection methods are also used outside of Mexico and Chile. For example, candidacies for municipal elections in Costa Rica are chosen using selection that is best characterized by Jones as "decentralized" and "elite-dominated." The exception is the Partido Liberación

Nacional, which selected candidates in 2002 via direct primary, though "even this competition was between lists drafted by elites" (Jones 2004: 1207).

In the cases analyzed here, decision making was typically in the hands of one or two local party elites. Chile's RN used exclusive-decentralized selection, as did two of the Mexican parties. The PRI used exclusive-decentralized candidate selection in the small town of Pueblo Viejo, while the PRD used these kinds of selection methods in Amanalco.

As mentioned in Chapter 4, it is not uncommon for selection processes to be something other than what they seem. Magdalena Huerta García and Eric Magar Meurs discovered that in 74 districts PRI candidacies were nominally chosen via primary; however, in these districts there was a single candidate competing in the primary (of these 74 candidates, 69 were men)[5] (2006: 259–260). While in Mexico evading the quota law provides an added reason to be disingenuous about candidate-selection procedures (an issue discussed in detail in Chapter 8), these processes routinely differ in practice from what is claimed on paper across Latin America. Parties prefer to appear more "modern" and "democratic" and therefore will claim to be using primaries or, at the least, deny their use of *dedazos*. Roza (2010a) found evidence that party candidate-selection procedures routinely differed from their written regulations. The second half of this chapter presents some cases that fall into this category.

The Renovación Nacional in Chile

The RN is one of the two significant parties of the Chilean right. The two historic parties of the right, the Liberals and the Conservatives, had merged in 1967 as the National Party. The National Party virtually disappeared in 1973, after hewing to the dictatorship's call for an end to all party activity. By 1984, the right had regrouped as three distinct entities: Gremialismo, Frente Nacional, and Unión Nacional (Moltedo 1998), which officially formed the RN in 1987. The following year, the Unión Demócrata Independiente (UDI) emerged from a break within the RN (Valenzuela and Scully 1997; Navia 2004).

The party's position on the role of women in society is stated in its Declaration of Principles:

> National Renovation values the functions and virtues of women as the carriers of life, the nuclei of the family, and the transmitters of values, morals, and traditions. National Renovation defends equal rights in all the fields in which women work alongside men, without

compartmentalizing these activities with their functions as mothers and educators of their children.[6]

There were more women members than male members in the RN—by the late 1990s, 52 percent of the militancy was female (Moltedo 1998). The party's directorate was 13.3 percent female in 1998. The RN had a woman president in 1988 and a woman vice president in 1990. In 2004, the RN had 17 male deputies, 2 female deputies, and 2 male senators in Congress. Of the 40 female mayors in the country in 2003, 13 represented the RN. The RN is firmly opposed to the use of gender quotas.

Though a councilman of the RN (perhaps inadvertently) described his party as "a party of gentlemen" (Interview, October 4, 2002), women in the party uniformly agreed that they faced no discrimination, or as one woman RN local party vice president said, "There are no limitations for women [in the party]" (Interview, September 30, 2002). One woman mayor from the RN said that the challenge of being a woman in politics was "breaking the myth" about women's capabilities (Interview, December 4, 2002). A council-woman from the party declared, "I'm not a feminist. Do I think women have the same capacities as men? Yes" (Interview, December 18, 2002).

For congressional elections, the RN uses candidate-selection procedures that are considerably less centralized than those of the other party of the right, the UDI. The party's National Council is charged with ratifying all candidacies, but for the most part, the National Council simply rubber-stamps decisions taken at the district level. It appoints candidates only in spots where there is no local functioning party. Navia describes the process of becoming a legislative candidate as necessitating "firm control of the local level party apparatus. That can be accomplished either by winning control in an internal party election or simply by 'taking over' the local party appara-tus" (Navia 2004: 19). The following section explains the candidate-selection processes of the party for municipal elections, which mirror these procedures.

Candidate Selection for Municipal Office

A councilman representing the RN described how he was approached about running for office: "They went to my house to talk to me about running for the Renovación Nacional. The woman who went to talk to me was the sec-retary of a mayor [of a nearby town]. She's a councilor now too. She remem-bered me" (Interview, September 27, 2002). Candidate-selection decisions were exclusive-decentralized processes, typically involving only one or two local RN leaders. It was rare for the candidate chosen by these elites to face competition (Interview, July 10, 2002). Local party elites made decisions, which were then rubber-stamped in Santiago. According to one council member, the formal decision-making processes were overlooked and decision making by a couple of local elites was simply "undemocratic" (Interview, July 10, 2002). While other party members did not characterize the process of candidate selection as being undemocratic, they did agree that decisions were being made by a very limited number of party elites. The RN also grants incumbents automatic candidacy in the following municipal elections.

The selection process was biased in favor of RN members; although the exclusivity of the process eliminated the need for self-nomination, candidates were routinely chosen from the party's membership. This candidate-selection process, however, does not avoid the influence of local power monopolies. One RN local party vice president said, "If you don't have the money, you won't be running" (Interview, September 30, 2002). Being a part of the local elite is important to becoming a candidate of the party.

The lack of self-nomination proved important to increasing women's representation: a councilwoman from La Serena said that she had "no political ambition" and that she "didn't go looking for it" (Interview, December 18, 2002). The RN circumvents self-nomination, allowing women who might otherwise not run to participate in the process. By deciding on a candidate and then asking her to run, the RN has nominated more women candidates than would be expected of a party with neither gender quotas nor an ideological commitment to increasing women's representation.

The case of Adriana Peñafiel in La Serena is one in which self-nomination was wholly avoided—she was not only handpicked by the RN as the party's candidate in 1992 (and allowed to compete again in 1996 and 2000) but had also previously been appointed to the mayoral post by Pinochet. Peñafiel served continuously as mayor of La Serena from 1989 until 2004. La Serena, in Chile's fourth region, is one of the larger cities in the country, with a population of nearly 150,000. Its size and its beaches—which attract throngs of tourists during the summer months—make it an important city. In addition, La Serena is the capital of the region of Coquimbo and of the province of Elqui. Peñafiel is a native of La Serena and she is also a member of an influential political family. She is the granddaughter and niece of former mayors. After graduating from university in 1978, Peñafiel began working for the municipality, where she rose through the ranks before being appointed mayor. As the incumbent, she was well placed after the return to democracy to be her party's candidate, and she won her election despite her association with the authoritarian regime. Peñafiel explained that having been part of the military government was seen as a point against her and that Pinochet appointees had a difficult time winning their elections following democratization (Interview, December 4, 2002). Peñafiel's vote share in the first post-dictatorship elections tells a different story: she received more than twice as many votes as her nearest competitor.[7] While exclusive-decentralized candidate selection does not allow candidates to circumvent local power monopolies, Peñafiel was from an important political family in town and part of these power groups.

Despite the RN's lack of an ideological commitment to increasing women's representation and lack of quotas, 18.6 percent of the party's candidacies went to women in the 2000 municipal elections. This is the same percentage of women candidates as in the left-wing Partido por la Democracia (PPD), which actively encourages women's candidacies and has goals in place for increasing women's representation. The RN had a greater percentage of female candidates for municipal elections than it had in its national directorship (13.3 percent). The party's surprising ability to get women into municipal political positions demonstrates that exclusive-decentralized processes do avoid an important obstacle to women's candidacies.

The Partido de la Revolución Democrática in Mexico

The PRD emerged in 1989, the product of a broad coalition of leftist forces that had supported the presidential aspirations of Cuauhtémoc Cárdenas. Cárdenas, the son of Mexico's most revered president, abandoned the PRI; many of the earliest PRD members were PRI defectors. The enormous support that Cárdenas received in the 1988 elections meant that this party was a powerful force from its inception.

Like many leftist parties, the PRD espouses a clear commitment to women's rights. In its Declaration of Principles, the party states:

> The PRD is committed to fighting for gender equality in all human activities, for equality of opportunities and equality of condition for the access of women and men to the use, control, and benefits of the goods and services of society. Likewise, the party is committed to fighting for the equal participation of women in decision-making in all the areas of life: social, economic, political, cultural, and familial.[8]

Two women have headed the party: Rosario Robles was president from 2002 to 2003, and Amalia García presided from 1999 to 2002. The party took an early lead in pushing for greater female representation, but despite a clear rhetorical commitment to women's rights, it has not always produced results. The PRD's women's organization, for example, was recently subsumed under the newly formed Secretariat for Equity, which is charged with increasing not only gender equity but also the representation of young people (defined as under age 30) as party candidates. Furthermore, women's descriptive representation in both chambers of the legislature waxed and waned throughout the 1990s and 2000s, despite the use of gender quotas. As Rodríguez argues:

> Both the PRI and the PAN appear more committed to opening leadership opportunities to women than does the PRD, despite the PRD's litany of promises. It sometimes seems that as far as women are concerned, the PRD is resting on its laurels; after taking the lead in espousing more opportunities for women, it has now placed women's concerns on the back burner. (2003: 123)

Bruhn, however, believes that the PRD's efforts to promote women were hampered because PRD members are disproportionately men and because competition for candidacies was very strong within the party, owing in part to the fact that the legislature was open to parties of the opposition before Mexico fully democratized (2003). In other words, PRD candidates had a chance of winning seats in the legislature, whereas executive positions were overwhelmingly out of their reach. This may help explain women's congressional representation throughout the 1990s and 2000s. PRD women's representation in the Chamber of Deputies dropped from 24.3 percent in 1994 to 20.7 percent at the end of the 1990s, at a time when women's political participation was increasing. By 2005, women's share of seats had risen to 27.8 percent, but rose less than 2 percentage points over the next five years. The same pattern emerged in the Senate. Women's representation dropped from 26.7 percent in 1997 to only 18.7 percent in 2002. The PRD was the first party to mandate a quota for list positions, initially set at 20 percent, but shortly thereafter increased to 30 percent. By 2003, the quota was increased to 50 percent.

The women of the PRD may not be operating under conditions of equality within their party, but they are nonetheless likely to voice their political ambitions. When asked whether she aspired to higher office, a councilwoman answered, "Of course! I have certain ambitions. I love politics" (Interview, April 28, 2003). A woman mayor had fought a long and hard battle to become a candidate and, after losing her first electoral battle, nonetheless actively sought the candidacy for a second time (Interview, May 7, 2003).

The PRD aims for internal democracy: "The fact that the PRD was born of a rejection of the extremely 'vertical' decision making structure of the PRI would lead to a search for democratic rule-making procedures" (Langston 2008: 159). Many of its efforts have been aimed at producing highly participatory selection procedures. Throughout its short electoral history, the PRD has, despite some setbacks, moved increasingly toward selection processes that are inclusive and decentralized. The PRD used internal primaries in nearly half of the nation's 300 districts in 1991 but used none in 1994 (Bruhn 1997). The use of primaries in the 1991 elections led Bruhn to write that the PRD was using the most democratic procedures of any Mexican party. Consistent with the argument presented in this book, in those elections, the PRD nominated the fewest female candidates of any party. The primaries were in place (usually) for Senate seats, plurality seats in the Chamber of Deputies, and mayoral elections (Bruhn 1997). Presidential candidates were selected via closed primary for both the 1994 and 2000 elections, as were gubernatorial candidates (Wuhs 2006: 41). In 2001, the PRD further opened up its selection procedures by allowing the National Executive Committee to decide between open and closed primaries for selecting all candidates, except seats elected under proportional representation rules (Wuhs 2006: 42). By 2004, the party had gone a step further and began relying solely on open primaries.

During this time period, the PRD also began using polls to choose more competitive candidates. According to Wuhs, "While selection decisions were not made on the basis of those polls, party leaders used them to encourage some pre-candidates to seek the party's nomination (and to discourage others)" (2006: 42).

The party's efforts to democratize internally have been complicated by its organizational problems. As Wuhs writes, "The central party office of the PRD was sorely underdeveloped as a result of frequent turnover, repeated fiscal crises and corruption problems, and disagreements about whether party development would be a benefit or a liability. Its weak development extended to state and municipal party offices as well" (2008: 133). Both the national party offices and the municipal-level offices in municipalities in the states of Veracruz, Yucatán, and Mexico appeared underfunded, understaffed, and disorganized. Ancient-looking computers competed for desk space with mounds of paperwork at the national offices. The national party offices were willing but unable to provide me with data on women's representation in the party; they would e-mail and fax me data whenever they did find it, forwarding material over the course of months. The municipal-level offices were in even worse shape. The PRD barely functioned in Mérida. The party's selection methods have also been complicated by the use of reserved slots for popular movement candidates and quotas for women. The PRD's selection methods were often formulated to give an edge to party outsiders, unlike those of the PRI, which rewarded loyal membership. The PRD sought to increase the representation of popular movements and augment its own popularity by allowing nonparty members to participate in internal selection procedures and as party candidates (Bruhn 1997). At one point, the party set aside half of its candidacies for PRD members and reserved the other half for nonparty candidates (Bruhn 1997: 156).

Candidate Selection for Municipal Office

The PRD maintains that it uses inclusive-decentralized selection methods to choose its municipal candidates. In practice, the PRD often uses decentralized selection processes that are much more exclusive. One PRD mayoral candidate from a small town in the state of Mexico[9] explained to me that party elites told her that she would be the party's candidate even before the primary. Technically, there was a primary, but she had already been designated as the candidate (Interview, March 28, 2003). Although I was unable to confirm her assertion because I did no other interviews in that municipality, the cases of Pueblo Viejo and Tianguistenco follow this same pattern, lending credence to her story.[10] These cases fit less neatly into the category of either exclusive or inclusive selection; while in the town of Amanalco, the PRD was clearly using exclusive-decentralized processes.

The PRD's Exclusive-Decentralized/Inclusive-Decentralized Selection: A Primary in Pueblo Viejo?

In Pueblo Viejo, the PRD had wrestled power away from the PRI only in 2000, after the PRI's candidate-selection procedures had pushed the enormously popular Reyna Enith Domínguez Wong to run under the PRD banner. Pueblo Viejo, located in the northernmost corner of Veracruz, is separated from the large port city of Tampico by only a short boat ride. Domínguez Wong became both the first woman mayor and the first PRD mayor of Pueblo Viejo after unsuccessfully vying for the mayoral candidacy in the PRI. When she was refused the candidacy, Domínguez Wong left the party and ran as the candidate of a small leftist party in 1997. Her unsuccessful bid led her to the PRD.

Widely known as *la doctora*, Domínguez Wong was a longtime member of the PRI and wife of former PRI mayor Marcos Acevedo Rodríguez. People of all political stripes agreed that *la doctora* was highly regarded. An obstetrician, Domínguez Wong had helped deliver many residents in this city of 50,000. Her turn as First Lady of Pueblo Viejo had only increased her popularity.

It was not surprising, then, that the PRD would choose Domínguez Wong as their candidate. When she defected from the PRI, many of her supporters did as well. Her supporters were incensed by the PRI's decision, and many of them personally told Domínguez Wong that they would vote for her regardless of her political affiliation. Her tremendous popularity virtually assured the PRD an easy (yet historic) win. Domínguez Wong was chosen as the PRD candidate using decentralized selection procedures that are not easily characterized as either exclusive or inclusive. Although Domínguez Wong was the "consensus" candidate of the local party, the state office insisted on a primary, in part because Domínguez Wong was a candidate in search of a party rather than a committed Perredista (Interview, May 7, 2003). The primary was used to justify a local decision to state party elites, but the extent to which a real primary occurred was unclear (Multiple interviews): there was much confusion among PRD elites in Pueblo Viejo about whether a primary election "had even taken place" (Interview, May 7, 2003). With Domínguez Wong as their candidate, the PRD was for the first time able to beat the PRI, which had handily beat the PRD in 1997 (40 percent to 25 percent), in 1994 (68 percent to 20 percent), and in earlier elections (in which the PRI had always received a minimum of 85 percent of the vote).

The PRD's Exclusive-Decentralized/Inclusive-Decentralized Selection: The Case of Tianguistenco

Tianguistenco, a municipality of about 50,000 in the state of Mexico, obtained its name from the *tianguis* (market) that had long drawn people to the city and that still takes place every Tuesday. Tianguistenco was governed by PRI mayor Alejandro Olivares Monterrubio. The PRI also held all of the council seats elected via plurality. The PRD held 2 of the council seats (both proportional representation seats) of 10 total seats on the council. Although in the city of Mérida the PRD had used a legitimate primary to select its mayoral candidate, here the PRD used a primary only nominally. The primary was used to mask the more important selection decisions that had already been made. In Tianguistenco, the party did actually have a primary election, but only after stacking the odds in favor of the local party leaders' preferred candidate. The party members, aware of this preference, voted for the favored candidate in the primary (Interview, June 18, 2003). In the case of Tianguistenco, as in Pueblo Viejo, the primary was a sham that pitted one exceptionally strong candidate with the full backing of the party elite against a much weaker candidate (Multiple interviews).

The PRD's Exclusive-Decentralized Selection:
Handpicking a Candidate in Amanalco

The small municipality of Amanalco is less than 30 minutes north of Valle de Bravo, where moneyed Mexico City residents enjoy rustic weekend re-treats (and smog-free fresh air). But while the full-time residents of Valle de Bravo are employed in the tertiary sector, Amanalco's 20,000 residents re-main dependent on agricultural work and, more recently, on a robust trout-farming industry.

Despite the fact that candidate selection for mayoral positions was sup-posed to be done via primaries, the PRD also chose some municipal candi-dates using clearly less inclusive methods. This was the case in Amanalco. Amanalco had traditionally been governed by the PRI, and in 2000 the PRI's most serious competition came from the PAN. The PRD enjoyed little success in Amanalco and placed only one candidate on the council in 2000. For the 2000 municipal elections, the PRI received over 50 percent of the vote, while the PAN obtained 26 percent of the vote and the PRD received one-tenth of all votes. By 2003, however, the party benefited from the grow-ing disillusionment with President Fox and had become the most significant competition for the PRI. The party's traditional weakness in Amanalco may have been part of the reason why it made no effort to open up its candidate-selection processes to a larger group. There was no primary in Amanalco, nor even any pretense of having held a primary. Candidate selection took place locally, but decision making was done by only a couple of local party leaders.

The party's strong ideological convictions about the role of women in society are incongruent with the status of women in the party. The PRD has been unable to place many women in mayoral candidacies or in local positions of power. The PRD proposed a smaller percentage of women can-didates than the PRI. More importantly, the party's talk of parity is far removed from the current reality of local politics, in which not even 10 per-cent of the party's candidates for mayoral office are women.

The Partido Revolucionario Institucional in Mexico

From the four municipalities discussed in this book, the PRI used exclusive-decentralized selection solely in the case of Pueblo Viejo. The party relied on primaries to choose its local candidates in Amanalco and Tianguistenco and used a *dedazo* in Mérida (covered in Chapter 6).

The PRI's Exclusive-Decentralized Selection:
A Local *Dedazo* in Pueblo Viejo, Mexico

The changing Mexican political context forced the PRI to experiment with candidate-selection procedures. The party used three of the four possible forms of selection that I have outlined in this book to choose candidates for municipal elections. The PRI's use of primaries in the small towns of Amanalco and Tianguistenco were discussed in Chapter 4. Chapter 6 describes the use of exclusive-centralized selection in Mérida.

A short boat ride across the Rio Pánuco from Tampico, a city of more than three-quarters of a million people in the state of Tamaulipas, sits Pueblo Viejo, Veracruz. This municipality had been turned over to the PRD in 2000, after the popular Reyna Enith Domínguez Wong was prevented from running under the PRI party banner, as explained earlier in this chapter. The party elite ruled that it would not be appropriate for the PRI to allow Domínguez Wong to run for the mayoral position that her husband had earlier held. Dissatisfied with that decision, Domínguez Wong left the party to run for mayor in 1997 (unsuccessfully as a minor party candidate) before winning election in 2000 as a candidate of the PRD. The exclusive-decentralized selection decisions that the party used in Pueblo Viejo prevented Domínguez Wong from becoming the party's candidate and ultimately cost the PRI political control of the municipality.

Candidate-selection decisions were exclusive-decentralized, both in 1997 and for the 2000 elections that the party lost. Officially, the PRI chose its mayoral candidate by conducting a local survey to determine who the local population believed were the most qualified potential candidates for the position; the names of these individuals were then forwarded to the state-level PRI offices, where a decision was made (Interview, April 29, 2003). The reality of the situation was quite different: mayoral candidates were actually directly designated by the outgoing mayor (Multiple interviews), a continuation of the PRI's traditional *dedazo*. This deviation from the official process should not be considered an exceptional case. Langston explains:

> Even with the formal provisions for voting in the conventions, candidates for local deputies and municipal presidents were often chosen by the favoured method of forwarding a "candidate of unity", meaning no other potential candidate could even compete in the nomination. If there were no choice for the delegates, the "correct" candidate would always be nominated. This was (and is) done to by-pass the supposedly destructive, factional nature of the conventions by simply

not allowing several pre-candidates to campaign for delegate votes. (2001: 495)

In the case of Pueblo Viejo, there was speculation that the outgoing mayor had at least attempted to gauge popular demand and citizen attitudes before selecting a candidate in 2000 (Interview, May 9, 2003), but no polling of the population had taken place. The outgoing mayor had single-handedly wielded the authority to decide who the next PRI candidate would be. The party's candidate was then allowed to choose the candidates for council positions (Multiple interviews).

This system of candidate selection began to break down when Domínguez Wong refused to accept the decision of the sitting mayor. As mentioned earlier, Domínguez Wong's enormous popularity caused many PRI members to follow her to the PRD. When Domínguez Wong won the election, the system of candidate selection within the PRI in Pueblo Viejo was upended. The lack of an incumbent PRI mayor raised the question of who would designate the next mayoral candidate. Interviewees from the party were uncertain of what the party would do to choose its next candidate and feared that if they were unable to come to a consensus, they would be "forced" to hold a primary (Interview, May 9, 2003).

The use of selection procedures that are inclusive and centralized or exclusive and decentralized allows women to avoid one of the potential pitfalls discussed in Chapter 3, as the cases cited in this chapter demonstrate. Avoidance of even one of these obstacles—whether self-nomination or local power monopolies—is helpful to female aspirants and pre-candidates. Chapter 6 discusses the use of exclusive-centralized selection methods that allow potential female candidates to avoid both the pitfalls of self-nomination and the disadvantages posed by power monopolies. The chapter demonstrates that such exclusive-centralized procedures can prove advantageous.

6

"Less Democratic, but More Effective"

Exclusive-Centralized Selection

> The President invited me to participate as a candidate, but
> I said to him, "No, President, I can't be a candidate. I'm
> just not very good at speaking in town squares." Fujimori
> responded by saying to me, "Campaigns are different now.
> Besides, we need people we can trust in Congress."
>
> —MARTHA CHÁVEZ, who later became president of the Peruvian
> Congress (quoted in Alberto Adrianzén, Juan Rial, and Rafael
> Roncagliolo, *Países andinos: Los políticos*)

Through her own "personal force," Evita Perón was able to augment Argentine women's representation in Congress, making Argentina the world leader in women's congressional representation in the mid-1950s (Jones 1996: 77). U.S. President Lyndon B. Johnson significantly increased his appointment of women after hearing a woman whom he respected talk about discrimination against women (Freeman 2000). And President Carlos Menem of Argentina, like his Peruvian counterpart Alberto Fujimori, was personally responsible for ensuring the passage of a national quota law (Jones 1996: 78). When a personal commitment to increasing women's representation is coupled with exclusive-centralized selection procedures, women's representation can rise dramatically. As Chapter 3 explains, personal preferences can make a substantial difference in exclusive-centralized selection. Exclusive-centralized selection coupled with a bias against women would almost certainly result in fewer women candidates. However, even absent a preference for women, exclusive-centralized selection still proves advantageous to women because it allows women to avoid self-nomination and does not require that they gain the support of local power monopolies.

Candidate selection is centralized when "candidates are selected exclusively by a national party selectorate, with no procedure that allows for territorial and/or functional representation" (Rahat and Hazan 2001: 305). Selection is exclusive when the selectorate is limited to include only one or two individuals. Across Latin America, there is "evidence of the persistence in many parties of strong tendencies toward centralized decision making" (Zovatto G. 2007: 309). Determining whether parties are using exclusive selection methods is more complicated, in part because party documents may obscure who has true decision-making authority; real power can be "covered up" by formal procedures (Freidenberg 2003: 30). As Freidenberg notes, "It is very difficult to find in a party text that the election of a presidential candidate is done by a single person, like the party leader" (2003: 30). The same is often true of candidate selection for other political offices. Exclusive decision making continues to exist and is most likely the norm in certain types of political parties (Freidenberg 2003).[1] GEPPAL[2] data indicate that 17 percent of the largest parties in Latin America are using exclusive selection methods to select their legislative candidates (Roza 2010a: 131–132), but it is likely that this figure may underestimate just how regularly this form of selection is used.

Exclusive-centralized candidate selection has important parallels to appointment systems. Appointments are used to select officeholders for some political positions; for example, members of the judiciary and ambassadors are often appointed to their positions. These appointments are different from exclusive-centralized candidate-selection procedures in that appointments are intended to select an officeholder, while exclusive-centralized systems are used to select candidates who must then participate in an election to determine whether they will become officeholders. In appointment systems, decisions are usually being made at the top and by a small number of people, often by a single individual. Here, too, decision making can be said to be less democratic, and yet women are routinely better represented in appointed than in elected positions. The data in Graph 1.1 demonstrate as much: while women are 7.4 percent of mayors in the region and 20.5 percent of legislators, one of every four ministers in the region is a woman.[3] The data in Table 6.1 show that on average women are much more likely to be represented as governors in countries that use appointment rather than election. Examples of this phenomenon abound. The Nicaraguan legislature is illustrative of the effects of appointment; under the Sandinistas, the legislature was converted into an appointed body known as the Council of State. Women's share of seats was 9 percent in 1972, when this was an elected legislature, and 22 percent in 1980, when councilors were appointed. The figure dropped to 16 percent, however, when the legislature was once again popularly elected in 1995 (Saint-Germain and Chavez Metoyer 2008).[4] Five of the seven appointed governors in Costa Rica were women in the mid-1990s, while only 16 per-

TABLE 6.1. WOMEN'S REPRESENTATION AS GOVERNORS: APPOINTMENT
VERSUS ELECTION

Country	Number of Governors	Number of Women Governors	Percentage of Women Governors	Selection Method
Chile	13	6	46	Appointed
Honduras	18	6	33	Appointed
Panama	12	3	25	Appointed
Ecuador	22	4	18	Elected
El Salvador	14	2	14	Appointed
Brazil	27	3	11	Elected
Colombia	32	3	9	Elected
Guatemala	22	2	9	Appointed
Venezuela	24	2	8	Elected
Paraguay	17	1	6	Elected
Mexico	32	1	3	Elected
Argentina	24	0	0	Elected
Bolivia	9	0	0	Appointed
Cuba	15	0	0	Elected
Peru	26	0	0	Elected
Uruguay	19	0	0	Elected

Source: Data compiled from websites for individual countries.

Note: These were the most recent data available in October 2010.

cent of elected members of the Legislative Assembly were women (Craske 1999). Women have also been well represented in the judiciaries of Latin American countries, where appointed positions are common (Camp 1995, as cited in Craske 1999: 67).

Across the globe, scholars have found that women are better represented in appointed rather than in elected positions (Karnig and Walter 1975; Putnam 1976; Alterman Blay 1979; Karnig and Welch 1979; Welch and Karnig 1979; Darcy, Welch, and Clark 1994; Bruhn 2003). Four reasons have been proposed to explain this phenomenon (Darcy, Welch, and Clark 1994), yet none of these is useful in explaining the similar outcomes that we encounter in exclusive-centralized candidate-selection systems. First, women are better represented in appointment systems because those who do the appointing "will be expected to answer for their appointments" (Darcy, Welch, and Clark 1994: 157).[5] Although accountability can certainly explain why a president appointing her cabinet may strive to assemble a diverse group, it cannot help us to understand the benefits of an exclusive-centralized selection system, given that party rank and file are sometimes unable to identify the party selectorate. Second, in appointment systems, balancing appointments to avoid excluding any particular group is useful. This balancing has limited applicability to exclusive-centralized systems again because party leaders can avoid accountability; the selectorate may not feel it necessary to include as many groups as possible if its members are not receiving pressure and are unlikely to be blamed for a lack of representativeness. Third, some appointment systems are not true appointment systems; instead, positions are rotated within a group (for example, a city council will rotate the position of mayor among themselves), and hence women will be as likely as men to get a turn or will, at minimum, be represented in this position in the same proportion as they are represented in the group from which the position is chosen. This rotation method of selection is not useful to understanding exclusive-centralized selection since the selectorate would be too small for true rotation to take place. Fourth, scholars have pointed out that appointed positions are often less important than elected ones. Because these positions hold less power, elites are more willing to give them to women. This final explanation has no relevance to exclusive-centralized candidate selection since a range of political candidacies—ranging from the most important (the presidency) to those that are much less powerful (local council member)—has been chosen using this selection method.

Nonetheless, exclusive-centralized candidate-selection processes do mimic appointment systems in two important ways that can simultaneously explain why women are better represented in appointed rather than elected positions and why exclusive-centralized selection may advantage women. First, in both appointment systems and exclusive-centralized selection, the selectorate tends to be very small. For example, cabinet members are usually chosen by a single individual, typically the head of state. Similarly, in exclusive-centralized systems, as the cases described subsequently elucidate, the selectorate usually consists of one or two individuals. Second, both the appointment process and exclusive-centralized selection circumvent the process of self-nomination. Figure 3.1 depicted the typical process of becoming an officeholder. In both exclusive-centralized selection and in appointment, eligibles do not need to become aspirants in order to end up as officeholders. Instead, party elites approach eligibles and transform them into either candidates (in the case of elected positions) or into officeholders (in the case of appointed positions). The parallels to appointment systems are indispensable in understanding women's success in exclusive-centralized selection.

The story of Casimira Rodríguez Romero depicts this process and allows us to understand how appointment systems work in women's favor when the selectorate has no active bias against women. Rodríguez Romero became Bolivia's Minister of Justice in 2006. Like many other poor, indigenous women, Rodríguez Romero had left her parents' home to work as a maid in a large city while she was still a child. She joined a union of domestic workers and ultimately rose through the ranks of the union to hold the post of Secretary

General of the Confederation, which includes all Latin American countries. President Evo Morales, the first indigenous president of Bolivia, asked Rodríguez Romero to serve as Minister of Justice. She replied, "I don't want to be the Minister. I'm not even a lawyer" (Rodríguez Romero 2007). President Morales reiterated his request, and she accepted the opportunity to join his "historic cabinet." Not only had Rodríguez Romero never aspired to this position, in effect, she moved from being an eligible to becoming an officeholder because she was designated as such by President Morales.

The following sections of this chapter use cases from Chile and Mexico to demonstrate the ways in which exclusive-centralized candidate selection can benefit women. The Unión Demócrata Independiente (UDI) in Chile and the Partido Revolucionario Institucional (PRI) in Mérida were able to place many women into candidacies and ultimately in positions of power by handpicking candidates. Cases from Peru and Argentina are presented as well to further illustrate these processes.

The Unión Demócrata Independiente in Chile

The UDI occupies the position farthest to the right among the major Chilean parties and has been described as "a blend of neoliberalism and strongly conservative Catholicism" (Scully and Valenzuela 1993: 7). From its beginnings, the party identified itself strongly with the Pinochet regime and maintained support for the authoritarian enclaves created during the dictatorship (Garretón 2000). One of the party's founding fathers described the UDI as a party guided by three principles: first, it is a party committed to free market economic politics; second, it is a "popular" party aligned with the poor; third, it is a party defined by Christian values (Longueira Montes 2003: 28). The UDI is the fastest-growing party in Chile (Hinojosa 2009; Luna 2010). Its strength can be attributed to "the existence of a defined project, an iron discipline and a cohesive team" (Joignant and Navia 2003: 148).

At the national level, candidate selection for legislative candidates is "the most centralized candidate selection process among Chilean parties" (Navia 2008b: 111). The party's success in legislative elections has affected other political parties; these "other parties have underlined the apparently negative effects that promoting bottom-up mechanisms in the candidate selection process eventually bring about for the parties that do not centralize the candidate selection mechanism" (Navia 2004: 18). To select congressional candidates, the UDI maintains both an electoral commission that works to identify potential candidates and organizations devoted to preparing these candidates for their elections.

Considered the extreme party of the right, the UDI elects more women to municipal office than any other party in the country. The UDI also has the largest percentage of women members of any major party: 63 percent (Muñoz D'Albora and Wojciechowski Levine 1996). It proposed the highest percentage of women candidates for municipal office (nearly 24 percent), despite the fact that unlike three of the major parties of the Concertación, the UDI does not use gender quotas. Of the 40 women mayors in the country, 17 were UDI members, although the party's platform makes no mention of increasing female representation in politics (Hinojosa 2009).

The percentage of UDI women in local politics cannot be attributed to an ideological commitment to women's representation. As opposed to other parties, the UDI has no gender quotas and is ideologically opposed to their use. The party's constitution talks explicitly about the promotion of women but also focuses on allowing them to carry out their roles as wives and mothers. The following statement, part of its founding principles, conveys the party's position toward women:

> Unión Demócrata Independiente recognizes the importance of women in society, for the role that they have played throughout the long history of our country. Unión Demócrata Independiente will energetically uphold the principle of equal rights for women in all of their activities, in employment or otherwise, in which they serve alongside men; the party will work to open opportunities to women, and will oppose all forms of economic or social discrimination that women may face. Likewise, Unión Demócrata Independiente especially values the virtues and proper functions of women as carriers of life, nuclei of the family, and the principal transmitters of values, morals, and traditions. Consequently, Unión Demócrata Independiente will work so that women's work in society can be compatible with their proper functions, especially those related to maternity, child-rearing, and caring for their families.[6]

According to the UDI, the number of qualified women ought to determine the number of women in office, and so the current underrepresentation of women represents a lack of qualified women (Interview, July 29, 2002). UDI leader Julio Dittborn stated, "If there effectively were very few women participating in politics, that in and of itself would not seem problematic. It's not a matter of incorporating women just so that the statistics will indicate a greater number of parliamentarians or ministers" (quoted in Macauley 1993). UDI members see the deficit of women politicians as a result therefore of both this supply problem and what can be termed a gendered demand problem. The conventional wisdom in the party is that "women prefer to vote for men" because women are jealous of other women (Interview, July 29, 2002), a sentiment also voiced by nonpolitical UDI women.[7]

While women's representation in municipal politics is high, this is not the case for other levels of government or for party structures. Only 1 of the party's 11 senators is a woman, and only 3 of its 35 deputies are women. By contrast, the conservative Renovación Nacional (RN) also has three women deputies, though it elected only half the number of deputies as the UDI. In 1998, women made up just over 5 percent of the national directorate of the UDI—to put this into perspective, the RN's directorate was composed of more than 13 percent women, and in the four other important parties, women constituted between 13 and 29 percent of directorates. The UDI was the only major Chilean party that saw its percentage of women in party decision-making bodies decrease during the 1990s, from 7.7 percent to 5.8 percent (Rico 2000).

UDI members explained the high levels of women's representation in local politics either as a result of the lack of discrimination within their party or, alternatively, as a reflection of women's natural roles. The influential UDI mayor of an important municipality within the Santiago metropolitan area explained that the party's high proportion of women in municipal office was not a party strategy and did not reflect party goals; rather, he said, the party was focused on "choosing the best person [for each position], regardless of gender" (Interview, August 27, 2002). UDI women voiced their belief that discrimination did not exist within the party. One young councilwoman went so far as to state that "it's much easier being a woman; as a woman, doors are opened for you" and "there's an advantage because there are so few women" (Interview, July 29, 2002). When asked about the high percentage of UDI women serving as mayors and council members, a UDI regional president said that this was women's natural field because it was the "administration of the biggest house" (Interview, November 21, 2002). This belief echoes Elsa Chaney's *supermadre* theory, which linked women's political participation with their roles within the family unit.[8] Such an explanation, however, fails to address why these traditional roles have benefited UDI women in particular, and not women from other parties.

A UDI council member from the midsized city of Talagante noted that most of the leaders within neighborhood organizations are women and called them "the engine of the neighborhood groups" (Interview, October 4, 2002). One UDI councilwoman theorized that women's local representation in the UDI might be high because the party "had very solid principles," was "focused on the everyday problems," and offered "a simpler discourse" (Interview, July 29, 2002). Not only did members of the party attribute women's greater representation at the municipal level to their traditional social roles, but party women also eagerly announced that they were not feminists (Multiple interviews).

In its legislative candidate selection, the UDI has the "most centralized and top-down approach to candidate selection" (Navia 2008b: 111). It also exercises the most proactive approach to candidate recruitment, using "an electoral commission that works during nonelection years to identify and prepare potential candidates for districts where there is no UDI legislative representation. Similarly, in districts where the incumbent UDI deputy will likely seek a senate seat, or vacate the seat for whatever reason, the UDI works to identify an attractive new candidate" (Navia 2008b: 110). These processes mirror those used by the UDI for municipal-level elections, as I explain in the following section.

Candidate Selection for Municipal Office

Manuel Fuentes was mayor of Peñaflor, a medium-sized city about an hour away from Santiago in the Metropolitan Region. A former member of the Socialist Party, Fuentes was disappeared for three months during the Pinochet dictatorship. Because of his association with the left, he was unable to return to the job as a hospital administrator that he had held before 1973; after his detention by the government, he could find employment only as a waiter at a local restaurant. Eighteen years later, elections were once again held at the municipal level. By then, Fuentes was well known in his hometown for his involvement in local sports teams (Multiple interviews). The UDI, recognizing his popularity, asked him to run for mayor in 1996.

The UDI employed exclusive-centralized candidate selection. The official party statutes explain a rigorous process involving search committees and requiring that the local UDI office draw up a list of names according to strict profiles, but actual party practices are less formal. The process of candidate selection could be more accurately referred to as a *dedazo*. One unsuccessful candidate to the council in La Serena was asked to be a candidate directly by one of the most important national UDI politicians; candidate decisions, she said, "are decided over there in Santiago" (Interview, December 4, 2002). Although the process can vary, the UDI deputy or senator from a particular region decides who would be an ideal candidate; the final decision is then made by the Congress member and the UDI district president.

Of this process, one UDI councilman said, "It looks less democratic, but it's more effective" (Interview, September 12, 2002). This same council member felt that the UDI's selection processes allowed the party to choose the most qualified people as candidates. He also believed that this system was "more just" than that employed by other parties; he argued that although the Partido por la Democracia (PPD) has internal elections, "all that happens is that you take as many friends and family as you find down to vote for you" but "that's not democracy."

This exclusive-centralized selection allows the party to nominate outsiders, and nominating party outsiders is one reason why the UDI has so many women in municipal politics. Although one national-level UDI person explained that the party was looking for municipal candidates "who have been leaders within the party for many years," the UDI was much more likely than other parties to choose nonparty members as candidates, such as Manuel Fuentes (Interview, June 14, 2004). A UDI councilman explained that the UDI chose a nonparty member to be its privileged candidate over him, despite the fact that he had been an active member and held internal party positions for many years, because the privileged candidate was acknowledged to be a "person of the people" (Interview, September 17, 2002). The popularity of the privileged candidate and thus his ability to win the election were more important than service and long-term loyalty to the party.

Considering the party's ideological focus, it was surprising to find that the UDI not only selected people from outside the UDI rank and file for candidacy but also, at times, chose candidates who were ideologically at odds with the party. The party's exclusive-centralized selection procedures made this possible. One UDI councilor stated, "I'm an enemy of political doctrine" (Interview, September 12, 2002). A councilman from Talagante said that he ended up a candidate of the UDI "because it was easier to be a candidate of the right" than a candidate of the left and center-left parties. Because "the doors were closed" to his being a candidate of the Concertación, even though ideologically he was in line with the parties of the left, he chose to take the UDI up on its offer of a candidacy (Interview, September 12, 2002).[9] Manuel Fuentes, the UDI mayor described earlier, was very grateful that the party had taken a chance on him: "The UDI believed in me." Despite the fact that he was ideologically far from the UDI's position on important issues and was a former Socialist who had been tortured for his political beliefs, the UDI decided to ask this man to run for mayor because his popularity ensured a win (Interview, October 2, 2002). A female UDI mayor whose own lack of ideology was the subject of much talk in town deflected a question about her devotion to UDI principles by asking, "How could I not be of the right?" (Interview, December 16, 2002). Although reputedly not ideologically aligned with the UDI, she was willing to subvert her own convictions for the opportunity to be a candidate.

In addition to giving party outsiders candidacies, the UDI puts genuine effort into recruiting candidates. The UDI is known to use scientific methods, such as polling, to decide candidacies, leading a Partido Demócrata Cristiano (PDC) Congress member to state, "They take pragmatism to an extreme" (Interview, September 16, 2002). Strategic recruitment, however, is a necessity for any party using exclusive-centralized selection processes that wants to field strong candidates. As opposed to parties employing inclusive candidate-selection procedures, both exclusive-decentralized and exclusive-centralized parties, like the UDI, must seek out candidates since no functioning institution for self-nomination exists. The UDI mayor of Talagante explained her entrance into politics by saying, "I didn't get involved; they got me involved." She was asked to run and won (Interview, December 16, 2002). It is typical for the UDI party leaders to seek out people to run for office, in many cases going directly to their homes and asking them to be candidates (Multiple interviews).

The UDI is a disciplined party, in which candidate decisions made at higher levels are not questioned by the local rank and file.[10] Local power monopolies see their influence diminished because of this deference to the party leadership's authority. Decisions are made away from the nucleus of local power and are respected locally. The UDI prides itself on its internal discipline. Having more than one pre-candidate for municipal elections is rare (Interview, October 1, 2002). Part of the UDI's electoral strategy has been to run fewer candidates to avoid diffusing the vote (Interview, October 2, 2002; see also Hinojosa and Franceschet, forthcoming, for a discussion of this strategy). In the large city of La Serena, for example, the UDI regional president explained that although the party could have run eight people, it chose to run only four from the Alianza, the coalition of the right (Interview, November 21, 2002). This latter strategy requires incredible discipline within a party and a long-term strategy. One of the few benefits that parties can offer their members is candidacies. Limiting these should have important repercussions, but UDI members have maintained party discipline, and only rarely are party decisions questioned (Multiple interviews).

The UDI's exclusive candidate-selection procedures extend to candidacies for council members, which are decided by the party's designated mayoral candidate. The discretion that privileged candidates (those candidates informally viewed as mayoral candidates before mayor and council member elections were separated in 2004) within the UDI have to make their own candidate decisions for councils may be one of the reasons why the party has managed to get more women into local office. One young councilwoman made clear that she ended up in her position because the privileged candidate went to the UDI Youth offices looking for young people to add to her ticket. She was asked to be on the ticket and unexpectedly ended up on the council (Interview, July 29, 2002). The party ticket is composed in this manner, often with decisions being made solely by the privileged candidate. The privileged candidates, therefore, have the ability to increase women's representation when choosing their tickets.

The UDI's nomination of more women candidates than that of any other party is a reflection of selection that circumvents local power monopolies and self-nomination. Table 6.2 provides data on female candidates from all major parties in the 2000 municipal elections. Although the variation across parties may not appear dramatic, the difference in the percentage of female candidates between the UDI and all other major parties is statistically significant at the 0.005 level.[11] Women were 55 percent more likely to emerge as municipal candidates from exclusive-centralized selection procedures than from inclusive-decentralized methods. A simple logit regression revealed that candidates chosen via exclusive-centralized selection procedures were 55 percent more likely to be women than candidates in parties using inclusive-decentralized selection (see Hinojosa 2005 for more information). Candidates chosen via exclusive-centralized selection were also 37 percent more likely to be female than candidates in parties employing exclusive-decentralized selection. The differences in probabilities are significant at the 95 percent level. The difference in probabilities of women candidates between exclusive-decentralized

TABLE 6.2. FEMALE CANDIDACY IN THE 2000 MUNICIPAL ELECTIONS

Party	Number of Candidates	Number of Female Candidates	Percentage of Female Candidates
PDC	619	103	16.6
PPD	382	71	18.6
PRSD	278	41	14.7
PS	370	63	17.0
RN	515	96	18.6
UDI	364	87	23.9

PDC, Partido Demócrata Cristiano; PPD, Partido por la Democracia; PRSD, Partido Radical Social Demócrata; PS, Partido Socialista; RN, Renovación Nacional; UDI, Unión Demócrata Independiente.

Source: Author's data set (compiled from information available at http://elecciones.gov.cl/SitioHistorico/index2000_muni.htm).

Note: This table shows data for only the six major parties.

and inclusive-decentralized candidate-selection procedures is not statistically significant, indicating that exclusive-centralized candidate selection is most effective at eliminating obstacles to women's candidacies. In other words, the combination of exclusive selection and centralized selection is most potent.

Women can be advantaged when selection is both exclusive and centralized, as can other traditional political outsiders. The case of Manuel Fuentes indicates that exclusive-centralized candidate selection benefits not only women but also various categories of individuals who are unlikely to self-nominate or to have access to the local power monopolies that play an important role in local politics.

Party women were reluctant to project themselves as politically ambitious—the mayor of Talagante said, "I say that I'm not a politician" (Interview, December 16, 2002)—though they often mentioned that they would be willing to do "whatever the party asked" of them (Interview, July 29, 2002).[12] Such comments indicate that self-nomination would have been problematic for women candidates and that avoiding self-nomination contributes to the success of the UDI in getting women into local politics.

Unlike other parties, the UDI has the resources to finance municipal campaigns and, consequently, has been effective in getting its candidates elected. Women's candidacies then translate into political offices. This fact is reflected in the percentages of women municipal officeholders who are UDI members and affiliates.

The Partido Revolucionario Institucional in Mexico

As Chapter 4 mentions, candidate selection within the PRI has been undergoing dramatic changes in the last two decades, and the party continues to experiment with selection procedures, as evidenced by the methods used in Amanalco, Tianguistenco, Pueblo Viejo, and Mérida. The following section describes the selection processes in Mérida. Members of the PRI explained that the party technically can use four different candidate-selection practices: selection by an assembly; by a council; through a primary election; or through traditional, indigenous means of leader selection, referred to as *usos y costumbres*. As one council member was quick to admit, however, "In practice, [candidates] were handpicked and later this was covered up by having an assembly" (Interview, May 26, 2003). This comment indicates that *dedazos* were even more common. This more typical form of selection has historically produced mayors who were "unpopular with the general public, local politicians, and members of the ayuntamiento [town hall]" (Rodríguez 1997).

The PRI's Exclusive-Centralized Selection: Traditional Selection in Mérida

The PRI used the exclusive-centralized candidate-selection procedures that had made it infamous in Mérida, even though the party had been forced to adopt new practices for selecting candidates in many other municipalities. The governor chose Mérida's mayoral candidate (Multiple interviews); this could be seen as "a consensual designation, though in the end, the governor made the decision" (Interview, May 26, 2003). The incumbent PRI council members agreed that the mayoral candidate, though designated, "was the best person for the job" or felt that "no one else wanted to run" (Interview, May 16, 2003; Multiple other interviews). The conventional wisdom, however, was that even though the individual selected was the best possible candidate, this type of selection process might nonetheless be seen by some as an "imposition" (Interview, May 26, 2003).

The mayoral candidate was then allowed to choose the candidates to the city council who would run on his slate (Multiple interviews). While the mayoral candidate had tremendous leeway in making his decision, he nevertheless was strategic in giving various PRI sectors representation on the list (Interview, May 27, 2003). Of the more than one dozen council seats in this large city, half were apportioned to women. The mayoral candidate was likely to be acquainted with those he chose to place on his list, but he had not simply picked friends to be council candidates (Multiple interviews).

While some have argued that the traditional selection procedures used by the PRI have been detrimental to potential women candidates because they were so "closed" (Rodríguez 2003), I argue that these traditional selection procedures (exclusive-centralized) could benefit women because they allowed them to avoid self-nomination and local monopolies. Historically, the PRI proposed the greatest percentages of female candidates and, through exclusive-centralized selection methods, was able to place women onto party lists (Multiple interviews). The continuation of exclusive-centralized candidate-selection procedures with an increased supply and demand for female candidates may have actually allowed more women to attain municipal positions. Although the mayoral candidate chosen was male, he personally selected the slate of council candidates: half of these candidacies went to women. The PRI's gender quotas cannot explain his actions, since the party's 50 percent quota was set in November 2001, months after the new mayor and council were inaugurated.

Exclusive-Centralized Selection
in Comparative Perspective

Exclusive-centralized selection introduces more women into politics by obliterating the need for self-nomination and removing the influence of local networks. With data obtained by GEPPAL from 92 parties (those with the greatest representation in 18 Latin American countries), Roza used statistical analysis to test the effects of candidate-selection procedures on both the percentage of female candidates and the percentage of female legislators. She reported as follows:

> First, the candidate selection process has important consequences for the composition of candidate lists. Our findings indicate that women fare worse in primaries, both open and closed, compared to all other types of selection processes. This corroborates previous research which has found that the democratization of candidate selection processes can decrease the number of women included in electoral lists (Hazan 2002; Hinojosa 2005, 2009; Baldez 2004). . . . [E]xclusive (national) selection processes result in the selection of more female candidates than primaries.[13] (2010a: 165–166)

These powerful results give further credence to the argument that I am making here. Roza's analysis is important because it also demonstrates that these processes function in a similar fashion for other offices; in other words, while my work here has tested only the relationship between candidate-selection procedures and women's representation for municipal-level office, Roza proves that this is also true for national legislative elections.

In the following sections, I use several cases to illustrate my argument and to extend it beyond local-level politics. Important Latin American female politicians, including Cristina Fernández, have recently been chosen through exclusive-centralized candidate selection. I discuss the selection of women for significant political positions by Alberto Fujimori of Peru and Juan Perón of Argentina.

Handpicking Candidates in Peru

This book began with the story of Michelle Bachelet, who was handpicked for the presidency of Chile by then president Ricardo Lagos. While neither the Socialist Party nor the Concertación chose candidates via exclusive-centralized selection, Bachelet was clearly the outgoing president's choice, although she was not the top choice of the Socialist Party elite (Navia 2008a). Her selection, however, would not have been possible without his popularity and her undeniable strength in the polls. These are concerns that are inapplicable when exclusive-centralized selection is combined with authoritarianism, as was the case in Peru.

By 1990, when Alberto Fujimori became Peru's president, the traditional parties had been discredited. The party system breakdown allowed a self-professed outsider who had never held office to win the presidency. For the first couple of years of Fujimori's presidency, Peru could be described as an example of Guillermo O'Donnell's delegative democracy, but in April 1992, Fujimori's auto-coup ended Peruvian democracy (Cameron 1997). Fujimori continued in office until 2000.

During Fujimori's decade in power, domestic violence legislation was proposed and passed, the criminal code on rape was amended, a quota was adopted despite initial derision by Congress members, the law finally fully recognized grassroots women's organizations, changes to the judicial system resulted in half of new appointments going to women, two women (Martha Chávez and Martha Hildebrandt) served as presidents of Congress, the percentage of women in the legislature rose to 20 percent, the Ministry of Women and the Public Defender for Women were created, and at one point all four members of the Governing Council of Congress were women (Barrig 2001; Yáñez 2003; Schmidt 2006).[14] What explains these dramatic changes?[15]

Fujimori was able to place women into positions of power because his extraordinarily weak parties allowed power to be concentrated in his hands. As Schmidt explains, "Fujimori was the undisputed leader of his own personalistic movement and thus free to recruit female talent that would enhance his government's image" (Schmidt 2006: 161). Fujimori maintained complete control of his party structures, mainly by keeping his parties weak and transient. He created parties in time for elections and dissolved them immediately after; Change 90, New Majority, Let's Go Neighbors, and Peru 2000 were "disposable parties" that served only as personalistic vehicles (Levitsky and Cameron 2001). Having created his own parties, Fujimori could choose candidates himself. The selection procedures of Fujimori's parties allowed many women access to Congress (Schmidt and Saunders 2004).

The Fujimorista parties used exclusive-centralized selection; decision-making power resided with Alberto Fujimori. Potential nominees went through a rigorous process:

> Fujimori used methodical screening processes to select candidates
> for Congress. Prospective candidates were subjected to background

checks, public opinion surveys, and even psychological interviews. A similar process was used to scrutinize candidates for the position of minister and for other top bureaucratic posts. Although these recruitment methods may have been more appropriate for selecting corporate executives than public servants, they were more receptive to new female talent than were the old-boy networks of the established political parties and the newer opposition movements. (Schmidt 2006: 161–162)

Fujimori's first party, Change 90, included many women candidates because, "As a hopeless minor presidential candidate in early 1990, Fujimori had to round out the congressional lists of his . . . party with many marginal figures, some of whom were women" (Schmidt 2006: 153). While these candidates, both men and women, were unlikely to be elected, Fujimori continued to field female candidates with better results in future elections. For example, five of the seven women in the elected body charged with rewriting the constitution were members of Fujimori's party. In 1995, the president's party nominated a smaller percentage of women candidates than other parties, but these women were much more likely to be elected than men on the list (Schmidt 2006: 157). The adoption of a quota law meant that by 2000 women were nearly equally represented on all party lists, and "whereas female Fujimoristas were once again more likely to be elected than men running on the president's list, the chances of women on other lists were only about half those of their male colleagues" (Schmidt 2006: 160).

The political situation of Peruvian women changed dramatically during the years of the Fujimori government. Fujimori utilized exclusive-centralized selection procedures that allowed women's representation to increase tremendously during his decade in office.

The Case of the Peróns

This book also began with the case of Cristina Fernández, who became president of Argentina after first serving as First Lady. The *dedazo* that brought Fernández into the Casa Rosada had previously been used by Juan Perón.

Evita Perón, Juan Perón's second wife, obtained power through her relationship to her husband, but she was herself politically talented. Her influence was heightened by the Eva Perón Foundation, a charitable organization with assets of over US$200 million in 1950. The Foundation allowed her to improve the lives of the many thousands who received sewing machines, bicycles, clothing, or cash from the foundation (Zabaleta 2000: 231). Her political strength led for calls by the Women's Peronista Party[16] and the Confederation of Labor for a Perón-Perón ticket in 1951. Political pressures ultimately forced her to refuse consideration as Juan Perón's running mate (Zabaleta 2000: 261), and others have suggested that part of those pressures came from Juan Perón himself, who may have been afraid that Evita could pose a real challenge to him (Hollander 1974: 53).[17]

It was not, then, Evita Perón who became the first *presidenta* in Argentina's history. Instead it was Juan Perón's third wife, Isabel, who became president in 1974. Perón's handpicking of his wife as his vice presidential candidate in 1973 resulted in the unlikely rise of this woman to the nation's highest office. Isabel (her stage name) met her future husband shortly after joining a folk music ensemble that had her dancing throughout nightclubs in Latin America. During one of her performances in Panama, 25-year-old Isabel met the exiled former president. They married five years later in Madrid. In 1973, after 18 years in exile, Juan Perón was allowed to return to Argentina and shortly thereafter to the presidency. Perón chose his wife as his vice president because he was unwilling to share political power and fearful of antagonizing any elements of the Peronista Party immediately before the impending election. The sudden death of Perón, on July 1, 1974, pushed his widow into the presidency.[18] Isabel was thought by some to be "a woman completely without political talent, a person who was hopelessly out of her depth when great responsibility was forced upon her, a figurehead manipulated by unscrupulous men who were little more than gangsters" (Alexander 1979: 150). Isabel Perón was in office until a military coup removed her from power on March 23, 1976.

Exclusive-centralized candidate selection in this case was used by Juan Perón to maintain power in his own hands. Rather than select a vice presidential candidate from within the already-divided Peronista Party, Perón handpicked his wife. Two decades earlier, Perón could also have chosen Evita as his running mate, but he did not despite calls from two of the three sectors of his party to do so. While Evita Perón had been a formidable political force and an undeniably charismatic figure, Isabel Perón wielded no political power. She was a political neophyte who could not (and did not) challenge Juan Perón.

These situations highlight the fact that exclusive-centralized selection can produce varied results; while it can, as in the case of the Kirchners, bring an already qualified individual to office, it can just as easily be used to place someone like Isabel Perón in a political position. The same would be true if we were speaking of male politicians: politically talented men with strong backgrounds can be advantaged by exclusive-centralized procedures, as can politically inexperienced men.

This chapter demonstrates the potential advantages that exclusive-centralized selection can have for female candidates. Absent an active bias against them, women will benefit from exclusive-centralized selection because of the avoidance of self-nomination and local power groups. In situations of both democracy and authoritarianism, such selection methods can be beneficial to women. These selection methods, as the case of Fernández shows, do not prevent women from self-nominating. Women can forward themselves as candidates if they so please, but because there is no formal mechanism for postulating oneself and because the selectorate must actively seek out potential candidates, women do not have to self-nominate. Similarly, women do not have to be political outsiders to emerge from such a system. Women with membership in local power monopolies can and do become candidates when exclusive-centralized selection is used. In Chapter 7, I discuss political widows, wives, and daughters, women who are likely to be a part of power monopolies and who have a different path to politics.

7

Selecting Candidates
Closer to Home

Widows, Wives, and Daughters

> If my doctor died, I wouldn't want his wife to operate
> on me.
>
> —Constituent's response to the news that Governor Mel Carnahan's
> widow would serve out the term that he posthumously won (quoted in
> Katharine Mieszkowski, "Behind Every Dead Candidate . . .")

> Just don't be like that husband of yours.
>
> —Oft-repeated phrase directed at a Mexican mayoral candidate
> (Interview, May 7, 2003)

hapter 1 began with the story of Cristina Fernández, who succeeded her husband to become president of Argentina in 2007. Fernández had been active in politics since joining the youth wing of the Peronista Party in the 1970s. After the return to democracy in 1983, Fernández re-entered politics and was elected to the legislature of her home province of Santa Cruz in 1989 and again in 1993. She launched her national political career when she successfully contested a seat for the Senate in 1995. She would later be elected to the Chamber of Deputies and twice re-elected to the Senate (once while serving as First Lady). Néstor Kirchner, her husband, was elected president in 2003. She ran for that office in 2007 and won with over 45 percent of the vote, a 22 percentage point lead over her nearest rival—a woman—and enough to avoid a runoff. Despite her noteworthy political career, Fernández nonetheless was accused of gaining office solely because of her husband. Cristina Fernández has been outspoken about the fact that her political career is not merely a function of her husband's, and as reporters noted "she made a point of remaining in her assigned seat in the Senate chamber on the day he [Néstor Kirchner] donned the azure-and-white sash inside the National Congress rather than join him on the podium" (Contreras 2005).

This chapter takes an analytical look at political widows, wives (like Fernández), and daughters. While the widows, wives, and daughters are often the subject of discussion by citizens of Latin American countries, they have not received much academic attention.[1] But the family connections that I describe in this chapter aid our understanding of candidate selection in the region. The assumption is generally that *dedazos* create the conditions necessary for women with these familial ties to come to power. In other words, the assumption is that when a single individual unilaterally has the power to decide candidacies, he may place his wife in office (to extend his rule—i.e., to use his wife as a political puppet). The examples that I discuss in this chapter instead demonstrate that women who are related to politically powerful men can and do emerge from all forms of candidate selection. While *dedazos* have placed widows, wives, and daughters into power, so too have primaries. Exclusive-decentralized and inclusive-centralized processes have had the same results.

Why might this be the case? These family connections can eliminate obstacles important to women's candidacies: self-nomination and local power monopolies. These constraints on female candidacies are often nonexistent for political widows, wives, and daughters. The cases that I discuss subsequently demonstrate this point.

While little academic work has examined the importance of kinship ties to women's political paths, especially for Latin America, small studies nonetheless indicate that the anecdotal wisdom concerning the familial connections of female politicians has a solid basis in fact (Pinto 1994; River-Cara 1993, as cited in PROLEAD 2002; PROLEAD 2002).[2] In a limited study of Latin American congresswomen, 8 of 11 women felt that their family connections had helped their political careers (River-Cara 1993, as cited in PRO-LEAD 2002). The political biographies of the handful of women who have occupied presidential office in Latin America serve to reinforce the significance of kinship.

We must note, however, that examples of both men and women who have entered politics with family connections abound.[3] How different is Cristina Fernández from Martín Torrijos? Martín Torrijos, the son of General Omar Torrijos, became president of Panama in 2004. What similarities exist between Cuauhtémoc Cárdenas—who served as governor of Michoacán, was mayor of Mexico City, and ran for the presidency three times—and the current Argentine *presidenta*? He is the son of famed Mexican president Lázaro

Cárdenas and the father of Lázaro Cárdenas Batel, the governor of Michoacán from 2002 to 2008. What comparisons can we make between Fernández and Adán Chávez, the brother of President Hugo Chávez of Venezuela?
Since his brother's election in 1998, Adán Chávez has served as presidential secretary, ambassador to Cuba, and Minister of Education and is currently the governor of the state of Barinas.[4] Although many men who enter
politics have familial relationships to other men, women in politics are often
presumed to have made it into politics *because* of their personal relationships with men. This assumed relationship exists even absent family connections. As one mayor of the Partido Revolucionario Institucional (PRI) said of
women candidates, "If you're single, they assume you're involved with someone [who could have gotten you the candidacy] or that you already slept with
the governor" (Interview, March 25, 2003). She clarified that in the absence
of a family relationship, the default assumption is that a sexual relationship
can explain women's success.

The earliest forms of political legitimacy relied on hereditary rule;[5] while
true hereditary rule is now rare, a modern version of the practice survives
and remains commonplace.[6] Putnam discovered that approximately 10 percent of Congress members in the United States who served from 1790 to
1960 had relatives who had also served in Congress, as did about 14 percent
of French deputies between 1870 and 1940 and 43 percent of cabinet ministers in Holland from 1848 to 1958 (1976: 61). Clearly, family relationships
can be important for gaining access to politics across the globe. The most
thorough academic work on family connections in Latin America has been
performed by Roderic Camp, who found that nearly a third of all politicians
in Mexico from 1935 to 1980 had familial ties (1982: 850).[7]

Why does kinship continue to play such an important role in politics?
There are at least three reasons why familial ties continue to be relevant. As
Alfred Clubok, Norman Wilensky, and Forrest Berghorn state, first, "by
virtue of his [*sic*] family identity, the aspiring politician inherits his [*sic*] pre-
cursor's fame and influence," and second, "he [*sic*] has grown up in an environment conducive to the internalization of political values, awareness,
understanding and motivation" (1969: 1036). Third, the trust or confidence that accompanies family membership can be translated into political capital.

First, the "fame and influence" that kinship provides is important to
obtaining political office. The name recognition from being a family member of a current or former politician may be enough to win an election. Furthermore, kinship itself usually guarantees press coverage. It is certainly the
case that a "wife of" or "widow of" will gain media attention for her cam-

paign, but the daughter or son of a politician is also likely to receive greater media coverage simply because of the family connection. Being a part of a political family can also mean access to powerful networks of people, including potential campaign donors. Members of these families are likely to have more substantial personal resources to draw from.

A second reason why kinship continues to be important in politics is socialization. Those individuals who have grown up in political households are more likely to be interested in and knowledgeable about politics and to feel politically efficacious. As Honduran legislator Carmen Elisa Lobo de García noted, "In Central America, you begin to like politics in childhood because you hear about it in the home. My grandfather was a legislator, and then my father. Generally, it is a matter of heredity. Those who were leaders in the times of our grandparents, they were the parents of the leaders of the times of my parents, and now the grandchildren of those leaders are the leaders of my generation" (quoted in Saint-Germain and Chavez Metoyer 2008: 133). Peruvian Susana Villarán de la Puente, who was elected mayor of Lima in 2010, stated that "politics wasn't something that was outside the walls of my home" (quoted in Adrianzén, Rial, and Roncagliolo 2008: 427). Political discussions were a constant in her childhood.

Finally, membership in a particular family can make an individual seem trustworthy. Camp argues that family connections are important in Mexican politics and are "rarely nepotism, but rather are the result of a political culture, which encourages dependence on the family for the degree of trust and confidence necessary to establish close political relationships. Family ties are a passport, so to speak, allowing easy access into the highest political echelons" (1979: 430). In later work, Camp noted that while more institutionalized forms of networking are used, often other more informal contacts take precedence, like family, friends, and hometown (2002: 36). He has found that for elite Mexican politicians, linkages through family and friends predominated—70 percent of their contacts were based on family or friendship, while only 33 percent of contacts were through political or bureaucratic organizations (Camp 2002: 42).[8] Family members are seen as individuals who can be trusted and are therefore given greater political access. They have easy access to the types of networks discussed in Chapter 3.

Family plays an important role in Latin American politics today. Diana Balmori, Stuart Voss, and Miles Wertman's analysis of powerful Latin American families found that these groups have "had access to political and economic power by virtue of their large fortunes, their landholdings, and their names. To this day, they promote particular family members into positions of power" (1984: 14). Families are often able to maintain power for decades. Camp analyzed the mayoral record for the town of Espinal, Oaxaca, from 1882 to the present and found that four last names continued to reappear on the list of mayors. He concludes that these four families held the mayoral position 60 percent of the time for over a century (Camp 2010: 24). Power and Mochel describe just how important kinship can be to politics in Brazil: "In oligarchical states, the criterion for gubernatorial nomination is often membership in the clan—but when blood is unavailable, loyalty will have to do" (2008: 237).

Political power may be more likely to stay within the family in certain instances. Politicians may be more apt to depend on family members when political instability is commonplace. Scholars have hypothesized that kinship benefits women during unstable times because such instability "opens the door for a select group of women leaders by allowing for kinship, ethnicity, or charismatic leadership to play a pivotal role in politics" (Genovese 1993; Jalalzai and Hankinson 2008; Jalalzai 2010: 136).[9] Academic work has also suggested that kinship is more politically significant in situations of underdevelopment. Genovese, for example, states that kinship ties are more important for women in the less developed areas than for those in more developed areas (1993: 214), harkening to Putnam's early work, which argued that kinship politics was unlikely in more modern societies (1976). Camp has noted that kinship ties are more prevalent in certain regions of Mexico; he writes that in the less developed regions "traditional state and local political groups are logical choices to be overrepresented by politically active families who long have been entrenched in politics" (1982: 850–851). Political institutions can increase the incentives to keep political power in the family. Roces (1998) believes that the increased use of term limits will lead to greater numbers of political wives entering politics. She argues that incumbents forced out by term limits will turn to wives, daughters, and other family members to maintain their political control.[10]

Political Women, Political Families

Across the globe, women who have gained power have often been the family members of political men. Jalalzai's work revealed that among women who had served as either presidents or prime ministers of their countries, 30 percent had familial ties (2004). In the United States, 44 widows have succeeded their husbands into Congress, and on seven occasions, Senate terms have been finished out by widows (Mieszkowski 2000).[11] In Ireland,

Galligan found that family ties were twice as important for female politicians as they were for men. Eight of nine women elected to the Dáil between 1957 and 1969 were political widows. By 1992, only 25 percent of female deputies were related to former Dáil members (Galligan 1993: 149).

The problem for a women with kinship ties is that "observers with a conscious or unconscious interest in preserving gender bias in the political system can discount her as an anomaly unlikely to be repeated or attribute her success to family or spouse rather than her own skills or efforts" (Genovese and Thompson 1993: 5). Friedman notes that Latin American women who have gained political office and who are family members of male politicians are often referred to as "women of" these men. This reinforces sexist attitudes about the proper roles for men and women (Friedman 2000: 94) and implies that these women would have been incapable of obtaining political power absent their relations to these men. Genovese and Thompson suggest that when women's pathways to power more closely resemble those of men "the more difficult it is for observers to avoid interpretations that challenge exclusionary assumptions" (1993: 5).[12]

Are these political wives, widows, and daughters different from women who have made their way into office without family connections? Jalalzai's study of female presidents and prime ministers debunked the notion that women who enter office because of family ties are unqualified for office. Fifty-four percent of women executives with familial ties had high levels of political experience before entering office; only 2 of the 13 women, or 15 percent, had no prior political experience (Jalalzai 2004: 104; Jalalzai 2010).

One early study from the United States found that widows were different from other female Congress members: they had lower levels of education, represented different professional backgrounds, and lacked political experience (Bullock and Heys 1972). More recent widows are more like other female members of Congress. For example, political widows now serve as long as other female Congress members, "thus debunking conventional wisdom that political widows are merely benchwarmers sent in to serve out their husbands' terms only to politely step aside when the party brass had had sufficient time to groom a more acceptable male candidate" (Kessel and Olson 2002: 4). Jalalzai and Hankinson found that those widows who continued in politics (i.e., beyond finishing out their husbands' terms) did differ ideologically from their late husbands (2008: 420).

In the United States, Kessel and Olson (2002) also found that the sympathy earned by political widows could not explain their long tenures in office, while it might have explained their initial election and subsequent re-election. Women, therefore, who had initially been elected to office because of their relationships to men were able to earn sufficient voter support to keep getting re-elected.

Political Widows, Wives, and Daughters in Latin America

> Politics essentially has been part of an old boys' network, in which only a rare woman has participated. Often, if elected or appointed to a position, a woman got it through the influence of her husband, also a politician, who put her (along with other relatives) on the payroll. Sometimes a woman would succeed her deceased husband, using his name and her experience with him as political assets.
>
> —Thomas G. Sanders, "Brazilian Women in Politics"

Female politicians in Latin America are often the widows, the wives, and the daughters of politically important men. Saint-Germain and Chavez Metoyer (2008) found that the majority of the Central American female legislators whom they interviewed had family members in politics. While only 56 percent of their interviewees in Nicaragua came from political families, 92 percent of the women they interviewed in Costa Rica had family members in politics. Women in my small sample of mayors and council members in eight cities in Chile and Mexico were more likely than men to have relatives in politics. Of the women I interviewed in Mexico, four had family connections. Three had husbands in politics, and the fourth was the daughter of a previous mayor. In Chile, female interviewees were also more likely than male politicians to have a family member in politics. Two of the women in the Chilean group had family connections: one was a political widow and the other had a grandfather and uncle in politics (see Hinojosa 2005 for more information).

The discussion that follows provides examples of political widows and their paths to power. Two of the best-known examples are Isabel Perón and Violeta Chamorro. Mireya Moscoso's story in many ways best exemplifies political widowhood. These three women's stories are quite different, demonstrating in part the diversity of experiences that can be consolidated under the label of "political widow."

Argentina's first *presidenta* entered politics through Juan Perón. While Isabel Perón had never pursued office prior to her nomination for the vice presidency, she nonetheless stated, "We talked about politics the day we first met, and afterwards he trained me to be his political representative" (quoted in Moritz 1975: 313). Once allowed to return to Argentina and vie for the presidency, Perón chose his wife as vice president rather than share power and antagonize factions of his party. The Perón-Perón ticket garnered 61.8 percent of the vote and ushered Juan Perón back into the presidency. Juan Perón's death propelled his 43-year-old widow to the presidency.

Violeta Chamorro's path to power differed dramatically from Perón's. Chamorro's husband had never held elected office; she had to campaign for the presidency. Chamorro's husband, Pedro Joaquín Chamorro, was editor of the influential opposition paper *La Prensa*. Pedro Chamorro was assassinated in 1978. There was little doubt that the Somoza dictatorship was responsible. The dictatorship was overthrown by the Sandinista Revolution shortly thereafter, and Violeta Chamorro, in her capacity as a political widow, was initially given a position on the new governing junta. She resigned from the position shortly thereafter ostensibly because of a broken arm. While Chamorro had been called "politically illiterate" and had not exercised power during her brief tenure on the junta, she was nonetheless seen as a viable candidate by an organization of opposition parties; as one strategist commented, "Violeta wasn't chosen for her abilities as president. Violeta was chosen to win" (quoted in Saint-Germain 1993: 84). However, Chamorro's abilities were publicly doubted, and her nomination was far from a sure thing; "it took days of heated debate before a presidential nominee was selected" (Saint-Germain 1993: 84). Chamorro was seen as a candidate who could garner widespread support and serve as a reconciliatory force; after all, as she often mentioned, of her four children, two were Sandinistas and two were Contras. If she could keep her family united, she could do the same for the nation. Chamorro actively campaigned for the presidency in her role as a political widow, often stating, "I am not a politician, but I believe this is my destiny. I am doing this for Pedro and for my country" (quoted in Bourdreaux 1991, as cited in Saint-Germain 1993: 85).

Mireya Moscoso's rise to power most closely approximates that of the stereotypical political widow. Her husband, Arnulfo Arias, had been elected president of Panama on three separate occasions, but each time he had been removed from office. Moscoso entered politics after her husband's death in 1988, while they were living in exile in the United States. Moscoso returned to Panama and ran for the presidency under the banner of her husband's party, the Arnulfista Party, first in 1994 and then again in 1999. Some Panamanians saw the 1999 presidential elections as a race "between two corpses" (Navarro 1999b) because Mireya Moscoso, a political widow, was running against Martín Torrijos, the son of deceased strongman General Omar Torrijos. Moscoso addressed concerns about her preparedness for the presidency by declaring during her campaign: "Although they say Mireya doesn't have the capacity, although they say that because she is a woman she can't be president, I tell you here, I can wear pants just like the men in this country! And I know when to put on skirts and when to put on pants, too" (quoted in Navarro 1999a). As a political widow, Moscoso was forced to campaign with an eye toward both the past and the future: during her failed run in 1994 and in her successful bid for the presidency in 1999, she repeatedly drew on the memory of her deceased husband while simultaneously attempting to convince voters that she could provide a break from the past.

There are at least three types of political widows that have emerged in Latin America. The first type would be exemplified by Isabel Perón. These widows inherit their husband's seats. In the case of Perón, she had a constitutional right to the seat on the basis of her status as vice president, but there are cases in which the incumbent politician's seat is ceremoniously awarded to his wife upon his death. The second type of widow, like Violeta Chamorro or Mireya Moscoso, has no political experience[13] before her husband's death, but rather than inheriting a seat, she must campaign for it. The third type of widow is someone with political experience who campaigns for, rather than inherits, political office. Karen Olsen, widow of former Costa Rican president José Figueres Ferrer, exemplifies this final type. Olsen had been politically active before her husband's death but was elected to the legislature after his death (Saint-Germain and Chavez Metoyer 2008: 142).

The increase in women's political representation has led to the emergence of political widowers.[14] Israel Reyes Montes, who worked in construction in the United States, served out his wife's term as mayor in the small Mexican town of San José Estancia Grande. His wife, Guadalupe Ávila Salinas of the Partido de la Revolución Democrática (PRD), was assassinated while campaigning and elected posthumously (Thompson 2004b). This situation would not normally occur in Mexico, as alternates are elected alongside officeholders; however, the alternate refused to take over for the murdered PRD candidate. Ávila Salinas had been assassinated by the incumbent mayor, a member of the PRI, who committed his attack in the town's public health clinic (Infobae 2004).

Examples of political wives also abound. The most recent high-profile case is one that has already been discussed in this book: that of Cristina Fernández. Fernández is not the only Argentine who has managed to be First Lady and politician (nor is she the first to have held the offices of First Lady and president). Fernández's main rival for the Senate in 2005 was Hilda González de Duhalde. González is the wife of Eduardo Duhalde, a Peronista who served as interim president of Argentina from 2002 to 2003. González was first elected to the Chamber of Deputies in 1997 and was re-elected six years later. In 2005, she was elected to the federal Senate.

In Mexico, another First Lady toyed with the idea of her own presidential run. Marta Sahagún, wife of Vicente Fox (2000–2006), publicly announced that Mexico was ready for a woman president, setting off rumors that the First Lady intended to seek her husband's seat in 2006. Journalist Ginger Thompson reported, "In recent months, political wives at state and local levels have broken with entrenched macho traditions and started campaigns to follow their husbands into office. They call themselves leaders of a new feminist fight, seeking status for women who have little formal work experience of their own, but who have toiled hard and faithfully in the shadows of powerful husbands" (2004a). These women included the wife of the governor of the state of Tlaxcala, María del Carmen Ramírez García (who had to fight her party for permission to stand for her husband's seat); the wife of the governor of Quintana Roo (who sought the mayorship of the important tourist city of Cancún); and the wife of the governor of the state of Nayarit, Marta Elena García de Echeverria. Current First Lady Margarita Zavala is the wife of President Felipe Calderón (2006–2012). A longtime militant of the Partido Acción Nacional (PAN), she was representing her party in the Chamber of Deputies when Calderón was campaigning for the presidency.

Ex-wives, too, can use their tremendous name recognition to launch their political careers, though they lack the advantages that political spouses are privy to. Susana Higuchi, now ex-wife of Alberto Fujimori, contemplated running for mayor of Lima during her first couple of years as First Lady. Her later political aspirations, however, were seen as a personal vendetta against her husband. Higuchi repeatedly accused Fujimori of corruption and secretly planned to run against him in the 1995 presidential elections; when her intentions came to light, she was forced to move out of the presidential palace (Schmidt 2006: 156). Fujimori stripped his wife of the title of First Lady and divorced her in 1996. While Higuchi's candidacy was destined for failure, she nonetheless served as a threat to Fujimori "because Peruvians were inclined to believe her allegations, especially the charges of corruption" (Schmidt 2006: 157). Although Higuchi was disqualified from her presidential bid and also had her congressional aspirations blocked in 1995, she was able to run successfully for Congress in 2001. The First Lady's actions may also have spurred other women to enter politics; as Mirko Lauer, a political analyst, stated, "The reason we see so many women candidates in this race, especially for Vice President, is that there is a new notion among politicos in Peru that women are now more prone to vote for women candidates than in the past, and this idea is the direct result of Susana Higuchi's high-profile campaign as a woman" (quoted in Sims 1994).

The case of Susana Higuchi is not unique. A similar situation emerged in 2006 in Brazil, where a divorcing husband and wife were campaigning for Congress. Valdemar Costa Neto and Maria Christina Mendes Caldeira separated; shortly thereafter, Mendes Caldeira testified against her husband on charges of corruption and then launched her political campaign. Costa Neto had long held political office and rose to head the Liberal Party before the corruption scandal forced his resignation (Moffett 2006).

Political daughters have also served in office. Dirce Quadros and Márcia Kubitschek, both daughters of former presidents, served in the Brazilian Congress during the 1980s.[15] In recent years, the best-known political daughter is Keiko Fujimori. Fujimori's first political role was that of First Lady of Peru; after her parents' divorce, she was appointed to fill the role. Later, her father urged her to run for Congress. Keiko Fujimori was elected to Congress with the highest vote share of any candidate. She ran for the presidency in 2011 but ultimately lost in the second round (48.5 percent to 51.4 percent) to Ollanta Humala (Quigley and Murphy 2011).

In Chile, Carmen Frei Ruíz-Tagle, daughter of former president Eduardo Frei Montalva and sister of former president Eduardo Frei, is a senator. Isabel Allende Bussi is a Chilean deputy and daughter of former president Salvador Allende. Evelyn Matthei, a deputy of the Unión Demócrata Independiente (UDI), is the daughter of General Fernando Matthei, who was part of the military junta. Amalia García, one of Mexico's best-known politicians, also comes from a political family. Her grandfather was a member of Congress, and her father was governor of their home state of Zacatecas. But García broke away from the PRI, the party of her father and grandfather, early in her career. García has been president of the PRD and has served as governor, deputy, and senator[16] (Camp 2010: 264–265).

The preceding discussion demonstrates the enormous diversity among political widows, wives, and daughters. Some have obtained power because of political designation by powerful men (Perón, for example); others are usually considered to be "politicians in their own right." Determining whether political widows, wives, and daughters have obtained political success *because* of their relationships to male family members is complicated. It is worthwhile to note, however, that some of the women who have attained political positions because of their relationships to male political leaders are themselves qualified, but their family connections may "make them more trustworthy in the eyes of the political establishment" (Frohmann and

Valdes 1993, as cited in Friedman 2000: 272). While the case of Cristina Fernández seems clear-cut (i.e., she and her husband began their political careers at the same time, and she held high-profile positions long before he became president), Keiko Fujimori's situation is more convoluted. While she certainly benefited from immense name recognition, she has also felt the sting of that name. Her father was in jail for corruption and human rights abuses while she campaigned for the presidency. How do we interpret the case of Amalia García? She has become one of Mexico's most influential politicians, but because she broke away from her father's party, it is unlikely that she benefited from his political positions.

Political widows, wives, and daughters—as well as sons, nephews, and husbands—can emerge from any of the four types of candidate-selection processes that are detailed in Chapters 4 to 6. We can certainly find examples of women with important family connections who have emerged from each of these types. Isabel Perón's selection by her husband for the vice presidency illustrates how exclusive-centralized selection can work. Power and Mochel present the case of former governor Anthony Garotinho, who nominated his wife to his seat when he abandoned his post to run for the presidency of Brazil (2008: 236). This would be an example of exclusive-decentralized candidate selection resulting in a political wife coming into power. First Lady Margarita Zavala, wife of President Felipe Calderón of Mexico, was chosen as a candidate by the National Action Party using inclusive-centralized selection. María del Carmen Ramírez García was the wife of a governor; she emerged victorious from an inclusive-decentralized form of selection (specifically, an open primary).

Networks are insular groups. Often, incorporation into these groups is difficult. For women, sponsorship has been greatly eased when they are the family members of those already within these networks of power. Freeman relates that historically in the United States, even when men wanted to sponsor women into power-holding groups within parties, these relationships were seen as suspicious (2000). Family membership, as mentioned earlier in this chapter, makes individuals (appear) more trustworthy.

Because local power monopolies are often composed of individuals related by blood and marriage, family connections are most useful in contexts in which such networks are highly influential. As explained in Chapter 3, when decision making is done locally, networks have greater influence. Candidate selection that is centralized tends to avoid the power of networks, while decentralized procedures emphasize network connections. Gallagher also hypothesized that when candidate selection is done locally, this will "result in a higher proportion of deputies who are related to previous depu-

ties, as locally prominent families manage to pass a seat on from one generation to another" (1988: 14). Exclusive selection always puts decision making
in the hands of one or two people. If the selectorate is made up of a single
person, he can as easily choose his wife (Néstor Kirchner selecting Cristina
Fernández) as his mentee (Lula da Silva handpicking Dilma Rousseff).

We can expect, then, that the obstacles to political office will be different
for those women who follow more "standard" routes to power and those who
are the widows, wives, or daughters of important men.[17] The following section looks at one example each of political widows, wives, and daughters who
served as mayors in Chile or Mexico.[18] An analysis of the candidate-selection
procedures used to select these women allows us to see how being part of a
political family affected these women during the selection process. These
particular cases are mentioned in earlier chapters, but the analysis here is
intended to highlight how the family connections of these women altered the
candidate-selection processes that were in place and to illustrate in general
how family ties can alter the effects of decentralized and inclusive selection.

Fresia Faúndez: A Political Widow

Fresia Faúndez was the only woman I interviewed who favored primaries.
A primary had afforded her the opportunity to convince others in her party
that although she was a political widow, she was also qualified to be mayor
of her small town. Faúndez had always been active in politics—working as
a local bureaucrat, volunteering on political campaigns, and serving as party
secretary in the municipality of Maule, but she gained elective office only
after the tragic death of her husband. At 27, he had become the youngest
mayor in Chile, but his political career was cut short when he was killed in
a car accident. Although there was talk of Faúndez's being named interim
mayor, the position went to a member of the town council as mandated by
law. Over the next year, Faúndez was repeatedly asked to run for her husband's seat. Ultimately, Faúndez chose to do so.

Faúndez competed for the candidacy in a primary. She felt that this process proved that she was electorally competitive (Interview, November 7,
2002). The success that Faúndez achieved from inclusive-decentralized selection cannot be separated from her status as a political widow. Faúndez
inherited her husband's political networks and was supported by members
of the power monopoly, who had helped elect her husband. These influential community members encouraged her to pursue the mayoral post; some
had pushed for her to take over for her husband immediately after his death.
While inclusive-decentralized selection usually requires that an individual

self-nominate, Faúndez's special status as a political widow meant that individuals, including locally powerful individuals, were asking her to run for office. Although Faúndez did have to register for the primary, self-nomination was quite limited. She was financially secure and able to pay for her own campaign. As a political widow, Faúndez avoided the obstacles that typically accompany inclusive-decentralized selection.

Reyna Domínguez Wong: A Political Wife

The PRD was not able to undo the PRI's political hold in the town of Pueblo Viejo until 2000 and only then because of the popularity of Reyna Domínguez Wong. Domínguez Wong was a longtime militant of the PRI and the wife of former PRI mayor Marcos Acevedo Rodríguez. Domínguez Wong defected from the PRI in 1997, however, after the party refused to let her run for mayor shortly after her husband left that office. Candidate-selection decisions at the time were being made by a local *dedazo*: the outgoing mayor would choose who the next candidate would be. While the decentralization of this form of selection should have benefited Domínguez Wong, the sitting mayor was unwilling to allow her to run for the candidacy just three years after her husband had ended his term. Domínguez Wong refused to wait three more years and instead ran as the (unsuccessful) candidate of a small leftist party in 1997; she then won office as the candidate of the PRD in 2000.

The PRD used decentralized methods to choose Domínguez Wong. Although she was a doctor, not a career politician, she was nonetheless a political insider with a strong group of supporters (who followed her from the PRI to the PRD). As the wife of a former mayor, Domínguez Wong was part of a trusted group of elites. It was not clear whether the process used to select Domínguez Wong was inclusive- or exclusive-decentralized selection (see Chapter 5 for more details). Although a primary would have been problematic for many women, Domínguez Wong was in a privileged position given her status as a political wife. She was part of networks of power, so decentralized selection did not pose an obstacle to her candidacy. The inability to determine whether the processes were exclusive or inclusive in the case of Pueblo Viejo's mayor is irrelevant. Self-nomination, if it was necessary, would not have prevented *la doctora* from seeking the nomination. Inclusive designation would have certainly worked in Domínguez Wong's favor; she was a popular individual who had defected to the PRD, bringing numerous supporters with her. In the case of exclusive selection, Domínguez Wong would most likely have been a natural favorite for the PRD because of her popularity. PRD leaders eager to end the PRI's monopoly of political power over Pueblo Viejo would have been hard-pressed to choose a different candidate.

Adriana Peñafiel: A Political Daughter

Adriana Peñafiel served as mayor of La Serena from 1989 to 2004. La Serena, in Chile's fourth region, is a large and important city. Peñafiel is not only a native of La Serena but also a member of one of the city's influential political families. Peñafiel can be said to have been chosen twice for the mayoral post: first in 1989, when she was appointed by Pinochet to serve as mayor, and then in 1992, as the candidate of the Renovación Nacional (RN), which used exclusive-decentralized procedures. This selection method does not allow women to avoid local power monopolies. However, because of her familial relationships, Peñafiel was already a trusted member of these networks.

The advantages that political widows, wives, and daughters are afforded extend beyond name recognition, access to power holders and networks of influential people, and often greater personal financial resources. There are, however, also disadvantages that can come along with being part of a political family. Political scientist and feminist activist Jo Freeman writes that being a political widow is more advantageous than being a political wife because political widows have "the advantages of her husband's prior status, name and goodwill with the independence to forge her own path." Wives, she argues, are forced to "carry his baggage along with his name" (Freeman, n.d.). The same is true of political daughters.[19] This baggage may be hard to discard: "The difficulty with kinship ties is that while they are often strongest in maintaining a group association, they are the most difficult to break in order to disassociate yourself from a group in decline" (Camp 1982: 859).

Politicians with these political ties often find them detrimental to their own political careers. Domínguez Wong explained that while campaigning she often heard, "Just don't be like that husband of yours," though at other times was thanked for the work her husband had done while in office (Interview, May 7, 2003). A male PRI member who ran for mayor of Pueblo Viejo said that having an uncle in politics "hurt me a lot." He was certain that his campaign had been damaged because people mistakenly believed that he shared his uncle's political views and assumed that, if elected, he would be under the political influence of his uncle (Interviews, April 28–29, 2003). Others worried that they would not be seen as serious politicians. One councilman from Mérida voiced the reservations he had prior to running for office. Because his father was a federal deputy, he was concerned that people would assume that he had obtained the position because of his father or that he would be acting as a puppet for his father if elected. He also worried that his father would be criticized for his performance in politics (Interview, May 27, 2003).

Limits on Keeping It in the Family

The political careers of widows, wives, and daughters—and, of course, countless sons and brothers—can be limited. As Table 7.1 demonstrates, more than half of the countries in the region legally prohibit relatives of the incumbent president from succeeding him or her in office. Susana Higuchi's presidential bid, for example, was cut short by such a law, preventing her from seeking Fujimori's seat even though they were in the midst of an acrimonious divorce.

These laws alter candidate selection by removing certain individuals from the pool of eligibles. While the laws detailed in Table 7.1 are constitutionally mandated and apply specifically to the office of the president, such laws could be more broadly construed. In the following discussion, I describe the efforts of a single party to dramatically alter candidate selection by limiting family members of incumbents from seeking elected office.

TABLE 7.1. LAWS PREVENTING FAMILY MEMBERS FROM CANDIDACY

Country	Family Ban?	Elaboration
Argentina	No	
Bolivia	Yes	Constitution, Article 89
Brazil	Yes	Constitution, Article 14
Chile	No	
Colombia	No	
Costa Rica	Yes	Constitution, Article 132
Dominican Republic	No	
Ecuador	Yes	Constitution, Article 166
El Salvador	Yes	Constitution, Article 152
Guatemala	Yes	Constitution, Article 186
Honduras	Yes	Constitution, Article 240
Mexico	No	
Nicaragua	Yes	Constitution, Article 147
Panama	Yes	Constitution, Article 187
Paraguay	Yes	Constitution, Article 235
Peru	Yes	Constitution, Article 107
Uruguay	No	
Venezuela	Yes*	Constitution, Article 238

Source: Data compiled from the constitution of each country (accessed online).

*The 1999 Constitution prohibits the president from selecting a family member for the vice presidency. The 1961 Constitution prohibited candidates related to the president from running for the presidency or vice presidency.

In an apparent reaction to the gubernatorial ambitions of María del Carmen Ramírez García of the Mexican state of Tlaxcala, the PRD passed a statute in 2004 preventing candidacies by relatives (either by blood or marriage) of incumbents for all elected political offices. The statute, which was adopted by the Eighth National Congress of the PRD on March 26–28, 2004, but was later struck down by the Federal Electoral Institute (IFE), would have limited the candidacies of women in particular (Hinojosa 2004).

The PRD statute, had it not been renounced by the IFE, had the potential to disqualify many women—not just Ramírez García—from pursuing political office. It was widely acknowledged that the party's statute was a response to Ramírez García, whose husband Alfonso Sánchez Anaya was then governor of their home state of Tlaxcala. The statute would have invalidated the candidacy of Ramírez García, a popular senator who was leading in the polls. The statute was most likely also a response to the rumored presidential candidacy of Marta Sahagún, the wife of then president Fox (although the PRD statute would not have applied to Sahagún, a member of the PAN).[20]

The reasoning behind the statute was simple: "After the revolution, Mexicans tried to protect themselves from dictatorships by prohibiting presidents and governors from seeking re-election. But there are no laws that prohibit spousal succession, and many see that as a loophole" (Thompson 2004a). The assumption, then, was that Ramírez García would serve as a puppet for her husband, allowing him to remain in power without staying in office. This statute, along with the laws currently in place in more than half of the countries of the region, assume that relatives of political incumbents are themselves unqualified to hold office and are being imposed on the population because of the whims of a power-hungry incumbent.

Because, as mentioned earlier in this chapter, kinship has been an important means for women to acquire political office in Latin America, critics pointed out that this statute would keep women out of politics. Many, however, agreed with Rossana Fuentes-Barain, the influential managing editor for the Spanish-language version of *Foreign Affairs*, who noted, "This is about nepotism, not feminism. It has nothing to do with passing on power to women" (quoted in Thompson 2004a).

The IFE declared that the reform violated not only the Mexican Constitution but also the party's own statutes. In effect, the new law would have extended to family members the country's existing ban on immediate re-election for all political offices, and would have the consequence of treating husbands and wives (as well as fathers and sons) as a single political entity rather than as separate individuals. In addition to violating the constitutional right to stand for office, the statute blatantly ignored the party's own guidelines. The PRD's internal rules dictate that the party will not discriminate on the basis of "gender, ethnicity, sexual identity or orientation, religious or personal beliefs, civil state, economic, social, or cultural condition, place of residency or origin, or for any other similar reasons." Some argued that beyond its discrimination on the basis of marital status or domestic partnership, the statute destroyed the spirit of the party's anti-discrimination rules by unfairly curtailing an individual's ability to run for political office (Hinojosa 2004).

While the PRD's statute was invalidated, similar laws exist in other countries, at minimum for the office of the president. If such a law had been in place in Argentina, Cristina Fernández would have been unable to even compete for the presidency. Article 107 of the Peruvian Constitution prevented Susana Higuchi from attempting to wrestle away the presidency from Fujimori. In Brazil, Marta Suplicy's political ambitions were framed by those of her husband. In 2000, Marta Suplicy was married to Eduardo Matarazzo Suplicy (they divorced in 2001), who was a candidate for the Worker's Party presidential nomination. Had her then husband realized his presidential ambitions, Marta Suplicy would have been forbidden from pursuing that office herself—something that she publicly acknowledged she wanted to do—since Brazilian law would not have allowed her to succeed her husband in office. Her career had already overshadowed his; "there was a period in which I had the feeling that I was possibly being left behind" (quoted in Rohter 2000), acknowledged her husband. By 2000, she had already run for the governorship of São Paulo and had served as mayor of São Paulo. Since then, she has again served as mayor of São Paulo, Minister of Tourism, and federal senator representing the state of São Paulo.

More recently, in Guatemala, such a law was challenged by First Lady Sandra Torres. Torres divorced the president in April 2011 in an effort to legally run for office in the September 2011 elections (Lara 2011). The Guatemalan constitution prohibits family members of the incumbent president from seeking that office. Torres often stated, "I'm divorcing the president but I'm marrying the people" (quoted in Valladares 2011: 1). Although Torres was quite popular and obtained the nomination from a coalition between National Union of Hope (UNE) Party and the Great National Alliance (GANA) Party, she was ultimately disqualified from participating in the elections. Raquel Zelaya of the Association for Research and Social Studies (ASIES) said, "It doesn't seem ethical to get a divorce when the reason is not relationship break-up but just to qualify as a presidential candidate," though Torres insisted that she should have the right to stand for election (quoted in

Valladares 2011: 1). Torres and President Álvaro Colom had met because of their political activity and married in 2003.

This chapter contributes to creating an academic literature about the role of family connections for scholarship on women's representation and candidate selection. Divorcing a discussion of these family connections from academic studies of these two topics does the literature a disservice. As this chapter demonstrates, widows, wives, and daughters are a part of the story, and their experiences are useful to broadening our understanding of both women's representation and selection procedures and their effects. Women have come into power because of their relationships to politically important men; women have also come to power and happened to have had relationships to politically important men. The same is true of men, who have long benefited because of the political connections of their family members.

By presenting examples from several Latin American countries, I attempt to highlight the cross-national significance of this phenomenon. By also drawing examples from all levels of office, I highlight the diversity of these widows, wives, and daughters. These family connections may also be relevant to our understanding of how gender quotas function. Parties may sometimes meet quota obligations by placing party elites' female family members on party lists, thus allowing them to "fulfill the quota and guarantee loyalty" (Archenti and Tula 2008, as cited in Roza 2010a: 73; see also Franceschet and Piscopo 2008). Chapter 8 turns to the topic of gender quotas and analyzes how quotas have interacted with candidate-selection processes.

8

Altering Candidate Selection

The Adoption and Implementation of Gender Quotas

> Men feel like they are done once they have implemented quotas.
>
> —Rosa Ester Huerta, former governor of the province of Talagante (Interview, September 9, 2002)

More than two-thirds of Latin American countries have adopted gender quotas since 1991, radically altering selection procedures to set aside a portion of candidacies for women; well-written quota laws have had dramatic results. Table 8.1 provides information on nationally mandated quotas in Latin America. In addition to affecting women's representation, gender quotas have changed the candidate-selection procedures that parties use. The first section of this chapter discusses the forms that gender quotas can take, explains why they have been adopted across Latin America and around the globe, and analyzes both their successes and failures. The latter half of the chapter then turns to examining the interaction between gender quotas and selection procedures.

There are three types of gender quotas—reserved seats, internal party quotas, and national quotas—but recent academic studies of gender quotas predominantly focus on the final category (Jones 1996; Htun and Jones 1999; Baldez 2004a; Meier 2004; Krook 2009). While reserved seats do just that (they set aside a certain percentage or number of legislative seats for women), both internal party quotas and national quotas dictate that a certain percentage of candidates must be women. In addition to the national quotas that many Latin American countries have adopted, party quotas are common.

Quotas have been relatively successful in increasing women's representation. The earliest studies found that national quotas increased women's par-

TABLE 8.1. GENDER QUOTAS IN LATIN AMERICAN COUNTRIES

Country	Quota for National Legislature?	Year of Quota Adoption	Quota for Sub-national Elections?
Argentina	Yes	1991	Yes
Bolivia	Yes	1997	Yes
Brazil	Yes	1997	Yes
Chile	No		No
Colombia	Yes	2011	Yes
Costa Rica	Yes	1996	Yes
Dominican Republic	Yes	1997	Yes
Ecuador	Yes	1997	Yes
El Salvador	No		No
Guatemala	No		No
Honduras	Yes	2000	Yes
Mexico	Yes	2002	Yes
Nicaragua	No		No
Panama	Yes	1997	No
Paraguay	Yes	1996	Yes
Peru	Yes	1997	Yes
Uruguay	Yes	2009*	Yes†
Venezuela	No	1997‡	No

Source: All data compiled from www.quotaproject.org (accessed November 2011).

*Uruguay's quota law was adopted in 2009 but will not be implemented until 2014.

†The municipal quota will not be applied until 2015.

‡Venezuela passed a quota law in 1997, which was applied to the 1998 elections and then rescinded.

ticipation in national legislatures by 5 percentage points (Htun and Jones 1999), falling far short of their targets. More recently, quotas have had a more substantial impact on women's representation—10 percentage points on average, according to Htun (2005)—in part because of the adoption of placement mandates and better enforcement. The efficacy of a national quota depends on the existence of five factors: a closed party list, a placement mandate, a large district magnitude, stringent enforcement mechanisms, and cooperative parties (Htun and Jones 1999). If carefully implemented, quotas can greatly increase women's representation as candidates and officeholders, as has been the case in countries as diverse as Argentina, Costa Rica, the Dominican Republic, and Peru.

Why have quotas been passed? Krook (2009) synthesizes explanations for the emergence of quotas into four basic categories: because of the mobilization of women (sometimes from across the political spectrum), because quotas are in line with current norms about representation and equality, because of a transnational movement in favor of quota adoption, and/or because political elites believe that adopting quotas will have strategic benefit (i.e., they are a "visible method for parties to demonstrate support for women" [Caul 2001: 1226]).

Quotas are not always adopted in response to "principled concerns to empower women in politics" but are sometimes used strategically (Krook 2009: 32). Quotas have been adopted by elites who viewed them as a means of communicating a commitment to women's rights (Htun and Jones 2002). In some instances, elites push for quotas, believing that quotas will never be fully implemented and are unlikely to personally affect them (Krook 2009: 30). Krook explains that elites may adopt quotas because doing so allows them to "hand-pick 'malleable' women who will not question or challenge the status quo . . . , institutionalize procedures for candidate selection that enforce central party decisions . . . , build alliances with potential coalition partners . . . , manifest independence from other centers of government . . . , and—more broadly—establish the national and international legitimacy of a particular regime" (Krook 2009: 31).

The adoption of quotas may be easier in post-conflict societies, such as Rwanda, and in countries that are undergoing democratic transitions because in such cases the "the electoral systems are open for discussion" (Dahlerup 2006: 11). Quota adoption and implementation are also likely to be easier in countries like Costa Rica and Mexico, where prohibitions on immediate re-election eliminate the possibility that quotas will lead to the unseating of an incumbent.[1] Dahlerup 2006 notes that quota adoption is most likely easier in situations in which other quotas, such as ethnic or occupational ones, are already in use. The adoption of quotas can depend on the support of key political figures. In Argentina and Peru, Presidents Menem and Fujimori, respectively, were essential to the passage of quota laws, while in Costa Rica, the First Lady played a significant role in advocating for quotas during the 1980s (Araújo and García 2006: 93). It may be easier to adopt national quotas when several parties are already using gender quotas since there may be a mutual contagion effect (Meier 2004). In addition, the adoption of a national quota may propel sub-national units to pass their own quota legislation, as in Argentina (Htun and Jones 2002). One potential benefit of voluntary party quotas is that they too may be contagious. A party may be more likely to adopt gender quotas if one of its competitors is already using gender quotas (Matland and Studlar 1996; Caul 2001; Kittilson 2006). Caul found that party quotas were more likely to be adopted if (1) women are in positions of power in the party, (2) other parties in the country have already adopted quotas, and (3) the party is leftist (2001: 1225).

Five basic arguments have been lobbed against quotas: (1) quotas are discriminatory toward men, (2) quotas restrict the democratic processes by limiting voter choices, (3) quotas are unnecessary because "qualified women will rise to power on their own merits" (Htun and Jones 1999: 35), (4) quotas will allow unqualified women to enter politics (Htun and Jones 1999: 35; Ríos 2006; Krook 2009), and (5) quotas are stigmatizing to all women politicians[2] (because they foster the assumption that women who make it into positions of political power owe that success not to their own efforts, but to the quota laws). Chapter 9 expands on these arguments.

A young councilwoman from the Unión Demócrata Independiente (UDI) explained why she found quotas to be "super unjust." She felt strongly that the number of qualified women should determine the number of women in office. Her feelings clearly reflected the third argument: qualified women would make it into office (Interview, July 29, 2002). Similarly, a councilwoman from the Partido Revolucionario Institucional (PRI) in a large city explained that she had never experienced sexism and "had never agreed with the use of quotas" which she found "offensive." "I can get to where I want to go [without quotas]" (Interview, May 16, 2003). Although recognizing that the lack of gender equity in politics was a problem, a Partido Acción Nacional (PAN) politician pointed out that there was simply no need for a gender quota. He noted that his party's municipal committee was composed of 17 members, 8 of whom were women (Interview, May 21, 2003). Both men and women interviewed for this project often used an example of a politically prominent woman or a particular situation in which women were well represented as proof that quotas were unnecessary. Women, like the Priista councilwoman previously mentioned, were likely to use themselves as examples; these women emphasized that they had managed to get into political office without quotas.

The fourth argument—that quotas will allow unqualified women to enter politics[3]—is regularly offered up by parties claiming that there is a severe shortage of qualified women to run for office. They argue that this presumed shortage will result in unqualified women getting into office if a quota is implemented. Despite these concerns, the oft-heard refrain "There just aren't enough qualified women" seems to have little merit. As a female Partido Socialista (PS) functionary explained, it is easy to discriminate against women: "Men say, 'There are no qualified women'" (Interview, August 6, 2002). In theory, as demonstrated in Chapter 2, there are plenty of qualified women willing and able to participate in politics. In practice, we know that in countries as diverse as Argentina and Peru, parties have managed to find capable women to run for political office after the implementation of quotas. Evidence from outside the region indicates that parties do not have great difficulty in finding female candidates. A poll in France found that 78 percent of elites said that it was "easy to apply the parity law when drawing up their lists" (Sineau 2001, as cited in Krook 2009: 196).[4] Forcing parties to find qualified women in order to meet quota laws "compels elites to find new ways of locating prospective female candidates and persuading them to run for office, thus overcoming some of the important biases that result in fewer women standing forward and being chosen as candidates" (Krook 2009: 48). The requirement to find more female candidates may encourage parties to not only unearth new talent[5] but also recognize the discriminatory nature of earlier practices and the gendered implications of the recruitment and selection process.

Finally, a concern that is sometimes voiced is that a 30 percent quota will result in maximum representation of 30 percent rather than a minimum of 30 percent. A PS functionary explained that while she favored the use of quotas and other affirmative action measures for increasing women's representation, quotas often became a "ceiling instead of a floor." She elaborated that men sometimes abstain "from voting for women because they'll be elected anyway [because of the quota]" (Interview, August 6, 2002). In a similar vein, a female governor argued against quotas, saying that male party members felt that once quotas were implemented they were "done" (Interview, September 9, 2002).

The backlash against quotas can lead party elites to disguise their efforts to increase women's representation. In a comical moment, a local party president for the PAN who explained that the party tried to reserve at least one spot for women on its lists quickly added that this was most certainly not a quota (Interview, May 21, 2003).

Noncompliance is an enormous obstacle to the success of quotas (Htun and Jones 1999; Krook 2009). Their enforcement requires the existence of reasonably strong governmental institutions that can monitor and censor parties. Compliance with both national quotas and party quotas also necessitates the existence of strong parties. Baldez notes, "One PAN leader in Chiapas, for example, claimed that he 'did not share' the goal of the quota law and did not intend to comply with it—but PAN leaders at the national level made sure that the Chiapas candidates conformed" (2004b: 23). Party quotas are most likely to succeed in "rule-bound" societies (Norris and Lovenduski 1995: 204), that is, where party structures are strong and where there are enforcement capabilities (whether that is at the party or national level).

Even the enormously successful Argentine quota law faced noncompliance; "the passage and regulation of the law alone did not by any means automatically lead to the relatively high level of compliance with the law by the political parties" (Jones 1996: 79). For the first elections following adoption of the law, 5 of the 71 lists did not comply with the new law. One significant problem in ensuring compliance with the Argentine quota law was that only the woman who was being denied a position on the party list had legal recourse. The law was later amended so that any party member or the National Women's Council could contest a party list (Jones 1996; Waylen 2000). The Argentine case, while currently a clear-cut example of success, demonstrates the need for party compliance and a well-written quota law.

Part of the reason why national quotas have not had more of an impact is that they depend on the cooperation of parties, which are "notoriously reluctant to accept legal measures that interfere with their selection of candidates" (Meier 2004: 596).[6] Araújo and García document numerous instances of parties' failure to meet quota requirements. For example, in the Ecuadorian elections of 2002, party lists did not conform to the requisite placement mandates (Araújo and García 2006: 96).

More troubling is the fact that, in some instances, parties not only have refused to comply with quota laws but even have subverted the quota. In Bolivia, allegations emerged that male names were being recorded as female names to make it seem as if parties had complied with the gender quota (Llanos and Sample 2008: 21). In Mexico, the election of alternates (*suplentes*) alongside titleholders allowed female titleholders to renounce their seats so that their male alternates could take over; 16 women gave up their seats to male alternates shortly after the 2009 elections, leading to accusations that parties were using the *suplente* system to undermine the quota requirement (Notimex 2010; Martoccia and Camacho 2011). Similarly, in the Dominican Republic, candidate lists were altered after they had already been approved by the electoral tribunal; parties claimed that female candidates had resigned (Bueno 2007, as cited in Roza 2010a: 190).

Political parties often fail to meet not only national quotas but also their own self-imposed quotas, demonstrating "the distance that exists between political discourse and the real practices of parties" (Salinero R. 2004: 16). Roza (2010a) found that the presence of voluntary quotas for internal decision-making positions had virtually no effect on women's presence on party national executive committees.

Inadequacies in the quota laws can lead to less than stellar results. Poorly written quotas are unlikely to succeed. Absent a placement mandate, parties can meet quotas by placing women at the bottom of their lists or even on alternative lists. Quota laws without teeth (i.e., quotas that lack enforcement mechanisms) are much less likely to yield results.[7] And quotas can sometimes be incongruent with electoral rules in the country.

Examples abound of inadequate quota laws. Mexican parties have been guilty of meeting their own voluntary party quotas by placing women into alternate seats (Bruhn 2003). A 33-year-old councilwoman from Mérida who represented the PRI said, "We don't want to be alternates anymore" (Interview,

May 22, 2003). Bolivia is another country with a poorly written quota law. Parties can place women as alternates in order to meet the quota for Senate elections (Jones 2009).

In Honduras, a lack of sanctions for failure to comply with the quota law makes the quota ineffective (Araújo and García 2006: 97). Despite a 30 percent quota, women are only 18 percent of national legislators. Although Panama has had a quota law since 1997, women make up only 8 percent of the legislature. Panama, like Mexico, allows parties an exemption to the quota law when candidates are chosen via primaries. Panama requires that primary elections also adhere to a gender quota: 30 percent of candidacies in primary elections must go to women. The quota for primaries has failed not only because of the provision that exempts parties from meeting the quota if too few women register for the primary but also because primaries are relatively uncommon (Jones 2009).

In the Brazilian case, the national quota law stipulates that 30 percent of spots be reserved for women, but parties are not penalized for failing to meet the quota unless they nominate the maximum number of candidates allowed. Because parties can nominate 50 percent more candidates than there are seats in the district, failing to fill their slates has no real consequence (Htun 2005: 119; Samuels 2008: 84).

Poorly written quota laws can be altered. As Araújo and García have noted, quotas have often required tweaking; they point out that the first elections following the implementation of quotas often produce much less striking results than second elections because of "legislative improvements and a broadening support base for quotas within women's movements" (2006: 100). Quotas are often implemented without full understanding of potential obstacles to their success; it is only after quotas have been put into practice that problems become obvious. The Costa Rican quota has been extraordinarily successful, but it too has required revisions. The original (1996) quota law required that 40 percent of candidates on lists be women, but it contained no placement mandate. The Supreme Electoral Tribunal decreed in 1999 that women would need to be included in 40 percent of the electable spots (as determined by previous election results) on party lists (Jones 2004: 1207). Prior to the 2002 elections, then, parties were under no obligation to place female candidates in electable spots on their lists. A 2009 law called for parity, increasing the country's gender quota to 50 percent and requiring that male and female candidates be alternated on party lists.

Quotas may be more likely to be effective if party quotas are reinforced with national quotas. This is especially possible given how often party quotas are simply ignored, as my own interviewees indicated. National quotas and internal party quotas regularly coexist—as in the case of Mexico, where the Partido de la Revolución Democrática (PRD) and PRI had passed party quotas before the adoption of a national quota (in contrast, in Chile, a number of important parties have quotas, but no national quota has been passed). Meier provides a compelling argument that this situation "opens up the political forum to women more than would have been the case if either party or legal measures alone had been applied," since parties can demonstrate a superior commitment to gender equality only by setting a higher standard than that imposed by the national quota (2004: 596).[8] The data presented in Table 8.2 indicate the widespread use of party quotas in countries that do have national quotas, as well as in those countries that have not passed such a law.

Early work found that quota laws were more likely to succeed in combination with closed-list proportional representation than with open-list proportional representation systems (Htun and Jones 2002). The reasoning is straightforward: assuming that mechanisms guarantee compliance and there is a reasonable placement mandate, a quota in a closed-list system provides a guaranteed return, but in an open-list system, voters can vote against women. The case of Brazil, where open-list proportional representation coexists with a gender quota first adopted in 1997, lent much credence to this argument. Brazil's experience with a gender quota has been risible: women's representation has barely nudged since the implementation of the quota and stands at only 9 percent. More recently, however, scholars have discovered that open lists are not particularly disadvantageous (Schmidt and Saunders 2004; Matland 2006; Jones 2009: 76).

Quotas are more likely to be effective in multimember districts, since districts that elect only a small number of members tend to see only the party's top candidates, who are typically men, get seats (Htun 2005). For the same reasons, others have noted that party magnitude is important in explaining the success of quotas in increasing women's representation (Schmidt and Saunders 2004; Dador and Llanos 2007; Jones 2009).

The effectiveness of party quotas has been debated. Some scholars believe that party quotas are more effective because they have been voluntarily adopted by a party concerned with increasing women's representation rather than imposed on the party like national legislation (Lovenduski 1993). Others argue that national quotas are more efficacious because they are a legal requirement (Jones 1998; Meier 2004) and that party quotas are less effective because enforcement is done by the parties themselves (Jones 2004: 1213).[9]

Voluntary party quotas can be successful. The first elections following female suffrage in Argentina ushered 24 women into the legislature, making Argentina the world leader in women's political representation in the early

TABLE 8.2. PARTY QUOTAS IN LATIN AMERICA

Country	National Quota?	Political Party	Quota (%)
Argentina	Yes	Partido Justicialista	30–50
		Unión Cívica Radical	30
		Alianza para una República de Iguales	30
Bolivia	Yes	Unidad Nacional	50
Brazil	Yes	Partido dos Trabalhadores	30
		Partido Popular Socialista	30
Chile	No	Partido por la Democracia	30
		Partido Socialista	30–40
		Partido Demócrata Cristiano	20
Colombia	No	None	
Costa Rica	Yes	Partido Unidad Socialcristiana	40
		Partido Liberación Nacional	40
		Partido Acción Ciudadana	50
		Partido Movimiento Libertario	40
Dominican Republic	Yes	Partido Revolucionaria Dominicano	33
		Partido Reformista Social Cristiano	33
Ecuador	Yes	Partido Roldosista Ecuatoriano	25
		Partido Izquierda Democrática	25
El Salvador	No	Frente Farabundo Martípara la Liberación Nacional	35
		Cambio Democrático	30
Guatemala	No	Unidad Nacional de la Esperanza	40
		Unidad Revolucionaria Nacional Guatemalteca	30
		Partido los Verdes	50
Honduras	Yes	None	
Mexico	Yes	Partido Revolucionario Institucional	50
		Partido de la Revolución Democrática	30
Nicaragua	No	Frente Sandinista de Liberación Nacional	30
		Partido Liberal Constitucionalista	40
		Alianza de Movimiento Renovador Socialista	40
Panama	Yes	None	
Paraguay	Yes	Asociación Nacional Republicana/Colorado	30
		Partido Liberal Radical Auténtico	33
		Partido Unión Nacional de Ciudadanos Éticos	30
		Partido País Solidario	50
Peru	Yes	None	
Uruguay	Yes	Partido Socialista	Varies
		Vertiente Artiguista	33
Venezuela	No	Movimiento al Socialismo	25
		Acción Democrática	30
		Movimiento V República	50

Source: Data on party-level quotas compiled from http://www.quotaproject.org (accessed August 19, 2011). For more information, including details about placement mandates, see http://www. quotaproject.org. Additional data compiled from Beatriz Llanos and Kristen Sample, *Del dicho al hecho: Manual de buenas prácticas para la participación de mujeres en los partidos políticos latinoamericanos* (Stockholm: International IDEA, 2008), and V. Roza, B. Llanos, and G. G. de la Roza, *Partidos políticos y paridad: La ecuación pendiente* (Stockholm: International IDEA, 2010).

Note: The data presented here may be incomplete.

1950s. This feat was the result of the first use of party quotas in Latin America (Htun and Jones 2002), which were implemented at the urging of First Lady Evita Perón. She was said to have personally selected all female candidates (Martin 2000).

While party quotas can lead to a dramatic rise in women's representation, the use of voluntary party quotas is no guarantee that women's representation will increase, and even including sanctions may not prove helpful. Parties with quotas that included sanctions regularly failed to meet their quotas, while parties without sanctions written into their own internal selection rules did meet the quota (Roza 2010a: 118–119). In situations such as Mexico's, in which party rules can be legally registered with a national body (in the Mexican case, the Federal Electoral Institute), party-level quotas can be more rigorous, since national institutions may have the power to enforce party-level rules (Interview, February 20, 2003).

Considering how often party quotas fail to deliver, it is not surprising, then, that party members express concerns about the efficacy of party quotas. Women in Mexican parties "had doubts" that their political parties would meet the quota (Interview, May 22, 2003). A representative of the National Organism for PRI Women explained the use of quotas in her party but concluded, "It's not enough." She explained that "mechanisms for encouraging female candidates" were missing, as was a "real commitment" on the part of the party (Interview, February 13, 2003). When answering one of my questions about the use of quotas, a female PS functionary explained that while the party was not using quotas, "they were making an effort" (Interview, August 6, 2002).

The implementation of gender quotas can present logistical problems. Meeting a gender quota can be problematic for parties, whose creativity is tested in devising ways to maintain the candidate-selection methods that they have been using while simultaneously guaranteeing a set percentage of female candidates. Furthermore, quotas interact with other candidate-selection rules and procedures. Analyzing this interaction is important to understanding women's representation.

Baldez points out that in theory primaries and quotas are "incompatible" and notes that where primaries and quotas coexist parties may have to alter the results of the former in order to meet the latter, as is the case in Argentina (2007: 70). This inherent incompatibility is obvious in the Mexican case, in which political parties are under no obligation to meet their quota requirements when candidacies are chosen via primary.

Women's inclusion in Mexican politics was significantly boosted by the adoption of a national quota law in April 2002, which set a quota of 30 percent.[10] While an earlier quota law had been passed in 1996, it "recommended" only that women constitute 30 percent of candidacies and offered no mechanisms for promoting this suggestion.[11] The 2002 quota law added enforcement guidelines and addressed concerns that women's representation suffered because women candidates were placed in alternate positions and in unelectable positions on lists (Coordinación General 2000: 52–53; Fernández Poncela 2000; Rodríguez 2003: 181–182; Tarrés 2006). The existence of alternates who run alongside candidates is conventionally considered to have negative consequences for women who aspire to public office,[12] and all three major parties have been accused of relegating women to the alternate spots (Bruhn 2003; Hinojosa 2005). The 2002 quota could not be met by placing women in alternate positions. Female candidates were also required to be in electable positions on party lists: 1 of every 3 seats must be filled by a woman for the first 9 spots on each list of 40 (Baldez 2004b: 14). A party that failed to meet the quota faced immediate consequences—a party that did not comply would ultimately be disqualified from running candidates in that district.[13]

The interaction between gender quotas and selection methods is particularly pronounced in Mexico, where parties are exempt from meeting the quota when using primaries. Baldez documents that "when the bill was under discussion, quota supporters did not believe this primary election exemption would be a significant issue. They did not consider any of the parties to hold legitimately competitive and democratic primary elections, and they believed that the Federal Electoral Institute would support this interpretation" (2004a: 249). This was not the case: half of all candidates from the three major parties nominated in single-member districts in 2003 were chosen using primaries (Baldez 2004a). It is unclear to what extent the primaries that the parties are holding are true primaries (see Chapter 4 for more details). Baldez explains that the Federal Electoral Institute simply takes "parties at their word" that they are holding primaries (2007: 81). She convincingly argues that the quota unintentionally encouraged parties to begin using primaries. Primaries became a means to avoid implementing gender quotas and had the added benefit of reducing conflict between the national and the local levels (Baldez 2004a, 2007).[14]

Primaries and gender quotas are at odds with one another. Although both primaries and gender quotas are intended to

> enhance democracy within political parties, they do so in distinct
> and potentially conflicting ways. Primaries are democratic to the
> extent that they take the power of nominating candidates out of the

hands of party leaders and disperse it more widely among rank-and-file party members and ordinary citizens, thus ostensibly enhancing the connections between voters and elected officials. Gender quotas are democratic in the sense that they enhance the election possibilities of an historically underrepresented group, women. Gender quota laws remove barriers that limit women's chances to win elective office. The two reforms reflect distinct understandings of political equality: quotas facilitate equality of results, while primaries foster equality of opportunity. (Baldez 2007: 70–71)

Some have characterized primaries as an "escape hatch" that permits parties to avoid meeting their quota obligations (Maya 2003b and c, as cited in Baldez 2007: 88). Although some see primaries as a move toward further democratization in Mexico, proponents of greater female representation have tended to see them as another ploy to keep women out of office (Baldez 2007).

The Mexican case illustrates how the use of gender quotas can interact with candidate selection. Not only have quota laws had a significant impact on the use of party primaries—increasing their use and potentially increasing the use of the traditional *dedazo* (Zetterberg 2008: 456); primaries have also had an effect on the success of the quota. Understanding these effects is critical to devising policies to increase women's representation as candidates and as officeholders. The interaction between quotas and selection procedures, however, is not limited to primaries. The use of quotas affects inclusive and exclusive, centralized and decentralized candidate-selection processes.

Quotas are currently being used for sub-national elections in many Latin American countries, as demonstrated in Table 8.1. Taken together, the data in Graph 1.1 and Table 8.1 show that women are better represented in municipal councils when quotas are in effect for sub-national elections. Women's representation on councils in countries with sub-national quotas in effect was 25 percent, but only 17.7 percent where quotas were not in use. Neither Chile nor Mexico had sub-national quotas in effect during my field research.

Quotas have often forced parties to take a more proactive approach to candidate selection; the application of gender quotas has required that parties seek out potential female candidates to add to their lists rather than depend on self-nomination. This newfound emphasis on external nomination for both the highest elections and municipal elections would already be a boon to women. The need for party elites to seek out female candidates rather than depend on processes of self-nomination would prove beneficial to women even absent the requirement to nominate a set percentage of female candidates. In combination with this quota, such external nomination yields impressive results.

As the previous discussion indicates, quotas make selection more exclusive. Even when parties continue to use inclusive candidate selection, as in Argentina, where political parties still use primaries to select candidates, elites must then "adjust" the results of primaries to include more women on party lists. The process of choosing candidates in cases like that moves control into the hands of a small number of elites rather than a large selectorate. Quotas increase the power of the national level relative to the local level in the candidate-selection process. In other words, the use of quotas centralizes candidate-selection procedures. The centralization of candidate-selection processes can cause disagreements within parties. Centralizing candidate selection provides an opportunity to decrease the influence of local networks in the nominating process.

Quotas may also have a snowball effect. A study of Spain revealed that the presence and placement of women are strongly determined by the individual who leads the list and who acts as the main candidate selector (Verge 2010: 179–181).[15] Verge found compelling evidence that "old boy networks" resulted in a gender imbalance: "When a man looks for female candidates, he does not find that many because he tends to recruit candidates from his inner circle of confidence, who are basically in-group (male) candidates. Conversely, when a woman is the selector, she already knows a group of women with whom she shares party activities and personal networks, so the lists are more balanced" (2010: 181). Verge's research on the Spanish case reveals that women are "letting the ladder down to other women" and allowing other women through the recruitment and selection process (2010: 181). The use of gender quotas can place women into positions in which they become the selectorate and provide these women with the opportunity to select female candidates.

The legal requirement that parties nominate a set percentage of women has, when properly enforced, introduced huge numbers of women to party lists and correspondingly to political office. In those countries with properly functioning quotas, women are guaranteed access to party lists. The question is no longer *Will there be women?*, but rather *Which women will make it onto the list?* and *Where will they be placed on the list?* New work is starting to address these questions. As the conclusion to Chapter 7 indicates, Archenti and Tula have noted the role that female relatives may play in meeting quota requirements. They have also begun to explore women's placement on lists, to determine whether parties meet placement requirements in only the most minimal way. The requirement that women be placed on "every third spot on the list" has prevented women from being pooled at the bottom of the list, but it appears that it has also prevented women from occupying the top slot (Archenti and Tula 2009).

Despite the impressive effects that gender quotas can have, some believe that quotas can do only so much. As Gabriela Vega et al. write:

> All the legal guarantees in the world will not help a chronically exhausted woman to enter politics. . . . Few legislatures in Latin America have instituted "family friendly" policies or included services—such as on-site child care—that make it feasible for women to have a family and a political career at the same time. And the financial resources required to launch and sustain any kind of political activism are prohibitive in most countries. Men starting out in politics rely on well-established networks of business contacts or associates in labor unions or political parties to finance a campaign. Women do not usually have the same degree of access to these networks. (2000: 9)

A former deputy of the Partido Demócrata Cristiano (PDC) attributed the lack of female candidates from his party not to discrimination but rather to the *triple jornada*: women simply cannot be talked into taking on yet another responsibility in addition to their work both inside and outside the home (Interview, September 23, 2002). The *jornada* refers to the workday, and the *doble jornada* refers to the reality of many women's lives: they end their paid workday only to begin their unpaid labor at home. The *triple jornada* adds a third workday to women's lives, since their political work too contributes to their many burdens. Scholars have noted that the *triple jornada* may keep women from participating politically (Craske 1999: 134).

Not all quotas have worked as well as Argentina's, and not all have been as irrelevant as Panama's. Cases of quotas that have had no effects or minimal effects on women's representation are not reason to dismiss quotas altogether, but it is necessary to examine these failures to understand how quotas interact with other political institutions and with candidate-selection procedures. Quotas can be redesigned to increase their effectiveness, as in Argentina and Costa Rica.

Jones characterizes quota adoption in the region as "an elite-dominated process, with little popular involvement in the crafting, debate, and implementation of these reforms" (2009: 79n10). In other words, quota adoption has not been a particularly inclusive process. The lack of knowledge about quota laws in countries of Latin America (see, for example, findings about Panama on ignorance of the quota law [UNDP 2007]) is disturbing in light of the tremendous effects that quotas have on the candidates presented to voters.

In addition to the impediments to women's participation that remain regardless of the existence of quota laws, it is noteworthy that quotas have rarely been intended to permanently alter candidate selection (Htun 2004; Schmidt and Saunders 2004); for example, the 2002 Mexican quota law included language that ensured its continuity only through the 2015 elections (Baldez 2007: 92n12). The potentially transient nature of quotas makes it important to understand the effects of other candidate-selection processes. Quotas have sometimes been revoked instead. This was the case in the Dominican Republic, when in 2002 the gender quota for the Senate was removed (Araújo and García 2006: 96). The most obvious example, however, comes from Venezuela. A 30 percent quota was adopted in 1997 but overturned by the National Electoral Council in 2000. The quota therefore was applied in only the 1998 elections (Araújo and García 2006: 97).[16]

Dahlerup observed, "Contrary to what many supporters of quotas believed or hoped for, in quite a lot of countries conflicts over quotas for women seem to return again and again with each electoral cycle" (2005: 152). Especially in light of the fact that quotas can—and have been—revoked, it is important that we examine other strategies that can be used to increase women's representation. Furthermore, the limited application of quotas (for example, some countries use them for national legislative elections, but not for sub-national elections) and the lax enforcement of them require that we look to other possible ways of promoting female candidacies. Chapter 9 provides a number of suggestions.

9

Candidate Selection and Women's Representation in Latin American Politics

> For women, it's pretty much a constant that they'll have this deep-rooted reluctance to promote themselves, because they think it's "in poor taste" and because they are afraid to be thought of as ambitious. For this reason, they avoid demonstrating their interest or lobbying on their own behalf, and they prefer to wait to be asked to be candidates.
>
> —MARÍA FERNANDA CAÑETE, "Las vicisitudes de la aplicación de la cuota electoral en los partidos políticos"

> There is a serious problem and that's that even though women are very well prepared [to enter politics], the parties are not preparing women [for candidacies].
>
> —SUSANA VILLARÁN DE LA PUENTE, mayor of Lima (quoted in Alberto Adrianzén, Juan Rial, and Rafael Roncagliolo, *Países andinos: Los políticos*)

This book began with the stories of Cristina Fernández's and Michelle Bachelet's paths to the presidencies of their respective nations. These accounts illustrate that candidate selection is instrumental to understanding women's representation: the selection stage can be more important than the election stage. Candidate selection is important. Selection processes are "not simply arcane details of a political system: they affect the substance of politics through their effect in determining who will (and who will not) govern the country" (Morgenstern and Siavelis 2008: 391). As demonstrated in the previous chapters, selection procedures have enormous effects on women's abilities to become candidates and officeholders.

By using data from across Latin America to assess the viability of arguments that "there just aren't enough qualified women" (supply side explanations) and that "voters just won't cast their ballots for women" (demand side
explanations), I demonstrate that women's underrepresentation in politics is
caused by bottlenecks at the candidate recruitment and selection stages. The
two dimensions that I have used to categorize candidate selection (exclusivity versus inclusivity and centralization versus decentralization) determine
the types of obstacles that potential female candidates will face. Selection
processes are grouped into one of four types on the basis of their position
along these two dimensions: inclusive-centralized, exclusive-centralized, inclusive-decentralized, and inclusive-centralized. Exclusive processes avoid
self-nomination, and centralized selection moves decision making away from
local power monopolies. By circumventing the two most important hurdles
that potential female candidates face, selection processes best characterized
as *dedazos* often prove advantageous to women. On the other hand, selection methods that are inclusive and decentralized can be problematic because they force women to put forward their own candidacies and advantage
members of local power groups. This latter form of selection includes primaries; although heralded as the best form of selection, such procedures can
encumber women, making it difficult for them to become aspirants or candidates. Processes that appear inclusive in process may not be inclusive in
outcome.

The cases studied in this book—the major parties in Chile and Mexico in the eight municipalities in which I conducted fieldwork—provide significant variation not only in the types of candidate-selection procedures
that are used but also in results. Women's nomination rates exhibited important variation. The empirical chapters demonstrate that efforts by the
parties of the left in Chile to increase women's representation have been undermined by inclusive-decentralized candidate selection. Alternatively, the
parties of the right, and in particular, the Unión Demócrata Independiente
(UDI), have experienced unexpected success. Despite lacking a desire to increase women's representation, the parties of the right as a group saw more
female nominees than the parties of the left. In the Renovación Nacional
(RN), potential women candidates avoid self-nomination, and in the case of
the UDI, women not only bypass self-nomination but also circumvent local
power monopolies; as a result, these parties have managed to produce more
female candidates than parties of the left. The use of inclusive-centralized
selection methods by the Partido Acción Nacional (PAN) showed mixed results. The Partido Revolucionario Institucional (PRI) and the Partido de la
Revolución Democrática (PRD) used a variety of selection methods across

the four municipalities. Although the PRI and the PRD also had voluntary party quotas in place, women suffered the effects of self-nomination and local power monopolies.

The next section of this concluding chapter briefly turns to the case of Cuba to illustrate the central arguments of this book. Here we see how variation in selection methods for different levels of office translates to variation in outcomes. The case highlights the gendered implications of different selection methods.

The Case of Cuba: Variation in Selection Methods, Variation in Outcomes

Cuban women have a long history of political representation that accelerated after Fidel Castro's revolution.[1] By the mid-1970s, 22 percent of National Assembly deputies were women. Those percentages have risen in the last three decades: nearly half of all national deputies are women (43.2 percent), but only 23 percent of municipal officeholders are women (Htun 2007; Inter-Parliamentary Union 2010). Women, then, are about half as likely to be municipal council members as deputies. Why would women be better represented in higher-level political positions?[2]

In local elections, the percentage of women in office has not always coincided with the government's commitment to equality or with the greater representation of women at higher levels of office. Local elections have more than a single candidate per seat, unlike National Assembly elections, in which "there is only one candidate for every seat in parliament. Thus, the gender—or any other characteristic of a particular candidate was not a factor in the voter's choice" (Luciak 2005: 252). In other words, national elections are noncompetitive, while local elections are competitive: there is only one party, but there are multiple candidates, and this difference affects the candidate-selection procedures used in different elections and explains the variation that we see.

The Communist Party's lack of overt controls in candidate selection for local representatives is quite different from its involvement at the national level. As Domínguez noted in the 1970s, "The degree of government and party control over all elections increases with the importance of the election" (1978: 503–504). Or as one of Luciak's interviewees noted, "We can control the composition of the provincial assembly and of the National Assembly better than the composition of the town councils" (2005: 253). This allows us to explain the higher proportion of women in national office than in local offices.

Here we see how the argument of this book plays out in the Cuban case. The process of candidate selection is considerably more centralized and exclusive for national-level elections (in which voters are not presented with a choice among candidates—there is a single candidate for each position) than for local ones. At the municipal level, "nominations and elections [are] the most direct" (Smith and Padula 1996: 47–48), "neighbors come together to nominate the candidates for local assemblies" (Luciak 2005: 245), and "voters actually exercise some choice" (Htun 2007: 132). Domínguez argues that the greater proportion of elected women in provincial than in local positions in the province of Matanzas "suggests a conscious government effort to increase women's share of those offices" (1978: 503–504).[3] As Htun points out, in the mode of election for deputies, the party has more discretion (2007). Although government officials deny the use of a gender quota, Luciak finds that the National Candidate Commission does consider gender when making candidate decisions (2005).[4] At the local level, the processes are less centralized and less exclusive, meaning that potential female candidates must overcome some of the obstacles posed by self-nomination and local power monopolies, just as women in the Chilean and Mexican municipalities did.

National-level elections in Cuba limit candidate selection in ways that prove beneficial to women. To begin with, self-nomination is not an option; all candidates have to be nominated at an official committee meeting (Domínguez 1978). Since self-nomination is one of the two problems that women face in becoming candidates, the absence of self-nomination increases women's representation. Additionally, there is no campaigning. The lack of campaigning eliminates the financial pressures that otherwise would exist. Because candidate selection is centralized, the Communist Party can also insert more women at the national level when it deems that there is insufficient female representation.

Local-level processes are both more decentralized and more inclusive, meaning that they present greater obstacles for potential women candidates, just as we saw in Chapter 4. The key to Cuba's success in getting women into office, then, is not communism, but rather candidate-selection procedures that eliminate self-nomination altogether and place decision making at the most central levels of the party.[5] An ideological commitment to women's equality is only a secondary explanation, considering that it is selection procedures that explain divergent outcomes in women's representation between the national and local levels.

The Cuban case highlights some of the main arguments of this book. But it also points to the fact that we need to be more aware of the gendered consequences of candidate-selection methods and to recognize that these methods have powerful effects.[6] These effects are often unintended and unexpected. The need to understand the gendered consequences of these processes is undeniable.

This book is not intended as an indictment of inclusive-decentralized candidate-selection processes, nor is it meant to encourage parties to revert to using exclusive-centralized selection. Rather, this work is aimed at revealing the gendered effects of selection procedures; like other political institutions, candidate selection can, at first glance, appear gender neutral. This book demonstrates that it is not. Selection procedures that are seen as being more "democratic" are the least hospitable to women's representation; the gendered effects of what may otherwise be preferred practices require analysis. A failure to reflect on the gendered outcomes of candidate-selection procedures can mean that parties end up selecting candidates with methods that subvert their intentions, just as the more leftist Chilean parties have chosen inclusive-decentralized procedures that undermine their own goals to increase women's representation. The current trend toward the adoption of primaries, discussed in Chapter 4, will have negative, if unintended, consequences for women's abilities to enter politics.

The ever-increasing academic literature on women's political representation ought to pay greater attention to the role that parties play both in enhancing opportunities for women's participation and (too often) in limiting women's political participation. Chapter 2 demonstrates that supply problems and demand problems cannot explain the severe underrepresentation of women in elected office, and that the recruitment and nomination stages impede women. Correspondingly, academics must turn their attention to understanding the effects of candidate-selection processes on women's representation.

The following sections provide some strategies that parties, civil society organizations, and governments can use to mitigate the effects of selection procedures that require women to self-nominate and increase the influence of local networks.

Strategy 1: Abandon the Use of Primaries

Since primaries pose a particularly large hurdle to women's representation, parties should consider abandoning their use. Primaries are not the only form of inclusive-decentralized selection. Parties can adopt other inclusive-decentralized selection methods in lieu of primaries or may choose to move to other systems of candidate selection altogether.

Primaries have become quite popular in recent years. One study indicated that half of Latin American parties had used primaries for at least some candidate selection by 2000 (Alcántara Sáez 2002). Primaries are viewed as truly democratic processes (see Rahat 2009 for arguments that contradict this widely held view), and because of this, the expectation is that parties would have a difficult time adopting alternative forms of candidate selection once they have already used primaries. This, however, is not the case.[7]

Parties have compelling grounds for abandoning primaries. Primaries come with a slew of problems, and it is common to hear complaints from Latin American politicians—both male and female—about primaries. In addition to limiting women's candidacies, primaries are known to divide parties because they pit pre-candidates and their supporters against one another, prevent parties from maintaining their programmatic profile, and consume valuable time and resources. Also, they do not appear to produce "better" candidates than other forms of selection.

In my interviews, politicians were most concerned with the divisiveness of primaries. A PRI municipal president said, "The problem is that we Mexicans are too passionate" and that means that primaries "split the party. . . . People from one group won't vote for a candidate of another" (Interview, May 9, 2003). While this local politician blamed Mexican culture, primaries appear universally to have the effect of decreasing party cohesiveness (Rahat and Hazan 2001). Interviewees in Mexico and Chile routinely voiced similar sentiments about primaries. Even politicians from parties not using primaries were quick to point out potentially negative effects on unity and emphasized the advantages of "not having to fight with anybody" (Interview, October 31, 2002).

Parties may also have reason to be concerned that "if candidates are chosen directly by voters or members, then the candidates, their views and preferences, could become more important than the programmatic profile of the party as a whole" (Pennings and Hazan 2001: 271). This may keep parties from presenting a "cohesive image" and from maintaining discipline (Rahat and Hazan 2001: 313). Parties may wish to use selection methods that foster greater control over candidacies.

Parties may want to discontinue the use of primaries for financial reasons. Primaries require that parties spend precious resources that instead could be used in the general election. The organizational capacity necessary to run effective primaries is often lacking in Latin American parties. For example, the PRD was forced to use open primaries because it had no comprehensive list of its members (Langston 2001: 510).[8] Furthermore, the inability to properly run primaries can have important effects. Wuhs points out that, "when well-run, primaries add transparency to the political process. When they are not (as is more often the case in Mexico, particularly in the PRD and PRI), they have deleterious effects on public confidence in political parties and political institutions more generally" (2006: 36). Bruhn argues that parties simply do not have the capacity to properly monitor primary elections and that because of this, "it has been common in PRD primaries for the losers to accuse the winners of cheating, often with evidence. These accusations undermine the very democratic legitimacy that primaries are supposed to provide" (2010: 27).

Primaries are not always the contested elections that we imagine. As discussed in Chapter 5, selection procedures are sometimes presented as primaries despite the fact that political elites have already chosen a candidate. Argentina's recent experiment with an obligatory national primary demonstrated as much: "All 10 main parties announced single candidates, leading critics to describe the process as a mere dress rehearsal—or a very expensive opinion poll" (BBC 2011). Instead of parties using this primary to select their candidates, the primary instead became an opportunity to assess President Fernández's likelihood of winning re-election.

One reason cited for using primaries is that they select more electable candidates. But research on primaries has indicated that they may be no more likely than other methods to produce winning candidates. An analysis of Latin American candidates found that those chosen via primary were no more successful than other candidates (Colomer 2002: 119, as cited in Zovatto G. 2006: 24–25), and data from elections outside the region have sometimes found that candidates selected by primary are less competitive (Rahat and Sher-Hadar 1999: 262–263).[9] Mexican party leaders did not agree that primaries produced more electable candidates (Bruhn 2010), nor did Chilean elites. A former PDC president explained:

> When closed primaries (or open primaries with very low levels of participation) are held, a small organized fraction of PDC militants can elect a local party leader, who lacks the skills and appeal beyond party militants to win enough support to clinch a seat. When only one party promotes democratizing the selection of candidates, other parties can benefit by strategically identifying stronger candidates who can then obtain more votes than the democratically elected PDC candidate. (Quoted in Navia 2004: 14)

For those parties concerned with finding the most electable candidate, primaries are not the only answer. Bruhn notes that Mexican parties have often used polls for the same purpose. These polls "do not have the public demonstration effects of primaries" (Bruhn 2010: 44) but are likely to produce similar results.[10] Polls have been used not only "to choose candidates but also, by political elites, to 'guide' party leaders in their candidate selection" (Bruhn 2010: 44).[11]

Proponents of primaries may argue that a move away from primaries will lead to a reduction in popular participation in the nomination process. Others may contend that abandoning primaries will return nomination to "smoke-filled rooms," where the preferred candidate of a small (and presumably unrepresentative) elite emerges triumphant. A move away from primaries does not imply a move away from democracy. Abandoning primaries does not mean "closing" the process. Other forms of candidate selection, such as caucuses or nominating conventions, can be open to large populations, and parties can take steps to increase participation in these events. These alternate forms of selection can attempt to bring together the most valuable elements of primaries. Parties may oppose the abandonment of primaries because they feel pressure from their own aspirants to hold such elections. The push to remove primaries can be interpreted as a sign that party leaders—or a single party leader—are trying to gain control of candidate selection.

However, the malleability of candidate selection in Latin America today presents an opportunity to refrain from using processes that limit women's opportunities. The "movement toward primaries is not invariably a one-way street" (Carey and Polga-Hecimovich 2006 535); as Chapter 4 documents, parties have experimented with myriad selection methods. The move away from primaries and toward other inclusive-decentralized methods or other forms of selection would most likely be far from controversial in Latin America given the tremendous variation in the types of selection processes in use and the oft-repeated concerns about primaries.

Strategy 2: Limit Primary Spending

Because of "women's exclusion from certain circles of power and moneyed networks" and "their own actual economic status, which is documented to be inferior to that of men" (WEDO 2007: 4), women are significantly disadvantaged by the costs that primaries entail. Party women are well aware of these disadvantages. The head of the National Organism for Women of the PRI stated that women "participate in conditions of inequality" because they have more limited access to financial resources than men (Interview, February 13, 2003). As discussed in Chapter 3, women are considerably less likely to belong to the networks that can provide campaign financing. Women also continue to earn less than men, which constricts their efforts to self-finance campaigns. A councilwoman from La Serena felt that using primaries led to a situation in which "whoever has the most cash gets the most votes" (Interview, December 2, 2002). Although women may be disproportionately affected by the financial costs associated with primaries, men also noted that the cost of primaries was problematic. Primaries "wear us out" and "weaken us financially before the election," according to one councilman from Mérida (Interview, May 28, 2003).

Since women are less likely to have personal financial resources for campaigns and less likely to have access to local power monopolies, which can help fund their political endeavors, setting and enforcing clear limits on primary spending will increase women's access to politics.[12] Getting on the ballot requires "building reputation and recognition" within the electoral district, which is not without cost. Communication (telephones, cell phones, computers and Internet access, fax machines, postage) is essential to setting up a campaign office. Transportation costs can be significant, especially in large or rural districts or in cases in which the candidate lives outside the district. There are also hidden costs for those eager to get on the ballot: appropriate clothing, attendance at party events, and family-related expenses, such as child-care costs (WEDO 2007: 5). As opposed to general election costs, the price of winning the primary is shouldered entirely by the candidate. Reducing these costs will have gendered consequences.

Even in general elections, candidates in Latin America often foot a significant portion of the bill.[13] In the 2006 legislative elections in Mexico, one-third of PAN candidates and more than one-quarter of PRD candidates indicated that they financed "most" of their campaigns. Among Panistas, another 25 percent said that they had paid for a "good part" of their campaigns; 23 percent of Perredistas said the same (Bruhn 2010: 42–43). Financing both a primary campaign and then a general election campaign within a short span of time is likely to discourage many from participating.

Primary spending limits should be clear and should not be subsumed under general campaign spending limits; these are separate elections, and separate guidelines should be established for each. Other countries have used limits on primary spending. In addition to the effects on women's political access, limiting primary spending can be important for other reasons. The PAN opted to cancel all primaries in the northeastern state of Tamaulipas because of concerns over the influence of drug money: "In the case of Tamaulipas, everybody knows the possible influence of crime in candidate selection," explained PAN's national chairman, César Nava (quoted in Casas-Zamora

2010). Parties may want to limit spending to increase the amount of funds that can be used in general elections. Limiting primary spending may have the added benefit of decreasing media coverage (because of the high cost of television advertising spots). Although parties certainly want more media coverage of general election campaigns, they are likely to appreciate a cap on media coverage of primary campaigns, which disseminate negative information about potential candidates months before the general elections.

Just as campaign finance laws can be difficult to pass, setting limits on campaign spending is likely to inspire heated debate. Limiting campaign spending is viewed by some as a limitation on the freedom of speech. Some may say that limiting campaign spending restrains the dissemination of information about candidates. Limiting the primary campaign season could similarly be said to reduce the amount of time that individuals can learn about candidates. In a discussion of campaign spending limits, it is important to keep in mind that those parties that are wealthiest or best able to drum up campaign support are least likely to want to impose limits on campaign spending. Policymakers may want to turn their attention to successful efforts in campaign finance reform to craft bills that are more likely to be passed. For example, Mexico was able to adopt significant campaign finance reforms while the PRI still held the presidency. Penalties were put into place, such as small fines for lesser transgressions and large fines and cancellation of the party's official registration for the most severe infractions (Peschard 2006). Shortly after the passage of this new legislation, the PRI was severely penalized for illicit donations from a state agency to its presidential candidate, proving the effectiveness of the law. Proponents of primary campaign spending caps may want to frame this policy effort as another element of campaign finance reform; campaign spending reform legislation can even be seen as a point of pride: "gain[ing] entrance to the community of modern nations," as was the case for Mexico (Peschard 2006: 87).

The implementation of primary spending limits may also be difficult. Governments may buckle under the administrative burden of monitoring primary elections. The enforcement of campaign finance laws (which govern general election financing) is often very weak, but all Latin American countries except El Salvador have campaign finance laws in place (Casas-Zamora 2005, 2010). Effectively limiting primary spending will require the existence of institutions to monitor parties and sanctions to discourage noncompliance, but parties already submit financial reports to governmental institutions on general election spending in all Latin American countries except El Salvador (Casas-Zamora 2010). Capping primary spending will also be more complicated in federal systems, like Mexico's. Supervisory agencies at the state level may be unwilling to work collaboratively with federal agencies. This practice has been problematic in Mexico, where the Federal Electoral Institute has been able to obtain cooperation agreements with state-level institutes in only two-thirds of the country's states (Peschard 2006: 97).

Because policing primary spending can be problematic, an alternative approach to decreasing the amount of primary spending, and therefore the disadvantages faced by women seeking to enter politics, would be for parties or governments to limit the amount of campaigning time devoted to primaries. It is an easier proposition to limit the time period in which electioneering can take place,[14] and decreasing the amount of time devoted to primary campaigns would reduce the costs associated with these contests.

Strategy 3: Earmark Funds for Women

Since financing primary campaigns is problematic for women because cross-nationally women have less money and less access to networks that can provide money (Ballington 2008: 22), parties that can afford to do so should consider earmarking funds for female candidates to spend on primary elections. Parties should also encourage the formation of groups to raise money specifically for women's primary campaigns. Similarly, because some women may be reluctant to become candidates because of the prohibitive cost of general elections, parties that can do so should set aside funds for women candidates to use in general elections or should encourage outside groups to raise such funds. For the reasons outlined in Chapters 2 and 3, women have less access to campaign financing than men;[15] this is even more alarming in light of the fact that women may need more money than men just to become viable candidates (Baker 2006). Franceschet documents Chilean politician's Adriana Muñóz's thoughts on the problem of election financing: "Men have access to circles or networks where money is lent—they are friends with bank managers. But we are not supported this way. For us, it's pretty complicated, this arena of power and money. . . . Because even if the party accepts you and you are a candidate, how do you get elected if you have no money?" (quoted in Franceschet 2005: 89–90).

Two primary obstacles emerge to explain why parties may not earmark funds for women. The first is a lack of funds; scant resources may make it impossible for some parties to set aside funds for women. The second reason is that they may be ideologically opposed to "preferential" treatment for female candidates. There seems to be little hesitation to offer training for women; data collected for GEPPAL indicate that 77 percent of the 82 most significant parties in Latin America provide women with training and 65 percent offer training programs specifically for female members. One-quarter of parties set aside some portion of their budget for women's training (Roza 2010a: 125). The willingness of parties across the region to adopt training programs for women makes it likely that many parties would also agree to set aside funds to increase women's political access.

Unfortunately, in Latin America, parties often have limited resources. They cannot set aside money for men or women to use to finance their primary campaigns and may provide only meager funds to general election candidates. But the existence of such funds could have tremendous results. Funds designated for financing general election campaigns may encourage women who lack financial resources to nonetheless enter politics. Even small investments may allow women to participate; for example, the New Democratic Party in Canada reimburses child-care expenses incurred by women seeking candidacies (Young 2005: 137). This same party sets aside small sums of money (about $500) for women and minority aspirants to cover their travel expenses within large districts and to offset costs from seeking a candidacy in a district where an incumbent party member is stepping down (WEDO 2007: 16).

Because of the limited resources that Latin American parties generally have, it is important that parties encourage the formation of organizations—both within and outside the party—that provide financial support, training, or services to women candidates and encourage its female members to seek the support of such organizations. In the United States, political action committees like EMILY's List have provided financial backing and support to pro-choice women running for office. EMILY's List is an acronym that references the saying "Early money is like yeast; it helps the dough rise." The organization works to provide early financial support to candidates in order to encourage other donations and to fend off challengers (who will be less likely to run against formidable opponents). EMILY's List has been so successful that it has been replicated in Australia and the United Kingdom. Nongovernmental organizations in Ethiopia encouraged political parties to nominate women by providing extra allocations of goods and services to parties fielding female candidates (Sidhu and Meena 2007: 31).

To reinforce the efforts of parties and organizations interested in increasing women's political representation, government can play a key role in limiting the financial burden of elections for women via the passage of appropriate campaign finance legislation. Governments with the resources to do so should also encourage parties to nominate and elect female candidates by providing financial and in-kind incentives.

In addition, governments can provide benefits to parties that nominate and elect women. Canada offers tax credits to parties that nominate women and minorities; child care is also considered a deductible expense for candidates under Canadian tax law (WEDO 2007: 16). Governments can also lower election registration fees for parties that propose a set percentage of women candidates (WEDO 2007). In East Timor (as happens routinely in Latin America), the government provides free airtime to parties.[16] Political parties there that placed women in high positions on candidate lists were rewarded with extra media time.[17]

Similarly, where governments already provide funding to parties, they can reward extra funds to parties that nominate women or, alternatively, withhold funds to punish those parties that fail to nominate women. Governments that provide public financing for parties should insist that a certain percentage of these funds be designated for women, as has already been done in Costa Rica, Mexico, Panama, and Brazil (Llanos and Sample 2008).[18] Governments should require that parties account for how these public funds are used. Female candidates have expressed concern about the use of government funds. They argue that women are inequitably awarded funds by their own parties (WEDO 2007: 5). Parties can alleviate those concerns by providing information on their distribution of government funds. Parties can also go above and beyond the government requirements. In Panama, although the government requires that 10 percent of all public funding that a party receives be set aside for women's training, the Partido Arnulfista established a 30 percent rule (WEDO 2007: 16).

In addition to providing financial support for female candidacies, parties, civil society organizations, and government agencies should set aside funds to help women with other necessary campaign resources. Seeking support from external organizations may be necessary in order to provide these types of services to female aspirants and candidates in the region. Parties in Chile, Mexico, and other Latin American countries have already set up government programs that are charged with providing political training to women; however, these organizations are usually given inadequate budgets. Chile's National Service for Women (SERNAM) offered this kind of support; its regional offices ensured that this training was not limited to women in the capital city or those with the funds to travel to the capital to participate in workshops (Multiple interviews).

Civil society organizations can also provide this training. In the United States, the White House Project's Ms. President Class is an example of the type of aid that outside organizations can provide.[19] The Ms. President Class is a day-long seminar focused on fund-raising and communications strategies

for women who will be running for office. The National Democratic Institute, a nonprofit organization working to strengthen democracy worldwide,
provided political training to over 2,000 women in Bolivia in order to increase female candidacies in the 2004 municipal elections.[20]

Strategy 4: Actively Recruit and Nominate Women

Because women are less likely to self-nominate than men, parties should
work to identify and recruit potential female candidates. Parties can do this
by setting up search committees, creating databases of female members, giving women's sections within parties the resources to carry out related work,
and networking with civil society organizations. Furthermore, outside organizations can also play an active role in the recruitment of women candidates.

Parties can take a more aggressive approach to increasing women's representation by setting up search committees charged with identifying potential candidates. Those parties that actively recruit candidates, like the
UDI, whose exclusive-centralized selection process requires the identification and recruitment of potential candidates, have selected large numbers of
women. Parties that fail to recruit candidates, like the Partido Radical Social Demócrata (PRSD), which "waits for people to come to [it]" (Interview,
November 1, 2002), are likely to feel the gendered effects of self-nomination.
Those parties that actively seek to promote women, like the UDI, are even
more likely to have success in finding women candidates when they recruit.

Parties should also consider having specific groups (for example, labor
or women) nominate pre-candidates, while still allowing aspirants to propose their own candidacies. Alternatively, parties should consider constitut-
ing working groups that would be charged with proposing lists of nominees.
Data from Canada indicate that when parties use search committees, they
are more likely to choose women candidates (Erickson 1993: 76). The party
leadership should also broadly communicate its desires to identify and recruit women candidates to all levels. The national party leadership can, for
example, encourage local-level party offices to nominate or select women. A
study of Canadian parties found that encouragement of this sort may have
contributed to larger numbers of female aspirants and candidates (Erickson
1993: 78–79).

Parties can go beyond simply identifying potential female candidates
and train women (i.e., a "grow your own" strategy), as the Mexican PAN has
signaled that it will do. The party has adopted a 40 percent quota for municipal council candidates, which is meant to "train women in the party for
higher level office" and avoid a situation in which, as one Panista explained,

"You take the woman from her house so she can be a candidate, but she isn't prepared and you lose the election" (quoted in Piscopo 2011: 50).

Search committees need to be charged with instructions for avoiding bias. What one of Luciak's respondents termed "the false machismo of the compañeras" could otherwise emerge in these discussions. The respondent warned that decision makers had been known to think: "Poor Aidita, who has two little kids, for what reason are we going to involve her in this responsibility" (quoted in Luciak 2005: 253). Members of the selection committees should be instructed to propose candidates without regard to whether they believe that these potential candidates would want to participate. Similarly, selection committees must be explicitly told not to assume discrimination on the part of voters (imputed discrimination). One means to do this is to request that search committees come up with a set number of potential female candidates.

Parties can adopt practices to identify qualified women within their own ranks. Women are 51 percent of party members in the region (Roza 2010b), indicating that parties have a large pool of potential women to recruit from. In the Netherlands and Canada, databases were created to provide information on the backgrounds and careers of female party members to prevent elites from claiming that they were unable to find enough qualified female candidates (Erickson 1993; Leijenaar 1993: 226–227). This strategy can be used by women's organizations within a party and also by outside groups. Often, parties do not even maintain gender-disaggregated membership lists (Roza 2010a).[21] To actively recruit candidates from among their members, parties must be more thorough in their record keeping. Maintaining data on girls and young women active in their youth wings presents parties with another recruitment opportunity; this is especially important for parties like Mexico's PRD that have voluntary quotas in place to increase the representation of not only women but also young people.

Parties should actively recruit female members. While women's rates on average are comparable to men's (see Roza 2010a for specific data), there is party-level variation. Parties must rethink requirements for membership as well to encourage women to become members.[22] The PAN, for example, has onerous requirements for full membership.

Women's sections within parties can propose female candidacies and promote female candidates. Saint-Germain and Chavez Metoyer found mixed perceptions of women's sections but noted that women's sections can be instrumental in mobilizing women. For example:

the women's section of the centrist PLN party in Costa Rica was successful at mobilizing female party members to attend regional

and national nominating conventions to support their demands that
women candidates for the next elections in 1994 be nominated in
proportion to their numbers as party activists (roughly 15–25 percent), and that the party dedicate 15 percent of its financial support
to promoting the political participation of women. (Saint-Germain
and Chavez Metoyer 2008: 146–147)

Friedman (2000) has argued that separate women's bureaus in Venezuelan
parties served to incorporate as well as marginalize women, and Chaney
(1979) also reported marginalization. Women's sections have, however, undergone substantial changes in recent years, reorienting themselves to "serve
not as support staff but as advocates of female leaders" (Htun 2005: 115).

Women's sections, too, often suffer from inadequate funding. Nonetheless, they can still play an important role in pushing party elites to take action. Roza points out that party women should check that party documents
"reflect gender equality principles. These principles should be linked to the
ideological platform of the party. Even though these are rhetorical commitments, women can draw upon these principles when arguing their case for
greater inclusion and participation" (2010a: 211–212). She also proposes that
women can use the rhetorical commitments made in international agreements or conventions to push their parties to take action to increase women's
representation. Party women must be especially vigilant that the gains their
parties make in proposing female candidates are not undone by coalition-
level negotiation. Party elites, too, can then draw on principles both from
party statutes and from international conventions when negotiating coali-
tion-supported candidates.

In searching for female candidates, parties should draw from civil society
organizations. Women throughout Latin America have been active participants in social movements, but parties often fail to make connections with
these groups. One Ecuadorian woman active in civil society stated that after
the quota law went into effect, she and other feminist activists did not know
"how to participate, how to become candidates. . . . There is no permanent
contact between the party structure and popular organizations" (quoted in
Zambrano Macías 2004: 243). Building connections with these organizations could dramatically increase the supply of potential female candidates
available to parties.

Parties can also turn to neighborhood organizations, which have large
numbers of female leaders, to find new candidates. In Chile, women are
better represented than men in the leadership positions of these neighbor-

hood organizations (Hinojosa 2005). This pool of women is one that parties should draw from.

Outside organizations can also play a role in identifying and recruiting potential candidates. In El Salvador, Women '94, a group made up of several women's organizations, worked to increase women's representation in the 1994 elections. Among the group's actions was identifying potential women candidates and asking them to run (Silber and Viterna 2009: 334). In Sri Lanka, a group went beyond this basic model.[23] In addition to identifying potential women candidates, the group prepared videos on them for viewing by political elites. In a less formal measure, the White House Project in the United States allows individuals to send electronic postcards to women whom they would like to run for office.[24] These electronic postcards are meant to encourage women to consider entering politics. In Latin America, women's organizations, as well as parties, could also use electronic (or, where Internet access is more limited, traditional) postcards for the same purpose. These are low-cost strategies that are readily available to parties, women's sections, and other organizations across the region.

Strategy 5: Use Gender Quotas

The final strategy proposed here is to adopt gender quotas. As illustrated in Chapter 8, gender quotas—in the various forms of party quotas, legislated quotas, and reserved seats—have been adopted en masse in recent years. When gender quotas are well written, they can dramatically increase women's political representation.

A number of arguments have been offered against quotas. First, some contend that quotas are discriminatory toward men. In a similar vein, quota opponents often argue that women have the same opportunities as men, and because of this, quotas are inherently unfair. Both of these arguments assume a meritocracy. Women's historical and continued underrepresentation in politics indicates that this is simply not the case. Quotas are an effort to address the nonmeritorious situation that exists and to alleviate the long-standing systematic exclusion of women. Quotas are a means of eliminating discrimination. Gender-neutral language ("no more than 30 percent of either gender") in the discussion of quotas and in quota legislation may mitigate some of these concerns.

Second, some argue that quotas are inherently undemocratic because they do not permit citizens to vote for their desired candidate. In practice, however, voters already routinely vote from a list of candidates put together by parties. As noted in Chapter 3, it is political parties that choose: from a large number of eligibles, parties ultimately compose a short list to present to voters. Dahlerup turns this argument on its head: "Seen from a different perspective," she writes, "gender quotas may in fact expand the choices of the voters" (2006: 11).[25] By forcing parties to incorporate more women—in effect bringing the missing majority into politics—the use of quotas presents citizens with a much larger range of options.

Third, some opponents of quotas believe that quotas will simply introduce unqualified women into office, as Chapter 8 mentions. Works by Murray (2010) and Franceschet and Piscopo 2012 indicate that this is not the case. These recent studies suggest that women are as qualified as men, though they may have different qualifications than men. It is rarely mentioned, but important to consider, that unqualified men have gained political office. The presence of these unqualified men has not, however, led to wholesale doubts about all men. Some of my female respondents were concerned that if unqualified women were to enter politics because of quotas, then all women would be assumed to be unqualified.[26] Opponents of quotas may also believe that women who enter politics because of quotas are acting as mere puppets for male political elites. As Chapter 8 demonstrates, quotas certainly do change the candidate-selection process, but many forms of candidate selection (and especially in combination with certain electoral systems) make candidates—male and female—"depend on the political leadership for their (re)nomination" (Dahlerup 2006: 14).

A fourth argument that is often mentioned is that quotas undermine women. Citizens will presume that women needed quotas, that they were unable to make it on their own. Many of the women interviewed for this project called attention to the fact that they had managed to enter politics without quotas, and that therefore quotas were unnecessary. These women were worried that others would assume that they were the beneficiaries of quotas. However, introducing quotas actually provides women with an opportunity to demonstrate just how capable they are.

If the adoption of national gender quotas is not an option, informal practices should be adopted that can increase women's representation and/or prepare women for candidacies. For example, despite not having a quota in place for vice presidential positions, Costa Rica developed an informal practice that at minimum one of the vice presidential candidates would be a woman.[27]

If quotas are adopted, much can be done to make them successful. Chapter 8 notes that effective quota legislation demands an enforcement mechanism, like the penalties imposed in Mexico when parties fail to meet the quota. Penalties in the form of canceling lists (as in Mexico) may be more effective than fines (since, as Murray [2007] documents, parties may opt for a financial penalty to avoid meeting the quota). Chapter 8 uses Argentina to demonstrate that quota laws may evolve over time to become more effective; impediments to the proper application of quotas are sometimes unforeseen. Women's groups have already worked collaboratively to document the successes and failures of quota adoption processes (Krook 2009: 28). These organizations must continue their efforts after quota adoption to share information on increasing quota compliance.

Where quotas lack teeth, watchdog organizations should be set up by civil society organizations or by parties to monitor inadequate compliance. Where quotas do have appropriate enforcement mechanisms, watchdog organizations can be helpful in calling attention to minimalist compliance with quota legislation.

Parties that use voluntary quotas should set up internal groups to monitor their own compliance. Political parties should not feel they are "done" when they introduce a quota. Because parties regularly fail to meet their own voluntary quotas, as discussed in Chapter 8, it is especially important for parties to establish mechanisms to hold themselves accountable. Civil society organizations should also monitor political parties' voluntary efforts.

Quotas can be eliminated. Recently, for example, women's representation in Egypt dropped dramatically following the revolution. While reservations were in place for women prior to the revolution, since then women are not represented. Quotas have been eliminated under less dramatic circumstances as well. For example, Venezuelan quotas were ruled unconstitutional and were revoked in 2000, only three years after the initial quota legislation was passed. Quotas can dramatically affect candidate-selection processes, but they may not be permanent. For this reason it is imperative that we examine all candidate-selection processes through a gendered lens. Quotas may work to conceal the gendered effects of different candidate-selection procedures.

An advantage of the preceding strategies is that they make politics more accessible to not only women but also other underrepresented groups, such as lower socioeconomic groups and ethnic minorities. Primaries are not disadvantageous only to women, and campaign financing is an impediment for many who might otherwise enter politics. Parties can set aside funds for other groups that they believe are underrepresented and can work to recruit such individuals to run as candidates. Quotas can and have been used to increase the political representation of the indigenous or other marginalized groups.

Political parties, as female politicians readily acknowledge, have not done enough to promote women as candidates. Adriana Muñóz stated, "If you don't have the party president supporting you, they are going to give a district that won't help you, that you'll never win, even if you invest ten million dollars you are not going to win. . . . [We will succeed] only if there is a conscious will in the party that they want, for example, seven women deputies—*deputies* not candidates—and the party supports you by giving you districts you can win" (quoted in Franceschet 2005: 90). However, parties can adopt policies to increase women's candidacies, such as those outlined earlier. The opening quotation by successful Peruvian politician Susana Villarán de la Puente summarizes the current situation of Latin American women: Latin American women are prepared, but political parties are not doing enough for women.

Appendix A:
Latin American Women's
Representation by Party

	Female Legis-lators	Total Legis-lators	Percentage Female	Mean	Standard Deviation
ARGENTINA				40.7	37.1
Frente para la Victoria (FPV)	36	87	41		
Unión Cívica Radical (UCR)	9	43	21		
Peronismo Federal	9	2	32		
Coalición Cívica	11	19	58		
Propuesta Republicana (PRO)	7	11	64		
Frente Cívico por Santiago	3	7	43		
BOLIVIA				20.8	12.4
Movimiento al Socialismo (MAS-IPSP)	20	84	24		
Plan Progreso para Bolivia–Convergencia Nacional (PPB-CN)	8	37	22		
Movimiento sin Miedo (MSM)	1	4	25		
Unidad Nacional	1	3	33		
Alianza Social	0	2	0		
BRAZIL				4.9	5.9
(PMDB-PTC) Coalition	8	92	9		
Partido dos Trabalhadores (PT) ◄	8	79	10		
Partido da Social Democracia Brasileira (PSDB)	3	58	5		
Democratas	3	56	5		
(PSB-PCdoB-PRB) Coalition	10	46	22		
Partido da República (PR)	4	43	9		

	Female Legis-lators	Total Legis-lators	Percentage Female	Mean	Standard Deviation
CHILE				15.7	15.3
Unión Demócrata					
Independiente (UDI) ▶	6	39	15		
Partido Demócrata Cristiano					
(PDC)	1	9	5		
Partido por la Democracia					
(PPD) ◀	4	18	22		
Renovación Nacional (RN) ▶	2	18	11		
Partido Socialista (PS) ◀	2	11	18		
Independents	1	5	20		
COLOMBIA				16.4	27.1
Partido Social de Unidad Nacional	3	48	6		
Partido Liberal Colombiano (L)	6	38	16		
Partido Conservador					
Colombiano (C) ▶	6	36	17		
Cambio Radical (CR)	2	16	12		
Partido de Integración					
Nacional (PIN)	1	11	9		
Polo Democrático Alternativo					
(PDA)	1	5	20		
COSTA RICA				22.1	21.0
Partido Liberación Nacional					
(PLN)	11	24	46		
Partido Acción Ciudadana (PAC)	5	11	45		
Partido Movimiento Libertario					
(PML)	4	9	44		
Partido Unidad Socialcristiana					
(PUS)	1	6	17		
Partido Accesibilidad sin Exclusión					
(PASE)	1	4	25		
Partido Frente Amplio (FA)	0	1	0		
DOMINICAN REPUBLIC				13.7	12.3
Partido de la Liberación					
Dominicana (PLD)	25	105	24		
Partido Revolucionario					
Dominicano (PRD)	13	75	17		
Partido Reformista Social					
Cristiano (PRSC)	0	3	0		

	Female Legis- lators	Total Legis- lators	Percentage Female	Mean	Standard Deviation
ECUADOR				26.5	34.7
Alianza PAIS (PAIS)	20	59	34		
Partido Sociedad Patriótica 21 de Enero (PSP)	3	19	16		
(PSC-PMG) Coalition	5	11	45		
Partido Renovador Institucional de Acción Nacional (PRIAN)	0	7	0		
Movimiento Municipalista por la Integridad Nacional (MMIN)	0	5	0		
Movimiento Popular Democrático (MPD)	1	5	20		
EL SALVADOR				8.4	12.8
Frente Farabundo Martí para la Liberación Nacional (FMLN) ◄	11	35	31		
Alianza Republicana Nacionalista (ARENA) ►	4	18	22		
Gran Alianza por la Unidad Nacional (GANA)	1	16	6		
Partido de Conciliación Nacional (PCN)	0	10	0		
Líderes por el Cambio	0	2	0		
Partido Demócrata Cristiano	0	2	0		
GUATEMALA				13.3	25.8
Unidad Nacional de la Esperanza (UNE)	6	40	15		
Partido Patriota (PP)	5	30	17		
Independiente Libertad Democrática Renovada	4	27	15		
Gran Alianza Nacional (GANA)	1	14	7		
Independiente Bancada Guatemala (BG)	1	14	7		
Independientes (IND)	1	9	11		
HONDURAS				16.8	9.7
Partido Nacional de Honduras (PNH) ►	15	71	21		
Partido Liberal de Honduras (PLH)	8	45	18		
Partido Demócrata Cristiano de Honduras (DC)	1	5	20		
Partido Unificación Democrática (PUD)	1	4	25		
Partido de Innovación Unidad de Honduras (PINU)	0	3	0		

	Female Legis- lators	Total Legis- lators	Percentage Female	Mean	Standard Deviation
MEXICO				34.7	11.6
Partido Revolucionario Institucional (PRI)	50	239	21		
Partido Acción Nacional (PAN)	49	142	34		
Partido de la Revolución Democrática (PRD) ◄	20	68	29		
Partido Verde Ecologista de México (PVEM)	6	21	28		
Partido del Trabajo (PT)	3	13	23		
Convergencia (CONV)	4	8	50		
NICARAGUA*				18.5	13.5
Frente Sandinista de Liberación Nacional (FSLN) ◄	14	38	37		
Partido Liberal Constitucionalista (PLC) ►	2	25	8		
(ALN-PC) Coalition	2	22	9		
Movimiento Renovador Sandinista (MRS)	1	5	20		
PANAMA				8.3	10.6
Partido Revolucionario Democrático (PRD)	2	26	8		
Partido Panameñista (PP)	0	20	0		
Cambio Democrático (CD)	3	18	17		
Partido Unión Patriótica (UP)	1	4	25		
Movimiento Liberal Republicano Nacionalista (MOLIRENA)	0	2	0		
Partido Popular (PP)	0	1	0		
PARAGUAY				42.5	45.0
Asociación Nacional Republicana Partido Colorado (ANR)	2	30	7		
Partido Liberal Radical Auténtico (PLRA)	3	29	10		
Partido Unión Nacional de Ciudadanos Éticos (PUNACE)	2	15	13		
Partido Patria Querida (PPQ)	1	4	25		
Partido Democrático Progresista (PDP)	1	1	100		
Movimiento de Participación Ciudadana (MPE)	1	1	100		

	Female Legis- lators	Total Legis- lators	Percentage Female	Mean	Standard Deviation
PERU				29.7	12.6
Partido Aprista Peruano (PAP) ▶	11	36	30		
Partido Nacionalista Peruano	10	25	40		
Unidad Nacional	3	13	23		
Fujimorista	5	12	42		
Alianza Nacional	2	11	18		
Unión por el Perú (UPP)	1	7	14		
URUGUAY				9.7	7.9
Frente Amplio ◀	7	50	14		
Partido Nacional ▶	2	30	7		
Partido Colorado	3	17	18		
Partido Independiente	0	2	0		
VENEZUELA				13.8	9.6
Partido Socialista Unido de Venezuela (PSUV)	25	139	18		
Por la Democracia Social/ Frente Popular Humanista Coalition (UPP)	1	11	9		
Patria para Todos (PPT)	1	6	17		
Partido Comunista de Venezuela (PCV)	1	4	25		
Independents	0	4	0		

Source: The data were compiled from the individual websites for each country's lower house or single house of Congress. The data pertain to (1) the sitting legislative body beginning in October 2010 and (2) either the parties or coalitions, whichever were listed on the individual websites. The coding for left (◀) and right (▶) is from Manuel Alcántara Sáez, "Partidos políticos en América Latina: Precisiones conceptuales, estado actual y retos futuros," 2004, available at http://www.ucm.es/info/eid/cursodcd/IMG/pdf_Alcantara03.pdf. Only those parties that Alcántara Sáez listed as left or right, not those labeled as centrist parties, are identified here. This table includes only the six largest parties (defined as the six with the greatest number of representatives in the lower house or single chamber). I coded only those parties that went by the same name as when Alcántara Sáez identified them (i.e., any party identified by Alcántara Sáez that changed names in the past decade is not coded here). Please note that although Alcántara Sáez's coding is highly regarded, some country experts may not agree with all assessments. For example, whereas Alcántara Sáez codes both the PAN and the PRI in Mexico as centrist parties, other experts might identify the PAN as a party of the center right.

*The data for Nicaragua are for the 90 elected deputies only. The National Assembly is composed of 90 elected deputies, the country's most recent former president, and the second-place finisher among the presidential candidates.

Appendix B:
Interviews

All interviews were conducted by the author. The position listed for each interviewee is the position that he or she held at the time of the interview. To maintain anonymity, only one position for each interviewee is listed. For example, for an individual who was serving simultaneously as a council member and as vice president for his or her local political party, the listing would include the position as council member only. Furthermore, none of the names of council members are provided, in an effort to safeguard anonymity for a few. See Chapter 1 for full party names.

CHILE

July 10, 2002	RN National Office Functionary
July 23, 2002	La Morada Feminist Organization Representative
July 24, 2002	National Women's Ministry (SERNAM) Representative
July 25, 2002	PPD Party Elite
July 29, 2002	UDI Council Member
August 2, 2002	PPD National Office Functionary
August 2, 2002	PDC Party Elite
August 6, 2002	PS National Office Functionary
August 12, 2002	PDC Former Intendant
August 14, 2002	Academic (Ximena Rojas)
August 19, 2002	Academic (Teresa Valdés)
August 27, 2002	UDI Mayor
September 2, 2002	Municipal Office for Women Functionary
September 2, 2002	Foundation for Women's Promotion and Development (PRODEMU) Functionary
September 2, 2002	RN Council Member
September 3, 2002	President of Neighborhood Organization
September 10, 2002	President of Neighborhood Organization

September 9, 2002	PDC Council Member
September 9, 2002	PS Governor
September 9, 2002	PPD Council Member
September 10, 2002	PPD Party Elite
September 12, 2002	UDI Council Member
September 12, 2002	Institute for Development of Agriculture and Fishing (INDAP) Functionary
September 13, 2002	Municipal Office for Women Director
September 13, 2002	PPD Municipal Pre-candidate
September 13, 2002	PDC Municipal Party Vice President
September 16, 2002	PDC Congress Member
September 17, 2002	National Women's Ministry (SERNAM) Former Functionary
September 17, 2002	UDI Council Member
September 23, 2002	PDC Party Elite
September 27, 2002	RN Council Member
September 30, 2002	RN Municipal Party Vice President
September 30, 2002	PPD Municipal Party President
October 1, 2002	UDI Congress Member
October 2, 2002	UDI Mayor
October 2, 2002	UDI National Executive Committee Member
October 4, 2002	RN Council Member
October 4, 2002	UDI Council Member
October 7, 2002	PDC Municipal Party President
October 7, 2002	PDC Women's Front Functionary
October 8, 2002	PS Municipal Party President
October 10, 2002	PDC Party Elite
October 21, 2002	Academic (Alfredo Rehren)
October 24, 2002	PDC Council Member
October 24, 2002	PS Council Member
October 31, 2002	PRSD Council Member
November 1, 2002	PRSD Municipal Party President
November 2, 2002	PS Council Member
November 5, 2002	PDC Council Member
November 6, 2002	RN Council Member
November 6, 2002	PPD Council Member
November 7, 2002	PDC Mayor
November 8, 2002	National Women's Ministry (SERNAM) Maule Functionary
November 12, 2002	PS Municipal Party President
November 12, 2002	PDC Congressional Candidate
November 12, 2002	PS Municipal Party Leader
November 12, 2002	PS Municipal Party Leader
November 19, 2002	PRSD Council Member
November 21, 2002	Academic (José Enrique Novoa)
November 21, 2002	UDI Regional Party President
November 26, 2002	PRSD Municipal Party Vice President
November 28, 2002	PDC Provincial Party President
December 2, 2002	PDC Municipal Party President

December 2, 2002	PDC Council Member
December 2, 2002	PPD Provincial Party President
December 3, 2002	PS Council Member
December 3, 2002	PDC Council Member
December 4, 2002	RN Mayor
December 4, 2002	UDI Council Member Candidate
December 4, 2002	RN Council Member
December 9, 2002	PPD Municipal Party President
December 12, 2002	PDC Municipal Party President
December 16, 2002	UDI Mayor
December 18, 2002	National Women's Ministry (SERNAM) Regional Director
December 18, 2002	RN Council Member
December 20, 2002	PDC Council Member
June 14, 2004	UDI Party Elite
June 15, 2004	Association of Chilean Municipalities Functionary
June 18, 2004	UDI Legal Consultant
June 21, 2004	J. Guzmán Foundation Elite
June 23, 2004	UDI Party Elite

MEXICO

July 31, 2001	PRI National Executive Committee Member
January 13, 2003	Academic (Alejandro Poiré)
January 13, 2003	Academic (Federico Estévez)
January 13, 2003	Academic (Eric Magar Meurs)
January 13, 2003	Academic (Jeffrey Weldon)
January 14, 2003	Political Consultant (Gisela Rubach)
January 14, 2003	Political Consultant (Isabelia Ríos)
January 20, 2003	Academic (Dalia Isabel Barrera Bassols)
January 22, 2003	Academic (Gisela Zaremberg)
January 27, 2003	Academic (Rossana Fuentes-Berain)
January 29, 2003	PRD Secretariat for Cities and Municipal Governments Functionary
January 31, 2003	Interdisciplinary Group on Women, Work, and Poverty (GIMTRAP) Representative
February 13, 2003	PRI National Organism for PRI Women Functionary
February 18, 2003	Academic (Gisela Zaremberg)
February 19, 2003	Academic (Alejandra Massolo)
February 20, 2003	PRD Secretariat of Equity Functionary
February 20, 2003	PRD Secretariat for Cities and Municipal Governments Functionary
February 21, 2003	PAN Federal Deputy
February 24, 2003	PRI Political Elite
March 17, 2003	PAN Council Member
March 17, 2003	PRI Council Member
March 17, 2003	PCD Council Member
March 17, 2003	PRI Council Member

March 17, 2003	PRI Council Member
March 18, 2003	PRI Council Member
March 18, 2003	PRD Council Member
March 19, 2003	PAN Council Member
March 19, 2003	PRI Council Member
March 24, 2003	Center for Municipal Services (CESEM Heriberto Jara) Functionary
March 24, 2003	Center for Municipal Services (CESEM Heriberto Jara) Functionary
March 25, 2003	PRI Mayor
March 25, 2003	PRI Council Member
March 26, 2003	PRI Municipal Party President
March 27, 2003	PRI Council Member
March 27, 2003	President of Municipal Institute for Women
March 28, 2003	PRD Mayoral Candidate
April 28, 2003	PRD/PAN Council Member
April 28, 2003	PRD Council Member
April 28, 2003	PRI Council Member
April 29, 2003	PRI Council Member
April 30, 2003	PAN Council Member
May 1, 2003	PRD Council Member
May 7, 2003	PRD Municipal Party President
May 7, 2003	PRD Mayor
May 8, 2003	PAN Municipal Party President
May 9, 2003	PRI Municipal Party President
May 16, 2003	PRI Council Member
May 16, 2003	PRI Council Member
May 19, 2003	PAN Council Member
May 21, 2003	PAN Council Member
May 21, 2003	PAN Municipal Party President
May 22, 2003	PRI Council Member
May 22, 2003	PAN Council Member
May 26, 2003	PRI Council Member
May 26, 2003	PRI Municipal Party President
May 27, 2003	PRI Council Member
May 27, 2003	PAN Council Member
May 27, 2003	PRI Council Member
May 28, 2003	PRI Council Member
May 29, 2003	PRD Council Member
May 29, 2003	PAN Council Member
June 4, 2003	PAN Mayor
June 4, 2003	PAN Council Member
June 16, 2003	PRI Council Member
June 18, 2003	PRD Council Member
June 19, 2003	PRI Council Member
June 23, 2003	PRI Council Member
June 27, 2003	Academic (Dirk Zavala)

Notes

CHAPTER 1

1. Bachelet's primary opponent was Soledad Alvear. The Christian Democratic Party had chosen her via a primary, in which she had competed for her party's support against Adolfo Zaldívar. Both Alvear and Zaldívar were established politicians: Alvear was serving as Minister of Foreign Affairs in the Lagos administration, but had served as Minister of Women's Affairs and Minister of Justice in previous administrations; Zaldívar had been his party's president and a national senator.

2. While across the globe it is generally true that women are more likely to be represented at the local rather than at the national level (Lovenduski and Norris 1993; Darcy, Welch, and Clark 1994), this is often not the case in Latin America. The application of national gender quota laws can explain why this is currently the situation in many Latin American countries. There are also significant differences in women's abilities to gain executive (mayors) versus legislative seats (council members).

3. Matland and Studlar (1996), Caul (1999), Tremblay and Pelletier (2001), and Kittilson (2006) have focused on political parties and party-level differences to explain women's political underrepresentation.

4. The mean for the percentage of women in lower or single chambers of legislatures (the data are represented in Graph 1.2) is 20.5, with a standard deviation of 9.3. The data presented in Appendix A provide the means and standard deviations by country for the percentage of women in the lower or single chambers of legislatures by party. Of the 18 countries listed in the table, only 2 have standard deviations of less than 9.3. In other words, in all but 2 of these countries, in-country differences were more substantial than differences across countries. This analysis included all political parties with representation in the lower or single chamber of the legislature. In a separate analysis, I included only the six largest parties in the country. By excluding many small parties from the analysis, I found that in 5 of the 18 countries, the standard deviation was smaller than 9.3, indicating that cross-country differences were more significant in nearly one-third of countries. The exclusion of the smaller par-

ties made a tremendous difference in standard deviations in some cases. For example, in the Argentine case, although the mean percentage of legislators who were women increased only slightly (from 40.7 percent when including all parties in the legislative body to 43.2 percent when looking at only the six largest parties in the Chamber of Deputies), the change in standard deviation was striking: from 37.1 to 16 when using only the six largest parties. In the Bolivian case, however, there was no change since only five parties or coalitions had legislative representation. Note that 12 of the 18 countries in this analysis use gender quotas for the national legislature. I suspect that if this analysis had been done in 1995, before the mass adoption of gender quotas, that we would observe even more significant variations within countries than we see here.

5. I have chosen to use these examples because one has a gender quota (Peru) and one does not (Nicaragua). We, of course, expect to see more substantial variation across parties in countries with quotas. Of the quota and nonquota countries, these two were chosen because their standard variations are the closest to the mean standard variation for the region. The complete data are presented in Appendix A.

6. Norris and Inglehart believe that culture explains what modernization has not been able to do.

7. Chilean academic Teresa Valdés notes that incumbency can present a "vicious cycle" because women "don't have the political capital to be nominated as candidates, but this keeps them from obtaining the political capital as well. Therefore, they never break into the system" (quoted in Franceschet 2005: 88).

8. Rainbow Murray's 2007 analysis of the French case and Lisa Baldez's 2004a work on the Mexican case are extremely useful in understanding how party-level differences remain, even with the adoption of a gender quota law.

9. See Chapter 8 for a list of Latin American countries using gender quotas.

10. Argentina, Brazil, Costa Rica, El Salvador, Mexico, Nicaragua, and Uruguay prohibit independents from running for presidential, congressional, or municipal office. Peru allows independent candidacies for municipal positions but prevents independents from running for the presidency or for Congress. Panama prohibits independent candidacies for the presidency (Zovatto G. 2007: 184–185).

11. See Escobar-Lemmon and Taylor-Robinson's study (2008) for their thorough explanation of the challenges of studying the effects of selection procedures on women's political representation in Latin America. Roza (2010a) found that when it came to candidate selection, party rules and practices routinely failed to match up.

12. Norris and Lovenduski's pathbreaking book on the subject categorized selection procedures in Great Britain as localized/centralized and formal/informal. Formal systems will best be able to use affirmative action measures to increase women's representation. They see local selection as opening the door to self-recruitment from women but believe that centralized systems provide women with the opportunity to work their way up in the party and give the party leadership the leeway to promote women's candidacies if they so choose. Caul (2001) tested the relationship between centralization of candidate nomination and women's representation in national legislatures in 12 industrialized countries and found that lower levels of centralization were actually associated with greater percentages of female parliamentarians, contrary to expectations based on arguments by Norris and Lovenduski (1995). Roza tested whether formality proved beneficial to women in parties from across 18 Latin American countries.

She found that formal parties—those that had written rules in place—provided less of an opportunity for women's representation (Roza 2010a: 167). In contrast, Ballington and Karam had urged formalized procedures for candidate selection to increase women's representation (2005: 106). See also Escobar-Lemmon and Taylor-Robinson's study (2008) for their excellent treatment of the effects of candidate-selection procedures on women's representation as legislators and ministers in Argentina, Brazil, Chile, Colombia, Mexico, and Uruguay.

13. I explain the selection of municipalities subsequently.

14. Chile is composed of 13 regions; each has an intendant who is appointed by the president. The 13 regions are subdivided into 51 provinces, each with an appointed governor. Mexico, on the other hand, is composed of 31 states and the federal district. Each of these subnational units elects its own governor.

15. In addition to the differences noted here, the careful reader will also note that while Chile does not have a gender quota law, Mexico does. However, at the time that research was undertaken in Mexico, the national quota law had been passed but had not yet been applied to any elections (a very weak quota recommendation was in effect, but it had not increased women's representation). Furthermore, the national quota would not have been applicable to the municipal-level elections under study here.

16. There were two reasons for doing this. First, it was not possible to obtain a list of municipal candidacies in Mexico. In part, this was because of the federal system. Electoral lists for municipal elections were (presumably) maintained by state-level electoral institutes (often known as Instituto Estatal Electoral [IEE]). Each of the 31 states has an IEE, but the level of organization varies dramatically across states. Second, by examining only cases of successful candidates, I dramatically increased the chances that I would be able to locate and interview these individuals. In fact, despite repeated efforts in all municipalities in which I conducted fieldwork, only rarely was I able to conduct interviews with unsuccessful candidates (see Appendix B). Staggered elections in Mexico, which place each state on its own elections schedule, made finding data much more complicated. To highlight the difficulties that I had in obtaining quality information, before arriving in the municipality of Pueblo Viejo, I was unsure of whether it was indeed called Pueblo Viejo. The Federal Institute for Federalism and Municipal Development (INAFED) listed the municipality as Pueblo Viejo, whereas the National Institute for Women (InMujeres) officially listed it as Pueblo Nuevo.

17. At the time of case selection, there were 341 municipalities in Chile and 2,443 in Mexico. Municipal population size varied dramatically. In Chile, the smallest municipality had 215 inhabitants and the largest 444,593. In Mexico, the smallest population was 110 and the largest was 1,646,319. The mean population size was 45,299 in Chile and 36,696 in Mexico.

18. This hypothesis and the corresponding decision to maximize variation in population size were based on previous work that had asserted that women were better represented in municipalities with smaller populations than in larger cities (Blay 1979; Blay 1980; Massolo 1998, 1999; Craske 1999). Hinojosa (2005) reveals that women are proportionally represented across municipalities of different sizes; women simply appear to be better represented in smaller municipalities because there are more small municipalities than there are large ones, and hence more women mayors of small municipalities than of large municipalities.

19. Chilean municipalities are small. The largest of them contains less than 500,000 people. I defined a municipality as large if it had a population greater than 120,000, medium-sized if it had between 50,000 and 120,000 inhabitants, and small if it had a population of less than 50,000. Only 10 municipalities outside of the metropolitan region have a population greater than 150,000, and only 1 of these had a woman mayor. The situation was quite different in Mexico, where municipal size varies greatly, with the average population still under 40,000. I therefore categorized municipalities as small if they had populations of less than 30,000, medium if they had populations between 30,000 and 250,000, and large if they had populations upwards of one-quarter million.

20. This decision was practical: that is, I presumed that I would increase the odds of studying various selection procedures if I studied a larger number of parties, but it was also based on reading the limited material available at the time on candidate selection in Latin America. Langston (2001) was particularly helpful in this regard.

21. For example, in the case of Chile, of the 40 female mayors in the country, 16 were members of the UDI, 13 were from RN, and 7 were from PDC. The PS, PRSD, and PPD each had one female mayor, and another mayor was an independent aligned with the right. The situation was even more pronounced in Mexico, where the vast majority of female mayors were PRI members. (See note 25 for a full explanation of party names.)

22. Mexico's ban on immediate re-election, on the other hand, meant that no officeholders who were interviewed had been incumbents.

23. In Chile, all municipalities included in the study are found in the middle two-thirds of the country and represent the metropolitan, north-central, and south-central regions. In Mexico, the municipalities used in my research were located in the central regions and along the southern portion of the Gulf Coast. This hypothesis was based in part on the uneven distribution of female mayors. In Chile, for example, none of the 10 mayors in the eleventh region was a woman, but in the seventh region, 7 of 30 mayors were women.

24. The desire to obtain this geographical variation was based on academic work noting the role that cultural differences play in women's political representation (see, for example, Reynolds 1999; Inglehart and Norris 2003).

25. The major political parties are the Unión Demócrata Independiente (UDI), Renovación Nacional (RN), Partido Socialista (PS), Partido por la Democracia (PPD), Partido Radical Social Demócrata (PRSD), and Partido Demócrata Cristiano (PDC) in Chile and the Partido Revolucionario Institucional (PRI), Partido Acción Nacional (PAN), and Partido de la Revolución Democrática (PRD) in Mexico.

26. While I wished to expand the temporal borders of my quantitative study, I could not have done so without extensive qualitative data documenting that the six political parties that I studied continued to use the same selection methods across municipalities. No similar analysis could be undertaken for the Mexican case for two reasons: first, obtaining data on candidacies would have been a herculean task, most likely necessitating that I visit each of 31 states to obtain data directly from their electoral institutions. While the PAN national offices had thorough records, the PRI and PRD national offices did not. The PRD had a difficult time providing me with a list of PRD mayors. Second, in Mexico, selection procedures varied significantly. Parties

did not use a single type of selection process; they used a medley, not only from election to election but also from municipality to municipality. Part of the explanation for this is that Mexico is a federal country, while Chile is unitary. Furthermore, Mexico's (then very recent) authoritarian past coupled with political parties' desire to distance themselves from any mention of authoritarianism most likely compelled the parties to experiment with new selection methods.

CHAPTER 2

1. Part of the relationship expressed in Figure 2.1 is borrowed from Norris and Lovenduski (1995), who show the dynamic nature of each step in the recruitment process. For a more comprehensive diagrammatic articulation of the recruitment process, see Norris and Lovenduski 1995: 184. Other scholars studying candidate selection have provided diagrams that build off or represent elements of the diagram elaborated by Norris and Lovenduski.

2. Carroll (1985) notes how often this refrain is used by male political leaders in the United States. This is a common sentiment voiced by Latin American politicians. The comments of Ecuadorian politician Giovanny López Endara are typical: "We have to admit, that as a general rule, women don't get involved in politics, and those that do don't have the adequate preparation, making them incapable of becoming candidates with real electoral options (2004: 79). As former Ecuadorean deputy Cecilia Calderón remarked, "There's no preparation that is expected of men, but for us [women] there is because we're being 'tested out'" (2004). See also Cañete 2004: 171–180. This concern about qualified women may be a form of imputed discrimination. Norris and Lovenduski (1995) note that elites rarely say they do not want female candidates; instead they use possible voter discrimination to dismiss women.

3. As Paxton, Hughes, and Green (2006) point out, these structural factors have usually been found to have little explanatory power.

4. Gender-disaggregated data from universities on majors are not widely available. While there may be differences in law school enrollment rates across countries, we have no reason to believe that the Chilean data would be aberrant.

5. However, as others have noted, analyzing women's presence in certain professions does little to help us understand women's political representation. Scholars have noted, for example, that while in both Costa Rica and Guatemala women held about 15 percent of professional and technical occupations, women's legislative representation in these two countries was radically different (Saint-Germain and Chavez Metoyer 2008). We do know that certain professions tend to be better represented in politics: Macauley (1993) found that one-third of Chilean deputies and nearly half of senators were lawyers. See Camp for work that examines the biographies of Mexican politicians.

6. Schmidt (2006) cites data from Webb and Fernández Baca 2000 indicating that in Peru, by 1998 more than half of accountants, almost one-third (31.5 percent) of economists, and more than 37 percent of public prosecutors were women.

7. While a number of Latin American countries have mandatory voting laws, voting rates are still an important indicator of women's interest. Mandatory voting laws are not regularly enforced, but even in countries where there is enforcement, such as Peru, there are still individuals who do not vote.

8. Roza (2010a) provides the first thorough cross-national look at women's representation in Latin American political parties. She obtained membership data on more than 30 of the largest political parties in the region; the majority of political parties in the region did not maintain gender-disaggregated data. Women are equitably represented as party members in most parties. Cuba would be an exception (Roza does not provide data on Cuba); female membership in the party ranged from 22 percent in 1985 to just over 30 percent in 1997 (Luciak 2005: 258).

9. Camp earlier argued that because of women's participation in nongovernmental organizations (NGOs) and in unions, women would most likely benefit from democratization in Mexico (Camp 2010).

10. A thorough discussion of women's collective action efforts across Latin America is outside the scope of this book.

11. Research in the United States has used experiments to determine whether voter bias exists. The results of experimental matchups between hypothetical male and female candidates have indicated that some discrimination exists. Unfortunately, no such studies have been done in Latin America.

12. This poll revealed virtually no differences in willingness to vote for a woman mayor or a woman president. This is surprising but may be a result of the very minimal levels of voter bias exhibited. In other words, it may be only those individuals who are completely opposed to having women in politics who answered no to both questions.

13. Dolan notes that much of the academic literature on the public's willingness to vote for female candidates has been severely limited because surveys "create an artificial situation that, although successful in isolating reactions to candidate sex, fails to replicate the more complicated evaluations people must make in the real political world" (2004: 154). Similarly, I would argue that surveys taken in a context in which women are running or are likely to run for the presidency tell us more about people's willingness to vote for female candidates, given that respondents are not being asked questions about an "artificial situation" but about a very real possibility.

14. Ana María Yáñez of the feminist Peruvian NGO Manuela Ramos would almost certainly be one of these individuals. Yáñez provoked controversy when she commented on the all-female makeup of the leadership of Fujimori's Governing Council of Congress by saying, "I prefer four authoritarian women to four authoritarian men" (Barrig 2001: 29–35). Given her preference for authoritarian women over authoritarian men, it is likely that she would also embrace democratically elected women over democratically elected men!

15. In other words, these electoral data on female presidents are used only to demonstrate that voters will vote for women. These data are not evidence that voters are as willing to cast their ballots for women as they are for men, nor do they indicate that voters do not exhibit bias. New studies, such as the terrific study by Morales Quiroga (2008) on Bachelet's election, are using statistical analysis to assess voter bias both against and for (i.e., gender solidarity) female candidates in Latin America.

16. Roza warns that because coalitions were common, a lot of incomplete data were collected. She eliminated all data from parties that provided incomplete data. The ratios could not be calculated at all for the Dominican Republic, Honduras, Mexico, or Venezuela. Ratios were calculated for all other countries when at least

two political parties could provide complete data. See Roza 2010a: 125–127 for more information on methodology.

17. While women may face only limited discrimination in the voting booth, they are more likely to be made to feel uncomfortable on the campaign trail. Voters may treat a woman campaigning for office differently than they would treat a man because of social norms. A female mayor remarked that the area farmers did not know how to treat her since "they couldn't even invite [her] to have a beer with them, the way they would have with a man" (Interview, May 7, 2003). As this woman realized, social norms limited her campaigning abilities and proved to be a political liability.

CHAPTER 3

1. Camp believes that local elites may be more conservative than national elites and therefore more resistant to allowing women into positions of power (2010: 111). If this is the case, then we can expect that women would be doubly burdened by decentralized selection.

2. Despite the increased popularity of primaries in the region, Field and Siavelis find that parties in Latin America are more likely to be using exclusive processes when selecting their legislative candidates (2008: 622).

3. Decision making by one or two people is not uncommon, as shown in the cases detailed in this book. In addition, Jones (2008: 47) mentions that this is common in Argentine provinces.

4. Walsh, at the Center for American Women and Politics (Rutgers University), has identified the Barack Obama phenomenon (previously, the John Edwards phenomenon): "Having never held elective office, they run for Senate, then before finishing a first term decide they should be president. . . . While men are assumed to be qualified, women have to prove they are, or at least they believe they do" (Zernike 2008: n.p.).

5. Political encouragement can also be important to keeping women in politics. Peruvian politician Martha Chávez considered retiring from politics in 2000 but listened to those who told her that "the government needed people like me" (quoted in Adrianzén, Rial, and Roncagliolo 2008: 330).

6. In her groundbreaking work, Fowlkes (1984) outlined various sources for this counter-socialization. Clark et al. (1993) provide a necessary analytical distinction between sources of counter-socialization that affect both men and women and those that most affect women. The experience of having a politically active mother, in particular, was seen as an important source of counter-socialization for women. See Elder 2004 for hypotheses that explain the different political socialization that men and women, as well as boys and girls, receive.

7. These categories may be gendered. For example, women may be more likely to exhibit static ambition than men as a result of familial responsibilities that constrain their geographic mobility. Further, because women have traditionally entered politics at a later age than men, they may appear more likely to exhibit discrete ambition— that is, if a man enters politics at age 35 and a woman at age 55 and both opt to retire at age 65, he will have several decades in which to pursue higher office, while she will have only 10 years to make her way up the political ladder.

8. Power and Mochel describe how these networks are able to maintain themselves in power: "Even when the ruling oligarch loses elections, he manages to keep control of important political resources because of the personal sway he holds over many congress members, mayors, and allies whom he has infiltrated throughout the state apparatus. Typically, his group enjoys significant economic power in the state, too" (2008: 237).

9. See Warner and Lunt 1941 and Knoke 1993 for different definitions of networks.

10. Salinero R. (2004) describes a *club de Tobi* as run by a masculine logic that prevents women from full participation.

11. According to Hagopian, traditional elites have prevented full democratization in Brazil, Colombia, El Salvador, Guatemala, and Honduras (1996: 70).

12. The notable exception is Roderic Camp, who has long studied the role of networks in Mexican politics. Camp has found that Mexican networks are built upon "family, friends, place, and shared educational experiences" and not just upon traditional, institutionalized forms of networking based on career contacts (2002: 36). For politicians, family and friends accounted for 70 percent of their networks (Camp 2002: 42). In earlier work, Camp (1979) found that attending the national university (UNAM) was an important networking and recruitment tool for men and women, although women were less likely to attend university. Balmori, Voss, and Wortman (1984) provided a much-needed account of the role of important family networks in the history of the region from 1750 to 1900. Scholarly works have also examined the importance of economic networks of power in Latin America (see, for example, the work of Aldo Musacchio).

13. The selectorate, in the case of an open primary, could be made up of every citizen over the age of majority. However, the size of the selectorate can vary wildly when selection is inclusive. Open primaries in which 10,000 people are eligible to vote may draw only 400 participants. Closed primaries open to all party members in a town might attract only a dozen or so individuals. Specific data on participation rates are available in Chapter 5.

14. According to some, "the way in which political parties select their candidates may be used as an acid test of how democratically they conduct their internal affairs" (Gallagher 1988: 1). This idea is discussed in Chapter 4. Serra (2011) uses the terms *democratic* and *undemocratic* to classify selection procedures. Bille (2001), Alcántara Sáez (2002), Freidenberg (2003), Baldez (2004b), and Carey and Polga-Hecimovich (2006) have all noted that primaries are seen as indicative of internal party democracy. See also Rahat 2009 on the issue of democratization of candidate-selection procedures.

CHAPTER 4

1. GEPPAL data indicate that 30 percent of the largest parties in the region use primaries to select their legislative candidates (Roza 2010a: 131–132).

2. See Rahat 2009 for a discussion of how the term *democratic* can be applied to candidate-selection procedures. Other scholars have no such concerns about labeling candidate-selection processes as democratic. Serra (2011) explicitly categorizes candidate selection as either open (which he also calls democratic) or closed/undemocratic.

3. For an extraordinarily thorough list of primary usage for presidential elections across time, see Carey and Polga-Hecimovich 2006: 536. Freidenberg (2003: 22) details the de jure and/or de facto use of primaries for presidential elections across Latin America.

4. Chapter 8 discusses the fascinating interaction between gender quotas and so-called primaries.

5. Bruhn (2010) notes that parties are unable to police fraud in primary elections.

6. Serra (2011) argues that part of the reason why primaries produce stronger candidates is that primaries "open the door" to many more pre-candidates than other selection methods (Serra 2011: 23). However, considering the high cost of primary elections and the gendered implications of using primaries, I would argue that primaries do not in effect produce an open-door policy. Scholars have tried to assess whether primaries do produce stronger candidates by examining elections results. Carey and Polga-Hecimovich (2004) found an electoral advantage, but Colomer (2002) and Bruhn (2010) did not.

7. Bruhn (2010) examines both PRD and PAN selection methods for senatorial candidates in Mexico. She refers to these as internal elections. She categorizes the PRD's selection as a type of primary but does not believe that the PAN is having true primaries. Although she categorizes both the PRD's primary elections and the PAN's much less inclusive methods (she considers them to be an example of "moderate inclusiveness") as internal elections, she does note the large differences between the two. To illustrate, she points out that in the PRD there were 97.5 selectors for every 1,000 registered voters, while in the PAN there were 3.3 selectors for every 1,000 registered voters (Bruhn 2010: 33). For more information on the PAN's conventions, see Baldez 2004a and 2007. As discussed in Chapter 8, Baldez has perceptively noted that the PAN's practices are treated as primaries and therefore exempt from meeting the quota.

8. Other scholars do not see this as usurping power from elites; instead, they paint elites as willing to take over the "prickly task" of choosing candidates (Carey and Polga-Hecimovich 2006: 534).

9. Serra (2011) explains that parties often try to decide what type of selection process to use before they start talking about potential candidates. Candidate selection is, in other words, a serious concern for parties.

10. This point is addressed further in Chapter 9.

11. I know of no similar studies for Latin America, although anecdotal evidence indicates that the same situation occurs.

12. See Chapter 2 for data from Latin America indicating that this situation may be changing.

13. The assumption today is that primaries in Latin America largely attract an even number of men and women. In the United States, the adoption of primaries catapulted women's participation in candidate selection; while they had been about 5 to–10 percent of convention delegates, they were 40 percent of voters in the earliest primaries (Ware 2002).

14. The local parties have had their autonomy in this respect questioned. In August 2002, the PS held a conference on increasing local decision making after a number of incidents in which the candidate chosen by the party was replaced by party elites at higher levels (Interview, October 8, 2002).

15. See www.ppd.cl.

16. See www.prsd.org.

17. President Lagos, a Socialist, beat the PDC pre-presidential candidate in the 1999 Concertación primary. In 2005, the Concertación nomination once again went to a member of the PS. The Concertación candidacy was returned to the PDC in 2009: former president Eduardo Frei received the nomination.

18. Unable to compile a reliable list of party members, the PRI was forced to use open primaries.

19. Chapter 5 explains that the PRI's selection procedures in Pueblo Viejo may appear to be inclusive-decentralized on paper, but in practice, the process cannot be considered inclusive.

20. The PRI and PRD used various selection procedures; unfortunately, there is no source of reliable data on the processes for selection used in each of the nearly 2,500 municipalities across 31 states in Mexico. Nor would it be likely that if such data were available that it would accurately describe selection procedures. In-depth fieldwork is necessary to obtain reliable information on candidate-selection procedures, for the reasons outlined in Chapters 1 and 3. I therefore cannot perform the type of quantitative analysis that I did for the Chilean parties.

21. The differences in probabilities are significant at the 95 percent level. More information on this statistical analysis is presented in Chapter 6.

CHAPTER 5

1. See www.pan.org.mx.

2. This exemption has proved to be extraordinarily important. A thorough discussion of the Mexican quota law, this exemption, and its effects appears in Chapter 8.

3. As Baldez (2007: 74) notes, there is quite a bit of disagreement about just how "democratic" the PAN's candidate-selection processes truly are, with Lara Rivera (2006) on one end of the spectrum (very democratic) and Wuhs (2006) on the other (quite closed).

4. However, one PRD member was represented as a relative majority councilman as the result of a coalition between the PAN and the PRD at the state level.

5. Huerta García and Magar Meurs are reluctant to say that parties (and specifically the PRI) used these less than competitive primaries as a means of evading the quota, but nonetheless they "maintain their suspicions" (2006).

6. See www.rn.cl.

7. Complicated electoral rules forced Peñafiel to split the 1992–1996 term with the second-place finisher. See Hinojosa and Franceschet, forthcoming, for a review of the electoral rules that have been used for municipal elections in Chile since the return to democracy.

8. See www.prd.org.mx.

9. This town was not among the eight municipalities chosen for inclusion in this study.

10. Furthermore, while candidates may want to allege that they were chosen by primary when they were not (both because this makes their party appear democratic

and makes them appear to have substantial support), I can see no compelling reason to make the opposite claim.

CHAPTER 6

1. Freidenberg mentions that parties serving as personalistic vehicles for charismatic individuals are most likely to use exclusive-centralized selection. This form of candidate selection also is common under authoritarian regimes. The case of Peru under Fujimori is one example in which exclusive-centralized selection in a context of authoritarianism proved beneficial to women's candidacies.

2. GEPPAL, an acronym from the Spanish phrase for Gender and Political Parties in Latin America, is a database created by the Inter-American Development Bank, PROLEAD, and International IDEA. The GEPPAL data were collected from January to October 2009.

3. Argentina is an exception. While only a small percentage of the country's mayors are women (8.5 percent), women are well represented in the Chamber of Deputies (38.5 percent) and in the Senate (35.2 percent). The percentage of female ministers is much lower: 25 percent. As in many countries of the region, women did not make inroads into the Cabinet until the 1980s and 1990s. There was a female Minister of Labor and Social Affairs in 1952 and a female Minister of Justice in 1973, but women ministers in the 1980s primarily obtained traditionally "feminine" ministries, such as Education and the Environment. Perhaps to compensate for women's historic underrepresentation in ministerial posts, President Carlos Menem set up a shadow (advisory) cabinet composed exclusively of women in 1992 (Waylen 2000: 778). Since 2000 and especially under the Kirchner administrations, women have been appointed to more important ministries. Nonetheless, women's share of ministries is average for the region, while women's representation in national-level appointed positions has been extraordinary.

4. The ideology of the *Frente Sandinista de Liberación Nacional* certainly plays a role in explaining women's appointments to the Council of State. However, also consider that during the Pinochet dictatorship, more women mayors were appointed than have been elected during democracy (Craske 1999). In Cuba, Fulgencio Batista appointed more women to office than had ever previously been elected (Domínguez 1978). Neither Pinochet nor Batista was a leftist; ideology cannot explain those appointments.

5. Altman remarks that Chilean President Lagos introduced an "informal" affirmative action policy for his cabinet and for other appointed positions. On the basis of the emergence of two strong female presidential contenders for subsequent elections, Altman concludes that the policy was successful (2008: 263).

6. See www.udi.cl.

7. See Morales Quiroga 2008 for a thorough analysis that contradicts the UDI's conventional wisdom. He finds evidence of gender solidarity in Chile. Morales Quiroga demonstrates that, controlling for political parties, women were more likely to vote for Bachelet than men.

8. In her classic work, Chaney wrote, "A woman official most often defines herself as a kind of supermadre, tending the needs of her big family in the larger *casa* of the

municipality or even the nation" (1979: 21). This sentiment was mirrored in my discussions with UDI officials. Tying women's traditional roles to their participation in local-level politics might explain women's increased participation at this level of government generally. While the "administration of the biggest house" might make local politics more accessible to women, we would suppose that would mean all women. Even if we would assume that more conservative parties would nominate women for local politics because it is closer to the private sphere, we would nonetheless expect that parties such as the RN and even the PDC would also be affected by this phenomenon.

9. The UDI is not the only party willing to overlook its own ideology. One councilman remarked that while the Concertación parties had not wanted him as their candidate when he first entered politics, he says that now, after having twice been elected to the council, some of these parties had approached him about being a candidate (Interview, September 12, 2002). A second councilman, representing the Partido Radical Social Demócrata (PRSD), said that other parties were actively pursuing him; as he told me in "Chilean" Spanish, "*Hay otros partidos que me andan pololeando*" (There are other parties flirting with me) (Interview, October 31, 2002).

10. The UDI faced an internal squabble in one municipality when one female candidate was elected mayor even though she was not the UDI's privileged candidate, leading to a huge fight between her and the privileged candidate (Interview, December 16, 2002). For information on the informal institution of the "privileged candidate," see Hinojosa and Franceschet, forthcoming.

11. There are 2,528 observations in this data set, which was compiled by the author.

12. For more on this, see Hinojosa 2009.

13. Roza (2010a: 168) also determined that if she controlled for effective quotas (i.e., those with strong sanctions for noncompliance), then selection method lost statistical significance: "Stated differently, sanctions designed to enforce compliance with the quota law exert such a potent influence on the composition of party lists that party-level characteristics become less influential."

14. A group of feminists opposed to the authoritarian regime adopted the slogan "What isn't good for democracy isn't good for women" to demonstrate their lack of support for feminist policies emerging from a nondemocratic regime (Barrig 2001).

15. It is beyond the scope of this work to ascertain Fujimori's true commitment to women's rights. However, Fujimori was the only head of state to attend the Fourth World Conference on Women (known as the Beijing Conference), is routinely credited for the passage of the quota law (since when it was originally proposed both men and women from his party opposed it), and both appointed and nominated many women to political positions (Blondet 2000). Schmidt characterized Fujimori's leadership as "critical to progress toward gender equity" but notes that the country's economic situation, societal changes, and political effects of both the failure of political parties and the successful end to the war on terrorism "created a context that was favorable to political gains by women" (2006: 171–172).

16. The Women's Peronista Party (PPF) was founded by Evita Perón on July 26, 1949. The PPF was one of three branches of the Peronista movement, along with the Peronista Party and the Confederation of Labor. The existence of the PPF dramatically increased the number of women in the Chamber of Deputies and Senate; one-

third of candidacies were guaranteed to women (Del Campo 2005: 1722). The PPF disappeared after Juan Perón was removed from power in 1955.

17. Such concerns would not be unfounded. Evita Perón was officially designated "Spiritual Leader of the Nation" by Congress just weeks prior to her death from cancer in 1952, and since her death, she has been nominated for sainthood yearly by Argentines who remain devoted to her.

18. Unlike Evita Perón, who sought to extend women's rights and participation in government, Isabel Perón did not pursue feminist policies. While president, she banned the sale of contraceptives and vetoed a law that would have granted mothers and fathers equality in *patria potestad*, which refers to the "set of rights and duties of parents over the person and property of minor children" (Zabaleta 2000; Htun 2003: 47).

CHAPTER 7

1. Some of the exceptions are listed in the section that follows.

2. However, in a much larger study that was not limited to Latin America, Ballington (2008: 16) found that less than 10 percent of both men and women reported that family connections were their route to the legislature. Ballington's work depended on legislators to identify which factors had been most important for their entry into politics.

3. In his study of political elites in Mexico, Camp found that women were no more likely to have family connections than men (2010: 122).

4. Chávez's father was also elected governor and stayed in that position for a decade. Marisabel Rodríguez, then wife of Chávez, was elected to the Constituent Assembly that rewrote the Venezuelan Constitution shortly after Chávez entered the presidency. Following their divorce, Rodríguez became a critic of her ex-husband's administration and ran unsuccessfully for mayor of a large Venezuelan city.

5. Eileen McDonagh (2002) indicates that monarchies in which women can inherit the throne can result in greater female representation than in electoral democracies.

6. Kinship politics is more common in some countries. In parts of Asia, they are necessary for both men and women who aspire to politics. Kinship ties are seen as "a useful opening through which women have an opportunity to emerge into the political arena" and are so instrumental to women's entry into politics in South Asia that when women have no kinship ties, they enter into patron/protégé relationships with male politicians that in many ways mimic these familial relationships (Samarasinghe 2000: 195). According to Roces, kinship politics "has empowered women in post-war Philippines" (1998: 2). A study of the Sri Lankan parliament revealed that 90 percent of female parliamentarians serving in the late 1990s had kinship ties (Samarasinghe 2000: 200).

7. See Taylor, Botero Jaramillo, and Crisp 2008 for the frequency with which the children of former presidents themselves run for the presidency in Colombia.

8. Contrary to what Putnam (1976) might have predicted, Camp finds that politicians from the middle or upper classes are twice as likely as those from the working classes to have family ties (1982: 857).

9. Roces describes an interesting phenomenon, whose reach extends beyond the Philippines: "Male politicians encourage their wives to run for office . . . to facili-

tate the enactment of policy from the national level to the local level (with one in national office and the spouse in local office, as is often the case)" (1998: 112). A failed PRD candidate from the state of Mexico recounted that she had "forced" her husband to run for a local deputy position when she was campaigning for mayor of their hometown because she was worried that if she won she would be short of allies. His candidacy was also unsuccessful (Interview, March 28, 2003). None of my other interviewees with family members in politics admitted to such a motivation.

10. An example of this phenomenon from the United States would be Alabama's Lurleen Wallace, wife of George Wallace. Unable to overturn the prohibition on immediate re-election during his first term in office, George Wallace had his wife run for his seat. She served as governor of Alabama from 1967 until her death in 1968. Similarly, women often take over for husbands who have been imprisoned.

11. These figures may be a bit deceiving. Gertzog (2002: 96) points out that in only 14 percent of cases wives were nominated to succeed their dead husbands in Congress. Gertzog analyzed an 84-year period and excluded all cases in which there were no wives to succeed Congress members who died while in office (i.e., bachelors, widowers, and Congress members with infirm wives). Spousal succession, however, was much more common prior to the 1940s.

12. Genovese and Thompson ignore that men have also used kinship as a path to power. Also, studies of women's representation in the media seem to indicate that reliance on these "exclusionary assumptions" is commonplace. Murray (2010) provides cases from across the globe that contradict Genovese and Thompson's argument.

13. One aspect of kinship politics, and in particular of *mujeres de*, that requires discussion is the nontraditional political work done by these women. Although these women often do not hold political office or positions within their parties, they nonetheless do valuable (and frequently invisible) work. Roces discusses some of their efforts in the Philippines, where "a social event like a charity dance may be a site for negotiations by go-betweens—usually women" (1998: 8). Other scholars have long noted that to understand women's political work we may have to redefine political work. A councilwoman whose husband was an important politician said that she ran for a spot on her city council when her party asked her to because she realized that she had long been doing the same work but in an "unofficial" capacity (Interview, May 16, 2003).

14. The best-known case comes from Pakistan. Asif Ali Zardari became leader of his party (along with his son) days after the assassination of his wife, Benazir Bhutto, the former prime minister. Months later he became president of Pakistan.

15. These ties are not at all uncommon in Brazil. A report from the late 1980s notes that of the congresswomen in the country, three were senators' wives, two were the wives of former governors, one was the widow of a former senator, and the last was the wife of a mayor (Sanders 1987). The necessity of such ties was not unique to national-level politics. In the Brazilian gubernatorial elections of 1994, only three women proceeded to the second round of voting: two were the wives of former governors and the third was the daughter of a former president (Pinto 1994).

16. García's daughter has also run for Congress.

17. I place the word *standard* in quotation marks because, as earlier portions of this chapter demonstrate, family connections have been an important part of candidate selection across space and time.

18. As Chapter 1 mentions, fieldwork was conducted in eight municipalities (four in Chile and four in Mexico). Six of these municipalities had female mayors. Of these six women, four were from political families. One was a political widow, another was a political wife, and two were political daughters/granddaughters.

19. Camp found that having a husband in politics was considerably more significant than having a parent in politics (1979: 430).

20. The PRD apparently saw no irony in passing this statute while simultaneously considering the nomination of Cuauhtémoc Cárdenas as its presidential candidate. Cárdenas, the son of former President Lázaro Cárdenas, had been the party's presidential candidate on three occasions and had also served as governor of his home state and mayor of Mexico City. His son also entered politics and has been governor.

CHAPTER 8

1. Baldez's study (2004a), which provides a terrific explanation of factors that allowed for the adoption of the gender quota in Mexico, begins with an introductory quote by Groucho Marx: "I'd give up my seat for you if it wasn't for the fact that I'm sitting in it myself."

2. See Franceschet and Piscopo 2008 and Zetterberg 2008 concerning a potential backlash.

3. Murray tested this argument in France and found that women selected through quotas were qualified and there were "no distinguishable differences between them and their male counterparts or the deputies that preceded them" (Murray 2010: 116).

4. Krook (2009) even uncovered evidence that implementing the parity law had an unexpected benefit for party leaders—they could exclude councilmen whom they did not like from the party lists with the excuse that they needed to run women (Bird 2003, as cited in Krook 2009: 196).

5. In the Spanish case, parties even sought new talent from outside their own membership rolls, sometimes meeting the quota by selecting independents (Verge 2010: 176).

6. This is not unique to Latin America. The major political parties in France, for example, accepted fines rather than comply with the national quota (Murray 2007). In Spain, Verge (2010) found that covert forms of discrimination, such as in the placement of candidates, led to inequality despite the use of quotas. This strategic discrimination appears to affect parties regardless of ideology.

7. Roza (2010a, 2010b) and Jones (2009) categorize quota laws in Latin America and note which are poorly designed or have weak enforcement mechanisms.

8. However, in Mexico, PRI men favored the national quota law, since it would require only 30 percent female candidacies; the PRI had already adopted a 50 percent quota (Baldez 2004a).

9. Norris and Lovenduski (1995) also believe that noncompliance with party quotas is more likely when candidate selection is decentralized.

10. See Reynoso and D'Angelo 2006 for a discussion of the effective quota in the Mexican case.

11. In 2008, a new bill pushed the quota to 40 percent. This new quota was first applied in the 2009 midterm elections.

12. See Hinojosa and Vijil Gurdián (forthcoming) for an assessment of the effects of alternate positions on women's representation in Nicaragua, where there is no gender quota. Also, it is the case that women can end up in positions of power because of the alternate spots. A young Panista was placed in an alternate position by her party; when the titleholder ran for and won a different office, she became a deputy (Interview, February 21, 2003).

13. Parties that do not comply with the quota law are first given 48 hours to revamp their lists, and then they are issued a reprimand and given 24 more hours to alter their lists. They are barred from presenting any candidates in that district if the problem is not fixed in the time allotted.

14. Baldez (2004b) points out that while primaries were used to avoid quotas in single-member districts, in the proportional representation seats, many of the parties nominated more female candidates than required by the quota law.

15. This contradicts some of the findings on Canada presented by Tremblay and Pelletier (2001).

16. The law, despite the lack of appropriate provisions such as a placement mandate, nonetheless seemed to affect women's representation. Women's representation doubled after the 1998 elections but dropped in the elections following repeal of the quota (www.quotaproject.org).

CHAPTER 9

1. As was the case in the USSR, the Cuban party's central committee had an extraordinarily low percentage of women (about 5 percent) despite the much greater representation of women in electoral positions during the 1970s (Domínguez 1978). But women continue to be less well represented in the party structures than in the legislature. Women are 16 percent of the members of the Council of State, 8 percent of the Politburo, and 13 percent of the party's central committee (Smith and Padula 1996; Htun 2007). The much lower percentages of women in party positions indicate that women's high levels of representation cannot be attributed to ideology.

2. Luciak writes, "The excellent gender composition of Cuba's parliament is an apparent exception that confirms the following rule: The state of gender equality in Cuba's decision-making structures reveals an inverse relationship between the actual decision-making power of a particular institution and the presence of women" (2005: 243).

3. Since 1992, electoral rules have dictated that there be a single candidate for each provincial and national legislative seat.

4. Luciak (2005) argues that the use of these "corrective measures" explains the high rates of women's representation in the national legislature.

5. Luciak (2005) notes that it is not only the candidate-selection processes used at the national versus the local level that explain these differences but also the responsibilities and time commitment of each position and the role of machismo at the local level.

6. Although the Cuban case is nondemocratic, these processes of candidate selection still function on the island. Authoritarians often use exclusive-centralized selection procedures.

7. See Chapter 4.

8. When I went to the PRD's National Secretariat for Equity, officials were unable to provide me with a list of candidates for municipal office but showed me a series of faxes demonstrating that they, too, were trying to obtain the same information.

9. Carey and Polga-Hecimovich (2006) found, however, that there was a "primary bonus"—that is, that candidates chosen via primary were more likely to win the general election. Their analysis, though, was of presidential candidates only. Presidential primaries are likely to attract many more voters than other primary elections, and because of this fact, their results may not be applicable to other primary elections. We may not see the same type of bonus for other elections.

10. A scientifically conducted poll may actually produce better results than a primary. As Chapter 4 notes, primaries do not tend to attract a group that is representative of general election voters.

11. Bruhn (2010: 44) recounts that the Mexican political party Convergencia settled disputes over candidacies by hiring a polling firm to determine who the most electable candidate was. The party then required that the last-place finisher in these polls pay for the cost of the poll. While this did discourage "frivolous" candidates, as Bruhn's respondent noted, it would most likely also discourage all but the most confident or wealthiest from participating.

12. In one Canadian party, this approach has been used in tandem with financial subsidies for women pre-candidates to increase female candidacies (Erickson 1993: 80–81). Campaign finance laws and the primary campaign finance regulations that I am suggesting here would have the added benefit of creating data on women's and men's access to financing for both type of electoral contests. Data are woefully lacking.

13. While data are scarce, we do know that elections in Latin America can be quite expensive. In 1990, candidates for congressional campaigns in São Paulo spent between US$200,000 and US$5 million. Although Brazilian elections are said to be more costly than others in the region, these figures are nonetheless disturbing. Even in the small country of Uruguay, with a limited geographical expanse and a population of only about 3.5 million, the total spent on all elections in 1999–2000 was estimated at US$40 million (Casas Zamora 2002, as cited in Posada-Carbó 2008). Casas Zamora (2005) provides more data.

14. In countries like Honduras, for example, time limits are already used for general elections. Parties are fined if they begin advertising prior to the start of the campaign period (Casas-Zamora 2005).

15. A study conducted by International IDEA found that male candidates in Peru spent an average of 4.6 times the amount that women candidates spent on television, radio, and print media advertising (Dador and Llanos 2007).

16. See Casas-Zamora 2005 for more information on government-provided media time to political parties.

17. See iKnowpolitics.org.

18. The percentage of funds that must be set aside for women varies. In Panama, 10 percent of electoral funding is set aside for training women. In Mexico, parties must set aside 2 percent of public funds to promote women's participation (Llanos and Sample 2008).

19. See www.thewhitehouseproject.org.

20. See http://www.ndi.org/past_programs.

21. Roza (2010a: 111) found that only one-third of the most important parties in Latin America kept such records.

22. For almost three decades, Cuban housewives were ineligible for party membership (Luciak 2005: 259).

23. See http://www.unwomen.org/wp-content/uploads/2011/07/CAT-Women-and-Media-Collective-Sri-Lanka-Profile-July-2011.pdf.

24. See http://www.thewhitehouseproject.org/join/invite/.

25. Dahlerup also points out that other practices have similar effects but are rarely called quotas. She specifically mentions the use of "regional quotas" that assign a set number of legislators to a particular region of the country (2005: 148).

26. See Franceschet and Piscopo 2008 for an excellent analysis of this point.

27. The Costa Rican Constitution calls for the election of two vice presidents to serve alongside the president. From 1998 to 2002, both vice presidential positions were occupied by women. Matland and Taylor noted that by 1994 all parties were making an effort to have female representation on the executive ticket: of the seven political parties running presidential candidates, one nominated a woman presidential candidate and the other six all featured a female vice presidential candidate (1997: 189n3).

References

Adrianzén, Alberto, Juan Rial, and Rafael Roncagliolo, eds. 2008. *Países andinos: Los políticos*. Lima: International IDEA.

Agüero, Felipe. 2003. "Chile: Unfinished Transition and Increased Political Competition." In *Constructing Democratic Governance in Latin Americas*, edited by Jorge I. Domínguez and Michael Shifter, 292–320. Baltimore: Johns Hopkins University Press.

Alcántara Sáez, Manuel. 2002. "Experimentos de democracia interna: Las primarias de partidos en América Latina." In *Kellogg Institute for International Studies Working Papers*. Available at http://kellogg.nd.edu/publications/workingpapers/WPS/293.pdf.

———. 2004. "Partidos políticos en América Latina: Precisiones conceptuales, estado actual y retos futuros." Available at http://www.ucm.es/info/eid/cursodcd/IMG/pdf_Alcantara03.pdf.

Alexander, Robert. 1979. *Juan Domingo Perón: A History*. Boulder, CO: Westview Press.

Altman, David. 2008. "Political Recruitment and Candidate Selection in Chile, 1990–2006: The Executive Branch." In *Pathways to Power: Political Recruitment and Candidate Selection in Latin America*, edited by Peter Siavelis and Scott Morgenstern, 241–270. University Park: Pennsylvania State University Press.

Andersen, Kristi, and Stuart J. Thorson. 1984. "Congressional Turnover and the Election of Women." *Western Political Quarterly* 37:143–156.

Araújo, Clara, and Ana Isabel García. 2006. "Latin America: The Experience and the Impact of Quotas in Latin America." In *Women, Quotas and Politics*, edited by Drude Dahlerup, 83–111. New York: Routledge.

Archenti, Nelida, and María Inés Tula. 2008. *Mujeres y política en América Latina: Sistemas electorales y cuotas de género*. Buenos Aires: Heliasta.

———. 2009. "Partidos políticos, elecciones y género: Análisis de las listas partidarias en cinco distritos subnacionales, Argentina 2007." Paper presented at the International Congress of the Latin American Studies Association, Rio de Janeiro, Brazil.

Associated Press. 2003. "Several States Move to Cancel Primaries." *Washington Times*, November 9, 2003.

Atkeson, Lonna Rae. 2003. "Not All Cues Are Created Equal: The Conditional Impact of Female Candidates on Political Engagement." *Journal of Politics* 65 (4): 1040–1061.

Baer, Denise L. 1993. "Political Parties: The Missing Variable in Women and Politics Research." *Political Research Quarterly* 46, no. 3 (September): 547–576.

Baker, Ashley. 2006. "Reexamining the Gender Implications of Campaign Finance Reform: How Higher Ceilings on Individual Donations Disproportionately Impact Female Candidates." *Modern Americas* (Fall): 18–23.

Baldez, Lisa. 2002. *Why Women Protest: Women's Movements in Chile*. New York: Cambridge University Press.

———. 2004a. "Elected Bodies: The Gender Quota Law for Legislative Candidates in Mexico." *Legislative Studies Quarterly* 2 (May): 239–258.

———. 2004b. "Elected Bodies II: The Impact of Gender Quotas in Mexico." Paper presented at the Pathways to Power: Political Recruitment and Democracy in Latin America research symposium, Wake Forest University, Winston-Salem, NC, April 2–4.

———. 2007. "Primaries vs. Quotas: Gender and Candidate Nominations in Mexico, 2003." *Latin American Politics and Society* 49 (3): 69–96.

Ballington, Julie. 2008. "Equality in Politics: A Survey of Women and Men in Parliaments." In *Reports and Documents*. Geneva: Inter-Parliamentary Union.

Ballington, Julie, and Azza Karam. 2005. *Women in Parliament: Beyond Numbers*. Rev. ed. Stockholm: International IDEA.

Balmori, Diana, Stuart Voss, and Miles Wertman. 1984. *Notable Family Networks in Latin America*. Chicago: University of Chicago Press.

Barrera Bassols, Dalia, and Alejandra Massolo, eds. 1998. *Mujeres que gobiernan municipios: Experiencias, aportes y retos*. Mexico City: El Colegio de México, 1998.

Barrig, Maruja. 2001. "Latin American Feminisms: Gains, Losses, and Hard Times." *NACLA Report on the Americas: The Body Politic: Gender in the New World Order* 34, no. 5 (March–April): 29–35.

BBC. 2000. "Israeli Labour Party Cancels Primaries." *BBC Summary of World Broadcasts: Ma'ariv*, March 21.

———. 2011. "Argentine President Cristina Fernández Wins Primary." *BBC News*, August 15.

Beckwith, Karen. 1989. "Sneaking Women into Office: Alternative Access to Parliament in France and Italy." *Women and Politics* 9 (3): 1–15.

Bille, Lars. 2001. "Democratizing a Democratic Procedure: Myth or Reality? Candidate Selection in Western European Parties, 1960–90." *Party Politics* 7 (3): 363–380.

Blay, Eva Alterman. 1979. "The Political Participation of Women in Brazil: Female Mayors." *Signs: Journal of Women in Culture and Society* 5 (1): 42–59.

———. 1980. *As prefeitas: A participação política da mulher no Brasil*. Rio de Janeiro: Avenir Editora Limitada.

Bledsoe, Timothy, and Mary Herring. 1990. "Victims of Circumstances: Women in Pursuit of Political Office." *American Political Science Review* 84 (March): 213–223.

Blondet, Cecilia M. 2000. *Lessons from the Participation of Women in Politics.* Lima: Inter-American Development Bank.

Bourdieu, Pierre. 1986. "The Forms of Capital." In *Handbook of Theory and Research for the Sociology of Education,* edited by John G. Richardson, 241–258. New York: Greenwood Press.

Brewer-Carías, Allan R. 2008. "Reforma electoral en el sistema político en Venezuela." In *Reforma política y electoral en América Latina, 1978–2007,* edited by Daniel Zovatto G. and J. Jesús Orozco Henríquez, 953–1022. Mexico City: Universidad Nacional Autónoma de México.

Brill, Alida. 1995. *A Rising Public Voice: Women in Politics Worldwide.* New York: Feminist Press.

Bruhn, Kathleen. 1997. "The Seven-Month Itch? Neoliberal Politics, Popular Movements, and the Left in Mexico." In *The New Politics of Inequality in Latin America: Rethinking Participation and Representation,* edited by Douglas A. Chalmers, Carlos M. Vilas, Katherine Hite, Scott B. Martin, Kerianne Piester, and Monique Segarra, 144–169. New York: Oxford University Press.

———. 2003. "Whores and Lesbians: Political Activism, Party Strategies, and Gender Quotas in Mexico." *Electoral Studies* 22:101–119.

———. 2010. "Too Much Democracy? Primaries and Candidate Success in the 2006 Mexican National Elections." *Latin American Politics and Society* 52 (4): 25–52.

Bullock, Charles S., III and Patricia Lee Findley Heys. 1972. "Recruitment of Women for Congress." *Western Political Quarterly* 25:416–423.

Burns, Nancy, Kay Lehman Schlozman, and Sidney Verba. 2001. *The Private Roots of Public Action: Gender, Equality, and Political Participation.* Cambridge, MA: Harvard University Press.

Burrell, Barbara. 1992. "Women Candidates in Open-Seat Primaries for the U.S. House: 1968–1990." *Legislative Studies Quarterly* 17, no. 4 (November): 493–508.

———. 1998. "Campaign Finance: Women's Experience in the Modern Era." In *Women and Elective Office: Past, Present, and Future,* edited by Sue Thomas and Clyde Wilcox, 26–37. New York: Oxford University Press.

Calderón, Cecilia. 2004. "Intervención de Cecilia Calderón (ex-diputada de la República de Ecuador)." In *Reflexiones sobre mujer y política: Memorias del seminario nacional "Los cambios políticos en Ecuador: Perspectivas y retos para la mujer,"* edited by María Fernanda Cañete, 171–180. Quito, Ecuador: CEDIME.

Cameron, Maxwell A. 1997. "Political and Economic Origins of Regime Change in Peru: The Eighteenth Brumaire of Alberto Fujimori." In *The Peruvian Labyrinth: Polity, Society, Economy,* edited by Maxwell Cameron and Philip Mauceri, 37–69. University Park: Pennsylvania State University Press.

Camp, Roderic A. 1979. "Women and Political Leadership in Mexico: A Comparative Study of Female and Male Political Elites." *Journal of Politics* 41, no. 2 (May): 417–441.

———. 1982. "Family Relationships in Mexican Politics: A Preliminary View." *Journal of Politics* 44, no. 3 (August): 848–862.

———. 1995. *Political Recruitment across Two Centuries: Mexico, 1884–1991.* Austin: University of Texas Press.

———. 2002. *Mexico's Mandarins: Crafting a Power Elite for the Twenty-First Century.* Berkeley: University of California Press.

————. 2010. *The Metamorphosis of Leadership in a Democratic Mexico.* New York: Oxford University Press.

Cañete, María Fernanda. 2004. "Las vicisitudes de la aplicación de la cuota electoral en los partidos políticos." In *Reflexiones sobre mujer y política: Memorias del seminario nacional "Los cambios políticos en Ecuador: Perspectivas y retos para la mujer,"* edited by María Fernanda Cañete, 171–180. Quito, Ecuador: CEDIME.

Carey, John M., and John Polga-Hecimovich. 2004. "Primary Elections and Candidate Strength in Latin America." Available at www.dartmouth.edu.

————2006. "Primary Elections and Candidate Strength in Latin America." *Journal of Politics* 68 (3): 530–543.

Carroll, Susan, ed. 1985. *Women as Candidates in American Politics.* Bloomington: Indiana University Press.

————. 1994. *Women as Candidates in American Politics.* Bloomington: Indiana University Press.

————. 2001. *The Impact of Women in Public Office.* Bloomington: Indiana University Press.

Casas-Zamora, Kevin. 2005. *Paying for Democracy: Political Finance and State Funding for Parties.* Colchester, U.K.: European Consortium for Political Research Press.

————. 2010. "Dirty Money: How to Break the Link between Organized Crime and Politics." *Americas Quarterly* (Spring): 57–62.

Castles, Francis G. 1981. "Female Legislative Representation and the Electoral System." *Politics* 1 (2): 21–27.

Caul, Miki. 1999. "Women's Representation in Parliament: The Role of Political Parties." *Party Politics* 5 (1): 79–98.

————. 2001. "Political Parties and the Adoption of Candidate Gender Quotas: A Cross-National Analysis." *Journal of Politics* 63, no. 4 (November): 1214–1229.

Chaney, Elsa. 1979. *Supermadre: Women in Politics in Latin America.* Austin: University of Texas Press.

Clark, Cal, Janet Clark, and Bih-er Chou. 1993. "Ambition, Activist Role Orientations, and Alienation among Women Legislators in Taiwan: The Impact of Countersocialization." *Political Psychology* 14 (3): 493–510.

Clubok, Alfred B., Norman M. Wilensky, and Forrest J. Berghorn. 1969. "Family Relationships, Congressional Recruitment, and Political Modernization." *Journal of Politics* 31: 1035–1062.

Colomer, Josep. 2003. "Las elecciones primarias presidenciales en América Latina y sus consecuencias políticas." In *El asedio a la política: Los partidos latinoamericanos en la era neoliberal,* edited by Juan Manuel Abal Medina, 117–134. Buenos Aires: Altamira/Konrad Adenauer.

Constantini, Edmond. 1990. "Political Women and Political Ambition: Closing the Gender Gap." *American Journal of Political Science* 34 (August): 741–770.

Constantini, Edmond, and Julie Davis Bell. 1984. "Women in Political Parties: Gender Differences in Motives among California Political Activists." In *Political Women: Current Roles in State and Local Government,* edited by Janet A. Flammang, 58–81. Beverly Hills: Sage Publications.

Constantini, Edmond, and Kenneth H. Craig. 1977. "Women as Politicians: The Social Background, Personality and Political Careers of Female Party Leaders." In

A Portrait of Marginality, edited by Marianne Githens and Jewel L. Prestage, 178–195. New York: McKay.

Contreras, Joseph. 2005. "Latina Liftoff. From Tijuana to Tierra del Fuego, Women Are Raising Their Political Profile and Breaking New Ground." *Newsweek International*, August 22, 36–39.

Coordinación General de la Comisión Nacional de la Mujer. 2000. "Memoria: Mujeres en el poder." Paper presented at the Mujeres en el Poder conference, Mexico City, October 17.

Craske, Nikki. 1999. *Women and Politics in Latin America*. New Brunswick, NJ: Rutgers University Press.

Crisp, Brian F. 2001. "Candidate Selection in Venezuela (and Its Impact on Legislator Behavior)." Paper presented at the International Congress of the Latin American Studies Association, Washington, DC, September 6–8.

Cross, William. 2008. "Democratic Norms and Party Candidate Selection: Taking Contextual Factors into Account." *Party Politics* 14 (5): 596–619.

Dador, Jennie, and Beatriz Llanos. 2007. *La igualdad esquiva: Una mirada de género a las elecciones generales 2006*. Stockholm: Asociación Civil Transparencia and International IDEA.

Dahlerup, Drude. 2005. "Increasing Women's Political Representation: New Trends in Gender Quotas." In *Women in Parliament: Beyond Numbers*, edited by Julie Ballington and Azza Karam, 141–153. Rev. ed. Stockholm: International IDEA.

———. 2006. "Introduction." In *Women, Quotas and Politics*, edited by Drude Dahlerup, 3–31. New York: Routledge.

Darcy, R., Susan Welch, and Janet Clark. 1994. *Women, Elections, and Representation*. 2nd ed. Lincoln: University of Nebraska Press.

Del Campo, Esther. 2005. "Women and Politics in Latin America: Perspectives and Limits of the Institutional Aspects of Women's Political Representation." *Social Forces* 83, no. 4 (June): 1697–1726.

De Luca, Miguel, Mark P. Jones, and María Inés Tula. 2001. "Back Rooms or Ballot Boxes? Candidate Nomination in Argentina." Paper presented at the International Congress of the Latin American Studies Association, Washington, DC, September 6–8.

———. 2002. "Back Rooms or Ballot Boxes? Candidate Nomination in Argentina." *Comparative Political Studies* 35 (4): 413–436.

Dolan, Kathleen A. 2004. *Voting for Women: How the Public Evaluates Women Candidates*. Boulder, CO: Westview Press.

Domínguez, Jorge I. 1978. *Cuba: Order and Revolution*. Cambridge, MA: Belknap Press.

Domínguez, Jorge I., and James A. McCann. 1998. *Democratizing Mexico: Public Opinion and Electoral Choices*. Baltimore: Johns Hopkins University Press.

Dresser, Denise. 2003. "Mexico: From PRI Predominance to Divided Democracy." In *Constructing Democratic Governance in Latin America*, edited by Jorge I. Domínguez and Michael Shifter, 321–347. Baltimore: Johns Hopkins University Press.

Duerst-Lahti, Georgia. 1998. "The Bottleneck: Women Becoming Candidates." In *Women and Elective Office: Past, Present, and Future*, edited by Sue Thomas and Clyde Wilcox, 15–25. New York: Oxford University Press.

Duverger, Maurice. 1955. *The Political Role of Women*. Paris: UNESCO.

Easter, Gerald. 2000. *Reconstructing the State: Personal Networks and Elite Identity in Soviet Russia*. New York: Cambridge University Press.

Eisenstadt, Todd A. 2002. "Straddling Formality: The Shift from Informal to Formal Contestation of Electoral Fraud in Democratizing Mexico." *Informal Institutions and Politics in the Developing World*, April 6, 1–28.

———. 2004. *Courting Democracy in Mexico: Party Strategies and Electoral Institutions*. New York: Cambridge University Press.

Elder, Laurel. 2004. "Why Women Don't Run: Explaining Women's Underrepresentation in America's Political Institutions." *Women and Politics* 26 (2): 27–56.

Erickson, Lynda. 1993. "Making Her Way In: Women, Parties and Candidacies in Canada." In *Gender and Party Politics*, edited by Joni Lovenduski and Pippa Norris, 60–85. Thousand Oaks, CA: Sage Publications.

Escobar-Lemmon, María, and Michelle M. Taylor-Robinson. 2004. "Women Ministers in Latin American Government: When, Where, and Why?" Paper presented at the Pathways to Power: Political Recruitment and Democracy in Latin America research symposium, Wake Forest University, Winston-Salem, NC, April 2–4.

———. 2008. "How Do Candidate Recruitment and Selection Processes Affect the Representation of Women?" In *Pathways to Power: Political Recruitment and Candidate Selection in Latin America*, edited by Peter Siavelis and Scott Morgenstern, 345–368. University Park: Pennsylvania State University Press.

Ezra, Marni. 2001. "The Benefits and Burdens of Congressional Primary Elections." In *Congressional Primaries and the Politics of Representation*, edited by Peter F. Galderisi, Marni Ezra, and Michael Lyons, 48–61. New York: Rowman and Littlefield Publishers.

Farah, Barbara G., and Virginia Sapiro. 1980. "New Pride and Old Prejudice: Political Ambition and Role Orientations among Female Party Elites." *Women and Politics* 1 (June): 13–36.

Fernández Poncela, Anna María. 2000. "Candidaturas federales en la elección del 2000: Formalidades y realidades." In *La mujer en el proceso electoral 2000: Balance y prospectiva*, edited by Rosario Román Pérez, 33–42. Hermosillo, Mexico: Grupo Ciudadano por la No Violencia "Ania, Ania."

Field, Bonnie N., and Peter M. Siavelis. 2008. "Candidate Selection Procedures in Transitional Polities: A Research Note." *Party Politics* 14 (5): 620–639.

Fowlkes, Diane L. 1984. "Ambitious Political Woman: Countersocialization and Political Party Context." *Women and Politics* 4 (4): 5–32.

Fox, Richard L. 1997. *Gender Dynamics in Congressional Elections*. Thousand Oaks, CA: Sage Publications.

Fox, Richard L., and Jennifer L. Lawless. 2004. "Entering the Arena? Gender and the Decision to Run for Office." *American Journal of Political Science* 48, no. 2 (April): 262–280.

Fox, Richard L., and Zoe M. Oxley. 2003. "Gender Stereotyping in State Executive Elections: Candidate Selection and Success." *Journal of Politics* 65 (3): 833–850.

Franceschet, Susan. 2005. *Women and Politics in Chile*. Boulder, CO: Lynne Rienner.

———. 2006. "Bachelet's Triumph and the Political Advance of Women." *Nueva Sociedad* 202 (March–April): 13–22.

Franceschet, Susan, and Jennifer M. Piscopo. 2008. "Gender Quotas and Women's Substantive Representation: Lessons from Argentina." *Politics and Gender* 4 (3): 393–425.

———. 2012. "Gender and Political Backgrounds in Argentina." In *The Impact of Gender Quotas*, edited by Susan Franceschet, Mona Lena Krook, and Jennifer M. Piscopo, 43–56. New York: Oxford University Press.

Freeman, Jo. 2000. *A Room at a Time: How Women Entered Party Politics*. New York: Rowman and Littlefield Publishers.

———. n.d. "Political Wives and Widows." SeniorWomenWeb. Available at http://www.seniorwomen.com/articles/freeman/articlesFreemanWivesWidows.html.

Freidenberg, Flavia. 2003. *Selección de candidatos y democracia interna en los partidos de América Latina*. Lima: Asociación Civil Transparencia and International IDEA.

Friedman, Elisabeth J. 2000. *Unfinished Transitions: Women and the Gendered Development of Democracy in Venezuela, 1936–1996*. University Park: Pennsylvania State University Press.

Frohmann, Alicia, and Teresa Valdéz. 1993. *Democracy in the Country and in the Home: The Women's Movement in Chile*. Santiago: FLACSO Series Estudios Sociales no. 55.

Galderisi, Peter F., Marni Ezra, and Michael Lyons, eds. 2001. *Congressional Primaries and the Politics of Representation*. New York: Rowman and Littlefield Publishers.

Gallagher, Michael. 1988. "Introduction." In *Candidate Selection in Comparative Perspective: The Secret Garden of Politics*, edited by Michael Gallagher, 1–19. Beverly Hills: Sage Publications.

Galligan, Yvonne. 1993. "Party Politics and Gender in the Republic of Ireland." In *Gender and Party Politics*, edited by Joni Lovenduski and Pippa Norris, 147–167. Thousand Oaks, CA: Sage Publications.

Gallo, Adriana. 2006. "Participación electoral libre e igualitaria, democratización partidaria y legitimación de candidaturas: La trilogía de la reforma política en América Latina." *Debates Latinoamericanos* 4 (6). Available at http://www.rlcu.org.ar/revista/numeros/04-06-Abril-2006/documentos/adriana_gallo.pdf.

Garretón, Manuel A. 2000. "Chile's Elections: Change and Continuity." *Journal of Democracy* 11 (2): 78–84.

Gehlen, Frieda L. 1969. "Women in Congress." *Society* 6 (11): 36–40.

Genovese, Michael A. 1993. "Women as National Leaders: What Do We Know?" In *Women as National Leaders*, edited by Michael A. Genovese, 211–218. Newbury Park, CA: Sage Publications.

Genovese, Michael A., and Seth Thompson. 1993. "Women as Chief Executives: Does Gender Matter?" In *Women as National Leaders*, edited by Michael A. Genovese, 1–12. Newbury Park, CA: Sage Publications.

Gertzog, Irwin N. 2002. "Women's Changing Pathways to the U.S. House of Representatives: Widows, Elites, and Strategic Politicians. " In *Women Transforming Congress*, edited by Cindy Simon Rosenthal, 95–118. Norman: University of Oklahoma Press.

Grupo de Opinión Pública de la Universidad de Lima. 2010. Estudio 493 Barómetro Social: VIII Encuesta Anual Sobre la Situación de la Mujer en la Provincia de Lima y Región Callao meeting, Lima, February 13–14.

Hagopian, Frances. 1996. "Traditional Power Structures and Democratic Governance in Latin America." In *Constructing Democratic Governance: Latin America and the Caribbean in the 1990s—Themes and Issues*, edited by Jorge I. Domínguez and Abraham F. Lowenthal, 64–86. Baltimore: Johns Hopkins University Press.

Heath, Roseanna Michelle, Leslie A. Schwindt-Bayer, and Michelle M. Taylor-Robinson. 2005. "Women on the Sidelines: Women's Representation on Committees in Latin American Legislatures." *American Journal of Political Science* 49, no. 2 (April): 420–436.

Helmke, Gretchen, and Steven Levitsky. 2004. "Informal Institutions and Comparative Politics: A Research Agenda." *Perspectives on Politics* 2 (4): 725–740.

Hernández Valle, Rubén. 2008. "Reforma política en Costa Rica." In *Reforma política y electoral en América Latina, 1978–2007*, edited by Daniel Zovatto G. and J. Jesús Orozco Henríquez, 457–494. Mexico City: Universidad Nacional Autónoma de México.

High-Pippert, Angela, and John Comer. 1998. "Female Empowerment: The Influence of Women Representing Women." *Women and Politics* 19 (4): 53–66.

Hinojosa, Magda. 2002. "Municipales 2004: Se buscan candidatas mujeres." November. Available at www.electoral.cl.

———. 2004. "Las Prioridades del PRD." *Enfoque*, weekend supplement to *Reforma*, May 23.

———. 2005. "Sex and the Cities: Candidate Selection Processes and Women's Political Representation in Chile and Mexico." Ph.D. diss., Harvard University.

———. 2008. "¿Más Mujeres?: Mexico's Mixed Member System." In *Women and Legislative Representation: Electoral Systems, Political Parties, and Sex Quotas*, edited by Manon Tremblay, 177–190. New York: Palgrave Macmillan.

———. 2009. "Whatever the Party Asks of Me: Candidate Selection and Women's Political Representation in Chile's UDI." *Politics and Gender* 5, no. 3 (September): 377–407.

Hinojosa, Magda, and Susan Franceschet. Forthcoming. "Separate but Not Equal: The Effects of Municipal Electoral Change on Female Representation in Chile." *Political Research Quarterly* 1065912911427449, first published on December 5, 2011 as doi:10.1177/1065912911427449.

Hinojosa, Magda, and Ana Vijil Gurdián. Forthcoming. "An Alternate Path to Power? Women's Political Representation in Nicaragua." *Latin American Politics and Society*.

Hollander, Nancy Caro. 1974. "Si Evita viviera." *Latin American Perspectives* 1 (3): 42–57.

Hopkin, Jonathan. 2001. "Bringing the Members Back In? Democratizing Candidate Selection in Britain and Spain." *Party Politics* 7 (3): 343–361.

Htun, Mala. 2003. *Sex and the State: Abortion, Divorce, and the Family under Latin American Dictatorships and Democracies*. New York: Cambridge University Press.

———. 2004. "Is Gender Like Ethnicity? The Political Representation of Identity Groups." *Perspectives on Politics* 2 (3): 439–458.

———. 2005. "Case Study: Latin America. Women, Political Parties and Electoral Systems in Latin America." In *Women in Parliament: Beyond Numbers*, edited by Julie Ballington and Azza Karam, 112–121. Rev. ed. Stockholm: International IDEA.

———. 2007. "Gender Equality in Transition Policies: Comparative Perspectives on Cuba." In *Cuba's Democratic Transition: A Reader*, edited by Marifeli Pérez-Stable, 119–137. Notre Dame, IN: University of Notre Dame Press.

Htun, Mala, and Mark P. Jones. 1999. "Engendering the Right to Participate in Decisionmaking: Electoral Quotas and Women's Leadership in Latin America." Paper presented at the 95th Annual Meeting of the American Political Science Association, Atlanta, September 2–5.

———. 2002. "Engendering the Right to Participate in Decision-Making: Electoral Quotas and Women's Leadership in Latin America." In *Gender and the Politics of Rights and Democracy in Latin America*, edited by Nikki Craske and Maxine Molyneux, 32–56. New York: Palgrave.

Huerta García, Magdalena, and Eric Magar Meurs, eds. 2006. *Mujeres legisladoras en México: Avances, obstáculos, consecuencias y propuestas*. Mexico City: Instituto Nacional de la Mujer.

Huneeus, Carlos. 2008. "Reforma electoral en Chile." In *Reforma política y electoral en América Latina, 1978–2007*, edited by Daniel Zovatto G. and J. Jesús Orozco Henríquez, 353–390. Mexico City: Universidad Nacional Autónoma de México.

Infobae. 2004. "Triunfo póstumo de una candidata en México." *Infobae.com*, October 4. Available at http://www.infobae.com/notas/nota.php?Idx=143742&idxSeccion=0.

Inglehart, Ronald, and Pippa Norris. 2003. *Rising Tide: Gender Equality and Cultural Change around the World*. New York: Cambridge University Press.

Inter-American Development Bank. 2000. Politics Matter: A Dialogue of Women Political Leaders. Washington, DC, November 13. Available at http://www. thedialogue.org/PublicationFiles/Politics%20Matter.pdf.

International IDEA and Department of Political Science (ICP) of the University of the Republic. 2008. "La representación política de las mujeres y las cuotas: Aportes para el debate parlamentario. Encuestas: ¿Que piensa la opinión pública uruguaya sobre las mujeres en política?" Available at http://www.parlamento.gub.uy/ externos/parlamenta/descargas/dossier/Dossiercuota_opinion_publica.pdf.

International Labour Office. 2010. *Key Indicators of the Labour Market*. 6th ed. Geneva: International Labour Office.

Inter-Parliamentary Union. 2010. "Women in National Parliaments: World Classification." Available at http://www.ipu.org/wmn-e/classif.htm.

Jalalzai, Farida. 2004. "Women Political Leaders: Past and Present." *Women and Politics* 26 (3/4): 85–108.

———. 2010. "Madam President: Gender, Power, and the Comparative Presidency." *Journal of Women, Politics and Policy* 31 (2): 132–165.

Jalalzai, Farida, and Chad A. Hankinson. 2008. "Political Widowhood in the United States: An Empirical Assessment of Underlying Assumptions of Representation." *Journal of Women, Politics and Policy* 29 (3): 395–426.

Jaquette, Jane. 1989. *The Women's Movement in Latin America: Feminism and the Transition to Democracy*. Boston: Unwin Hyman.

Jennings, M. Kent, and Barbara G. Farah. 1981. "Social Roles and Political Resources: An Over Time Study of Men and Women in Party Elites." *American Journal of Political Science* 25 (August): 462–482.

Joignant, Alfredo, and Patricio Navia. 2003. "De la política de individuos a los hombres del partido: Socialización, competencia política y penetración electoral de la UDI (1989–2001)." *Estudios Públicos* 89 (Summer): 129–171.

Jones, Mark P. 1996. "Increasing Women's Representation via Gender Quotas: The Argentine Ley de Cupos." *Women and Politics* 16 (4): 75–98.

———. 1998. "Gender Quotas, Electoral Laws, and the Election of Women: Lessons from the Argentine Provinces." *Comparative Political Studies* 31, no. 1 (February): 3–21.

———. 2004. "Quota Legislation and the Election of Women: Learning from the Costa Rican Experience." *Journal of Politics* 66 (4): 1203–1223.

———. 2008. "The Recruitment and Selection of Legislative Candidates in Argentina." In *Pathways to Power: Political Recruitment and Candidate Selection in Latin America*, edited by Peter Siavelis and Scott Morgenstern, 41–75. University Park: Pennsylvania State University Press.

———. 2009. "Gender Quotas, Electoral Laws, and the Election of Women: Evidence from the Latin American Vanguard." *Comparative Political Studies* 42 (1): 56–81.

Kanthak, Kristin, and Rebecca Morton. 2001. "The Effects of Electoral Rules on Congressional Primaries." In *Congressional Primaries and the Politics of Representation*, edited by Peter F. Galderisi, Marni Ezra, and Michael Lyons, 116–131. New York: Rowman and Littlefield.

Karnig, Albert K., and B. Oliver Walter. 1975. "Election of Women to City Councils." *Social Science Quarterly* 56:605–613.

Karnig, Albert K., and Susan Welch. 1979. "Sex and Ethnic Differences in Municipal Representation." *Social Science Quarterly* 60, no. 3 (December): 464–481.

Katz, Richard S., and Peter Mair. 1995. "Changing Models of Party Organization and Party Democracy: The Emergence of the Cartel Party." *Party Politics* 1 (1): 5–28.

Kemahlioglu, Ozge, Rebecca Weitz-Shapiro, and Shigeo Hirano. 2009. "Why Primaries in Latin American Presidential Elections?" *Journal of Politics* 71 (1): 339–352.

Kenworthy, Lane, and Melissa Malami. 1999. "Gender Inequality in Political Representation: A Worldwide Comparative Analysis." *Social Forces* 78:235–269.

Kessel, Alisa, and Clark D. Olson. 2002. "Political Widow Rhetoric: From Historical Footnote to Distinguished Career." Paper presented at the American Political Science Association meeting, Boston.

Kittilson, Miki. 2006. *Challenging Parties, Changing Parliaments: Women and Elected Office in Contemporary Western Europe*. Columbus: Ohio State University Press.

Knoke, David. 1993. "Networks of Elite Structure and Decision Making." *Sociological Methods and Research* 22:23–45.

Krook, Mona Lena. 2009. *Quotas for Women in Politics: Gender and Candidate Selection Reform Worldwide*. New York: Oxford University Press.

Langston, Joy. 2001. "Why Rules Matter: Changes in Candidate Selection in Mexico's PRI, 1988–2000." *Journal of Latin American Studies* 33:485–511.

———. 2003. "Rising from the Ashes? Reorganizing and Unifying the PRI's State Party Organizations after Electoral Defeat." *Comparative Political Studies* 36, no. 3 (April): 293–318.

————. 2008. "Legislative Recruitment in Mexico." In *Pathways to Power: Political Recruitment and Candidate Selection in Latin America*, edited by Peter Siavelis and Scott Morgenstern, 143–163. University Park: Pennsylvania State University Press.

Lara, Julio F. 2011. "Sandra Torres queda fuera de la contienda electoral." Available at PrensaLibre.com

Lara Rivera, Jorge Alberto. 2006. "La organización y los procesos en el Partido Acción Nacional." In *Partidos políticos: Democracia interna y financiamiento de precampañas. Memoria del VII Congreso Iberoamericano de Derecho Constitucional*, edited by María del Pilar Hernández. Mexico City: Instituto de Investigaciones Jurídicas.

Latin American Public Opinion Project. 2008. "The AmericasBarometer 2008." Available at www.LapopSurveys.org.

Lawless, Jennifer L. 2003. "Women and Elections: Do They Run? Do They Win? Does It Matter?" Ph.D. diss., Stanford University.

Lawless, Jennifer L., and Richard L. Fox. 2005. *It Takes a Candidate: Why Women Don't Run for Office.* New York: Cambridge University Press.

Lawson, Chappell. 2000. "Mexico's Unfinished Transition: Democratization and Authoritarian Enclaves in Mexico." *Mexican Studies/Estudios Mexicanos* 16 (2): 267–287.

Leijenaar, Monique. 1993. "A Battle for Power: Selecting Candidates in the Netherlands." In *Gender and Party Politics*, edited by Joni Lovenduski and Pippa Norris, 205–230. Thousand Oaks, CA: Sage Publications.

Levitsky, Steven, and Maxwell A. Cameron. 2001. "Democracy without Parties? Political Parties and Regime Collapse in Fujimori's Peru." Paper presented at the Congress of the Latin American Studies Association, Washington, DC, September 6–8.

Llanos, Beatriz, and Kristen Sample. 2008. *Del dicho al hecho: Manual de buenas prácticas para la participación de mujeres en los partidos políticos latinoamericanos.* Stockholm: International IDEA.

————. 2009. *30 Años de democracia: ¿En la cresta de la ola? Participación política de la mujer en América Latina.* Miraflores, Peru: International IDEA.

Longueira Montes, Pablo. 2003. *Mi testimonio de fe: El servicio publico, el sentido de dolor.* Santiago: Random House Mondadori, S.A.

López Endara, Giovanny. 2004. "Intervención del delegado del Partido Democracia Popular." In *Reflexiones sobre mujer y política: Memorias del seminario nacional "Los cambios políticos en Ecuador: Perspectivas y retos para la mujer,"* edited by María Fernanda Cañete, 77–81. Quito, Ecuador: CEDIME.

Lovenduski, Joni. 1993. "Introduction: The Dynamics of Gender and Party." In *Gender and Party Politics*, edited by Joni Lovenduski and Pippa Norris, 1–15. Thousand Oaks, CA: Sage Publications.

Lovenduski, Joni, and Pippa Norris. 1993. *Gender and Party Politics.* Thousand Oaks, CA: Sage Publications.

Lublin, David, and Sarah E. Brewer. 2003. "The Continuing Dominance of Traditional Gender Roles in Southern Elections." *Social Science Quarterly* 84 (2): 379–396.

Luciak, Ilja A. 2005. "Party and State in Cuba: Gender Equality in Political Decision Making." *Politics and Gender* 1 (2): 241–263.

Luna, Juan Pablo. 2010. "Segmented Party Voter Linkages in Latin America: The Case of the UDI." *Journal of Latin American Studies* 42 (2): 325–356.

Macauley, Fiona. 1993. "Gender, Power and Parties in the Transition to Democracy in Chile." Ph.D. diss., University of Oxford.

Marsden, Peter V. 1987. "Core Discussion Networks of Americans." *American Sociological Review* 52:122–131.

Martin, Mart. 2000. *The Almanac of Women and Minorities in World Politics.* Boulder, CO: Westview Press.

Martoccia, Hugo, and Carlos Camacho. 2011. "QR: Impiden a diputada dejar cargo a suplente." *La Jornada*, June 24, 34. Available at http://www.jornada.unam.mx/2011/06/24/estados/034n2est.

Martz, John D. 2000. "Political Parties and Candidate Selection in Venezuela and Colombia." *Political Science Quarterly* 114 (4): 639–659.

Massolo, Alejandra. 1998. "Women in the Local Arena and Municipal Power." In *Women's Participation in Mexican Political Life*, edited by Victoria E. Rodríguez, 193–203. Boulder, CO: Westview Press.

———. 1999. "Defender y cambiar la vida: Mujeres en movimientos populares urbanos." *Cuicuilco: Revista de la Escuela Nacional de Antropología e Historia* 6 (17): 13–24.

Matland, Richard E. 1998. "Women's Representation in National Legislatures: Developed and Developing Countries." *Legislative Studies Quarterly* 23, no. 1 (February): 109–125.

———. 2006. "Electoral Quotas: Frequency and Effectiveness." In *Women, Quotas and Politics*, edited by Drude Dahlerup, 275–292. New York: Routledge.

Matland, Richard E., and David King. 2003. "Women as Candidates in Congressional Elections." In *Women Transforming Congress*, edited by Cindy Simon Rosenthal, 119–145. Oklahoma City: University of Oklahoma Press.

Matland, Richard E., and Donley T. Studlar. 1996. "The Contagion of Women Candidates in Single-Member District and Proportional Representation Electoral Systems: Canada and Norway." *Journal of Politics* 58, no. 3 (August): 707–733.

Matland, Richard E., and Michelle M. Taylor. 1997. "Electoral System Effects on Women's Representation: Theoretical Arguments and Evidence from Costa Rica." *Comparative Political Studies* 30, no. 2 (April): 186–210.

Maxfield, Sylvia. 2005. "Women on the Verge: Corporate Power in Latin America." Women's Leadership Conference of the Americas. Available at http://www.thedialogue.org/PublicationFiles/Women%20on%20the%20Verge.pdf.

McDermott, Monika L. 1998. "Race and Gender Cues in Low-Information Elections." *Political Research Quarterly* 51 (4): 895–918.

McDonagh, Eileen. 2002. "Political Citizenship and Democratization: The Gender Paradox." *American Political Science Review* 96 (3): 535–552.

Meier, Petra. 2004. "The Mutual Contagion Effect of Legal and Party Quotas." *Party Politics* 10 (5): 583–600.

Mellman, Lazarus, Lake, Inc. 1994. "Why Don't More Women Run?" National Women's Political Caucus, December 15.

Mieszkowski, Katharine. 2000. "Behind Every Dead Candidate . . ." Available at www.salon.com/mwt/feature/2000/11/09/jean_carnahan.html.

Mizrahi, Yemile. 2003. *From Martyrdom to Power: The Partido Acción Nacional in Mexico.* Notre Dame, IN: University of Notre Dame Press.

Moffett, Matt. 2006. "Unhappy Couple Run against Each Other for Congress in Brazil." *Wall Street Journal*, September 27, 1.

Molina, Natacha. 2000. "El derecho a elegir y a ser elegidas." *Perspectivas* 20:33–38.

Moltedo, Cecilia. 1998. *Experiencias de participación de las mujeres chilenas en los partidos políticos.* Santiago: Instituto de la Mujer.

Moncrief, Gary, Peverill Squire, and Malcolm Jewell. 2001. *Who Runs for the Legislature? Candidates and Recruitment in the States.* Upper Saddle River, NJ: Prentice-Hall.

Moore, Gwen. 1990. "Structural Determinants of Men's and Women's Personal Networks." *American Sociological Review* 55:726–735.

Moore, Gwen, and Deborah White. 2000. "Interpersonal Contacts." In *Gendering Elites: Economic and Political Leadership in 27 Industrialised Societies*, edited by Mino Vianello and Gwen Moore, 120–130. New York: St. Martin's Press.

Morales Quiroga, Mauricio. 2008. "La primera mujer presidenta en Chile." *Latin American Research Review* 43:7–32.

Morgenstern, Scott, and Peter Siavelis. 2008. "Pathways to Power and Democracy in Latin America." In *Pathways to Power: Political Recruitment and Candidate Selection in Latin America*, edited by Peter Siavelis and Scott Morgenstern, 371–402. University Park: Pennsylvania State University Press.

Moritz, Charles. 1976. *Current Biography Yearbook 1975.* New York: H. W. Wilson.

Moya, F. 2001. "Candidatas mujeres . . . ¿Cómo viene la mano?" Available at www.mujereschile.cl, www.mujereschile.cl/para_imprimir.php?opc=333.

Mueller, Melinda A. 2002. "Deciding to Run: Candidate Selection, Recruitment, and the Gender Gap in Illinois." Paper prepared for the Annual Meeting of the Midwest Political Science Association, Chicago, April.

Muñoz D'Albora, Adriana, and Scarlett Wojciechowski Levine. 1996. *Mujer y ciudadanía.* Santiago: Fundación IDEAS.

Murray, Rainbow. 2007. "How parties evaluate compulsory quotas: a study of the implementation of the 'parity' law in France." *Parliamentary Affairs* 60 (4): 568–584.

———, ed. 2010. *Cracking the Highest Class Ceiling: A Global Comparison of Women's Campaigns for Executive Office.* Santa Barbara, CA: Praeger.

Navarro, Mireya. 1999a. "Earnest Icon for Panama." *New York Times*, May 4, 6.

———. 1999b. "The Widow of Ex-leader Wins Race in Panama." *New York Times*, May 3, 8.

Navia, Patricio. 2004. "Legislative Candidate Selection in Chile." Paper presented at the Pathways to Power: Political Recruitment and Democracy in Latin America research symposium, Wake Forest University, Winston-Salem, NC, April 2–4.

———. 2008a. "¿Cuando se jodió la concertación?" *Revista Poder* 7 (November). Available at http://www.poder360.com.

———. 2008b. "Legislative Candidate Selection in Chile." In *Pathways to Power: Political Recruitment and Candidate Selection in Latin America*, edited by Peter Siavelis and Scott Morgenstern, 92–118. University Park: Pennsylvania State University Press.

Niven, David. 1998. "Party Elites and Women Candidates: The Shape of Bias." *Women and Politics* 19 (2): 57–80.

———. 2006. "Throwing Your Hat out of the Ring: Negative Recruitment and the Gender Imbalance in State Legislative Candidacy." *Politics and Gender* 2, no. 4 (December): 473–489.

Norris, Pippa. 1985. "Women's Legislative Participation in Western Europe." In *Women and Politics in Western Europe*, edited by Sylvia Bashevkin, 90–101. London: Frank Cass.

———. 1987. "The Gender Gap: A Cross-Cultural Trend?" In *Politics of the Gender Gap*, edited by Carol M. Mueller, 217–234. Newbury Park, CA: Sage Publications.

Norris, Pippa, and Ronald Inglehart. 2000. "Cultural Barriers to Women's Leadership: A Worldwide Comparison." Paper presented at the International Political Science Association World Congress, Quebec, August 3.

———. 2001. "Cultural Obstacles to Equal Representation." *Journal of Democracy* 12, no. 3 (July): 126–140.

Norris, Pippa, and Joni Lovenduski. 1995. *Political Recruitment: Gender, Race and Class in the British Parliament*. New York: Cambridge University Press.

Notimex. 2010. "Suplentes de Juanitas rinden protesta." *El Universal*, Feb. 2. Available at http://www.eluniversal.com.mx/notas/655822.html.

Palacios, Margarita, and Javier Martínez. 2006. "Liberalism and Conservatism in Chile: Attitudes and Opinions of Chilean Women at the Start of the Twenty-First Century." *Journal of Latin American Studies* 38:1–34.

Paxton, Pamela, Melody M. Hughes, and Jennifer L. Green. 2006. "The International Women's Movement and Women's Political Representation, 1893–2003." *American Sociological Review* 71 (December): 898–920.

Pearson, Kathryn, and Jennifer L. Lawless. 2006. "The Primary Reason for Women's Under-representation? Reevaluating the Conventional Wisdom." Paper presented at the Annual Meeting of the American Political Science Association, Philadelphia.

Pennings, Paul, and Reuven Y. Hazan. 2001. "Democratizing Candidate Selection: Causes and Consequences." *Party Politics* 7:267–275.

Pérez-Stable, Marifeli. 2007. "Bachelet, Fernández Push Politics beyond Gender." *Miami Herald*, November 8.

Peschard, Jacqueline. 2006. "Control over Party and Campaign Finance in Mexico." *Mexican Studies/Estudios Mexicanos* 22 (1): 83–106.

Peterson, V. Spike, and Anne Sisson Runyan. 1999. *Global Gender Issues*. 2nd ed. Boulder, CO: Westview Press.

Pinto, Céli Regina Jardim. 1994. "Donas de casa, mães, feministas, batalhadoras: Mulheres nas eleições de 1994 no Brasil." *Revista de Estudos Feministas* 2 (2): 297–313.

Piscopo, Jennifer M. 2011. "Gender Quotas and Equity Promotion in Mexico." In *Gender Quota Laws in Latin America: Policy Innovation, Regional Diffusion, and the End of a Wave*, edited by Adriana Crocker, 36–52. New York: Peter Lang Publishers.

Poiré, Alejandro. 2002. "Bounded Ambitions. Party Nominations, Discipline, and Defection: Mexico's PRI in Comparative Perspective." Ph.D. diss., Harvard University.

Posada-Carbó, Eduardo. 2008. "Democracy, Parties and Political Finance in Latin America." Working Paper no. 346. South Bend, IN: Kellogg Institute for International Studies.

Power, Timothy J., and Marília G. Mochel. 2008. "Political Recruitment in an Executive-Centric System: Presidents, Ministers, and Governors in Brazil." In *Pathways to Power: Political Recruitment and Candidate Selection in Latin America*, edited by Peter Siavelis and Scott Morgenstern, 218–240. University Park: Pennsylvania State University Press.

Praamsma, Wanda. 2005. "Chile's Bachelet Scolds Parties for Lack of Women Candidates: Concertación Presidential Nominee Says Progressive Parties Can Do Better." *Santiago Times*, August 22.

PROLEAD (Program for the Support of Women's Leadership and Representation). 2002. "Moving into Power: Changing the Rules of the Game."

Putnam, Robert. 1976. *The Comparative Study of Political Elites*. Englewood Cliffs, NJ: Prentice-Hall.

Quigley, John, and Helen Murphy. 2011. "Humala Claims Victory while Clinging to Lead in Peru Vote." *Bloomberg Businessweek*, June 6.

Rahat, Gideon. 2009. "Which Candidate Selection Method Is the Most Democratic?" *Government and Opposition* 44, no. 1 (2009): 68–90.

Rahat, Gideon, and Reuven Y. Hazan. 2001. "Candidate Selection Methods: An Analytical Framework." *Party Politics* 7 (3): 297–322.

Rahat, Gideon, and Neta Sher-Hadar. 1999. "The Party Primaries and Their Political Consequences." In *The Elections in Israel: 1996*, edited by Asher Arian and Michal Shamir, 241–268. Albany: State University of New York Press.

Ranney, Austin. 1981. "Candidate Selection." In *Democracy at the Polls: A Comparative Study of Competitive National Elections*, edited by David Butler, Howard Penniman, and Austin Ranney, 75–106. Washington, DC: American Enterprise Institute.

Reynolds, Andrew. 1999. "Women in the Legislature and Executive: Knocking at the World's Highest Glass Ceiling." *World Politics* 51 (4): 547–572.

Reynoso, Diego, and Natalia D'Angelo. 2006. "Las leyes de cuota y su impacto en la elección de mujeres en México." *Política y Gobierno* 13 (2): 279–313.

Rico, María Nieves. 2000. "Las mujeres chilenas en los noventa: Hablan las cifras." United Nations Economic Commission for Latin America and the Caribbean report. Available at http://www.eclac.org/publicaciones/xml/4/5494/LBC-57.pdf.

Ríos, Marcela. 2006. *Cuotas de género: democracia y representación*. Santiago: International IDEA and FLACSO.

Ríos, Marcela, and Andrés Villar. 2006. "Mujeres en el congreso 2006–2010." *Observatorio* 2 (January): 1–6.

Roberts, Kenneth. 1998. "Rethinking Economic Alternatives: Left Parties and the Articulation of Popular Demands in Chile and Peru." In *The New Politics of Inequality in Latin America: Rethinking Participation and Representation*, edited by Douglas A. Chalmers et al, 313–336. New York: Oxford University Press.

Roces, Mina. 1998. *Women, Power, and Kinship Politics: Female Power in Post-war Philippines*. Westport, CT: Praeger.

Rodríguez, Victoria E. 1997. *Decentralization in Mexico: From Reforma Municipal to Solidaridad to Nuevo Federalismo*. Boulder, CO: Westview Press.

————. 2003. *Women in Contemporary Mexican Politics*. Austin: University of Texas Press.

Rodríguez Romero, Casimira. 2007. "Presentation by Casimira Rodríguez Romero, Bolivian Minister of Justice." Paper presented at the Latin American Studies Association, Montreal, Canada.

Rohter, Larry. 2000. "Mayor Most Rare: Sexologist and Monied Marxist." *New York Times*, November 26.

Rosenstone, Steven J., and John Mark Hansen. 1993. *Mobilization, Participation, and Democracy in America*. New York: Macmillan.

Roza, Vivian. 2010a. "Gatekeepers to Power: Party-Level Influences on Women's Political Participation in Latin America." Ph.D. diss., Georgetown University.

————. 2010b. "Report on GEPPAL (Género y Partidos Políticos en América Latina)." Paper presented at Partidos Políticos y Paridad: La Ecuación Posible, a conference organized by the Inter-American Development Bank, UNIFEM, and International IDEA, in Lima, Peru.

Rule, Wilma. 1981. "Why Women Don't Run." *Western Political Quarterly* 34:60–77.

————. 1987. "Electoral Systems, Contextual Factors, and Women's Opportunity for Election to Parliament in Twenty-Three Democracies." *Western Political Quarterly* 40:477–498.

Saint-Germain, Michelle A. 1993. "Women in Power in Nicaragua: Myth and Reality." In *Women as National Leaders*, edited by Michael A. Genovese, 70–102. Newbury Park, CA: Sage Publications.

Saint-Germain, Michelle A., and Cynthia Chavez Metoyer. 2008. *Women Legislators in Central America: Politics, Democracy, and Policy*. Austin: University of Texas Press.

Salinero R., Mónica. 2004. "La experiencia de las mujeres en los procesos de nominación de las candidaturas al interior de los partidos políticos chilenos: Los casos del partido socialista y por la democracia." Study funded by Fundacion Instituto de la Mujer, Santiago. Available at http://www.fesgenero.org/uploads/documentos/participacion_politica/estudio_final_instituto_de_la_mujer_2004.doc.

Samarasinghe, Vidyamali. 2000. "Subverting Patriarchy? Leadership and Participation of Women in Politics in South Asia." *Ethnic Studies Report* 18 (2): 193–213.

Samuels, David. 2008. "Political Ambition, Candidate Recruitment, and Legislative Politics in Brazil." In *Pathways to Power: Political Recruitment and Candidate Selection in Latin America*, edited by Peter Siavelis and Scott Morgenstern, 76–91. University Park: Pennsylvania State University Press.

Sanbonmatsu, Kira. 2006a. "Do Parties Know That 'Women Win'? Party Leader Beliefs about Women's Electoral Chances." *Politics and Gender* 2, no. 4 (December): 431–450.

————. 2006b. "State Elections: Where Do Women Run? Where Do Women Win?" In *Gender and Elections: Shaping the Future of American Politics*, edited by Susan J. Carroll and Richard L. Fox, 189–214. New York: Cambridge University Press.

Sanders, Thomas G. 1987. "Brazilian Women in Politics." *UFSI Reports* 6 (14): 1–7.

Sandoval, Ricardo. 2000. "Women Gain Clout in Mexican Politics." *Miami Herald*, March 28.

Schmidt, Gregory D. 2006. "All the President's Women: Fujimori and Gender Equity in Peruvian Politics." In *The Fujimori Legacy: The Rise of Electoral Authoritarianism in Peru*, edited by Julio F. Carrión, 150–177. University Park: Pennsylvania State University Press.

Schmidt, Gregory D., and Kyle L. Saunders. 2004. "Effective Quotas, Relative Party Magnitude, and the Success of Female Candidates: Peruvian Municipal Elections in Comparative Perspective." *Comparative Political Studies* 37, no. 6 (August): 704–724.

Schwindt-Bayer, Leslie A. 2006. "Female Legislators and the Promotion of Women, Children, and Family Policies in Latin America" Background paper prepared for UNICEF's State of the World's Children Report. Available at http://www.unicef.org/french/sowc07/docs/schwindt_bayer.pdf.

Scully, Timothy, and J. Samuel Valenzuela. 1993. "From Democracy to Democracy: Continuities and Changes of Electoral Choices and the Party System in Chile." Working Paper no. 199. July. Helen Kellogg Institute for International Studies. Available at https://www2.nd.edu/~kellogg/publications/workingpapers/WPS/199.pdf.

Seltzer, Richard, Jody Newman, and Melissa Voorhees Leighton. 1997. *Sex as a Political Variable: Women as Candidates and Voters in U.S. Elections*. Boulder, CO: Lynne Rienner.

SERNAM (Servicio Nacional de la Mujer). 2001. *Mujeres chilenas: Estadísticas para el nuevo siglo*. Santiago: Empresa Periodística "La Nación S.A."

Serra, Gilles. 2011. "Why Primaries? The Party's Tradeoff between Policy and Valence." *Journal of Theoretical Politics* 23 (1): 21–51.

Setzler, Mark. 2006. "Creating a Critical Mass or Fragmenting the Vote? Intra-Gender Competition and the Election of Women in Brazil." Paper presented at the American Political Science Association Conference, Philadelphia, August.

Siavelis, Peter, and Scott Morgenstern. 2008. "Political Recruitment and Candidate Selection in Latin America: A Framework for Analysis." In *Pathways to Power: Political Recruitment and Candidate Selection in Latin America*, edited by Peter Siavelis and Scott Morgenstern, 3–38. University Park: Pennsylvania State University Press.

Sidhu, Gretchen Luchsinger, and Ruth Meena. 2007. "Electoral Financing to Advance Women's Political Participation: A Guide for UNDP Support." In *Primers in Gender and Democratic Governance*. No. 3. New York: United Nations Development Programme. Available at: http://www.undp.org.ir/gender/electoral%20financing-EN-EBOOK.pdf.

Silber, Irina Carlota, and Jocelyn Viterna. 2009. "Women in El Salvador: Continuing the Struggle." In *Women and Politics around the World: A Comparative History and Survey*, edited by Joyce Gelb and Marian Lief Palley, 328–351. Santa Barbara, CA: ABC-Clio.

Sims, Calvin. 1994. "In the Macho World of Peru, 8 Women Muscle In." *New York Times*, December 7, 4.

SISESIM (Sistema de Indicadores para el Seguimiento de la Situación de la Mujer en México). 2004. Available at http://dgcnesyp.inegi.gob.mx/sisesim/sisesim.html?c=1416.

Smith, Lois M., and Alfred Padula. 1996. *Sex and Revolution: Women in Socialist Cuba*. New York: Oxford University Press.

Smith, Peter H. 1979. *Labyrinths of Power: Political Recruitment in Twentieth-Century Mexico*. Princeton, NJ: Princeton University Press.

Stoloff, Jennifer A., Jennifer L. Glanville, and Elisa Jayne Bienenstock. 1999. "Women's Participation in the Labor Force: The Role of Social Networks." *Social Networks* 21, no. 1 (January): 91–108.

Stone, Walter J., and L. Sandy Maisel. 2003. "The Not-So-Simple Calculus of Winning: Potential U.S. House Candidates' Nomination and General Election Prospects." *Journal of Politics* 65, no. 4 (November): 951–977.

Studlar, Donley T., and Ian McAllister. 1991. "Political Recruitment to the Australian Legislature: Toward an Explanation of Women's Electoral Disadvantage." *Western Political Quarterly* 44:467–485.

Tarrés, María Luisa. 2006. "The Political Participation of Women in Contemporary Mexico, 1980–2000." In *Changing Structure of Mexico: Political, Social, and Economic Prospects*, edited by Laura Randall, 406–423. Armonk, NY: M. E. Sharpe.

Taylor, Steven L., Felipe Botero Jaramillo, and Brian F. Crisp. 2008. "Precandidates, Candidates, and Presidents: Paths to the Colombian Presidency." In *Pathways to Power: Political Recruitment and Candidate Selection in Latin America*, edited by Peter Siavelis and Scott Morgenstern, 271–291. University Park: Pennsylvania State University Press.

Taylor-Robinson, Michelle M. 2001. "Candidate Selection in Costa Rica." Paper presented at the International Congress of the Latin American Studies Association, Washington, DC, September 6–8.

Thompson, Ginger. 2004a. "Mexican Politicos Won't Stay Home and Bake Cookies." *New York Times*, October 11.

———. 2004b. "Mexican Town Refuses to Abandon Fallen Hero's Dream." *New York Times*, November 7.

Tremblay, Manon, and Réjean Pelletier. 2001. "More Women Constituency Party Presidents: A Strategy for Increasing the Number of Women Candidates in Canada?" *Party Politics* 7 (2): 157–190.

Tripp, Aili M., and Alice Kang. 2008. "The Global Impact of Quotas: On the Fast Track to Increased Legislative Representation." *Comparative Political Studies* 41 (3): 338–361.

Trotter, R. T., and J. J. Schensul. 1998. "Methods in Applied Anthropology." In *Handbook and Methods in Cultural Anthropology*, edited by Russell H. Bernard, 691–736. Walnut Creek, CA: Altamira Press.

Tuesta Soldevilla, Fernando. 2008. "Reforma política en Perú." In *Reforma política y electoral en América Latina, 1978–2007*, edited by Daniel Zovatto G. and J. Jesús Orozco Henríquez, 821–864. Mexico City: Universidad Nacional Autónoma de México.

UN DESA (United Nations Department of Economic and Social Affairs), Population Division. 2008. "World Marriage Data." Available at http://www.un.org/esa/population/publications/WMD2008/Main.html.

UNDP (United Nations Development Programme). 2007. "Diagnostico sobre la participación de las mujeres en la política: Panamá." Available at http://www.fonamupp.org/diagnostico%20sobre%20la%20participacion%20politica.pdf.

UNESCO (United Nations Educational, Scientific and Cultural Organization). 2009. Institute for Statistics Database (UIS). Available at http://www.uis.unesco.org.

UNIFEM (United Nations Development Fund for Women). 2001. "Goals for Women Still Unmet," Women's Wages as Percentage of Men's Wages in Industry and Services chart. Available at http://www.lapress.org/articles.asp?art=2262.

UNIFEM/CONMUJER (United Nations Development Fund for Women/Comisión Nacional de la Mujer). 2000. "El enfoque de género en la producción de las estadísticas sobre participación política y toma de decisiones en México." Available at http://www.undp.org.mx/spip.php?page=publicacion&id_article=1071.

United Nations. 2004. *Statistical Yearbook for Latin America and the Caribbean, 2004*. Available at www.eclac.cl/cgi-bin/getProd.asp?xml=/publicaciones/xml/4/28074/P28074.xml&xsl=/deype/tpl-i/p9f.xsl&base=/tpl-i/top-bottom.xsl.

Valdés, Leonardo. 2001. "La selección de candidatos y el cambio del sistema de partidos políticos en México." Paper presented at the Latin American Studies Association Conference, Washington, DC, September 6–8.

Valdés, Teresa, and Enrique Gomáriz. 1995. *Mujeres latinoamericanas en cifras: Tomo comparativo*. Santiago: Instituto de la Mujer de España and FLACSO.

Valdés, Teresa, Ana María Muñoz, and Alina Donoso. 2005. "1995–2003: Have Women Progressed? Latin American Index of Fulfilled Commitment." Facultad Latinoamericana de Ciencias Sociales report. Available at http://www.unrol.org/files/ICC_rev_eng.pdf.

Valenzuela, J. Samuel, and Timothy R. Scully. 1997. "Electoral Choices and the Party System in Chile: Continuities and Changes at the Recovery of Democracy." *Comparative Politics* 29 (July): 511–527.

Valenzuela, María Elena. 1998. "Women and the Democratization Process in Chile." In *Women and Democracy: Latin America and Central and Eastern Europe*, edited by Jane S. Jaquette and Sharon L. Wolchik, 47–74. Baltimore: Johns Hopkins University Press.

Valladares, Danilo. 2011. "Ethics and Politics Get Divorced in Guatemala." Inter Press Service News Agency, May 19.

Vega, Gabriela, Ana Maria Brasileiro, Vivian Roza, and Cristen Dávalos. 2000. "Women in Power: Changing the Rules of the Game." PROLEAD Inter-American Development report.

Vengroff, Richard, Zsolt Nyiri, and Melissa Fugiero. 2003. "Electoral System and Gender Representation in Sub-National Legislatures: Is There a National–Sub-National Gender Gap?" *Political Research Quarterly* 56 (2): 163–173.

Verba, Sidney, Kay Lehman Schlozman, and Henry E. Brady. 1995. *Voice and Equality*. Cambridge, MA: Harvard University Press.

Verge, Tània. 2010. "Gender Representation in Spain: Opportunities and Limits of Gender Quotas." *Journal of Women, Politics and Policy* 31 (2): 166–190.

Ware, Alan. 2002. *The American Direct Primary: Party Institutionalization and Transformation in the North*. New York: Cambridge University Press.

Warner, W. Lloyd, and Paul S. Lunt. 1941. *The Social Life of a Modern Community*. New Haven, CT: Yale University Press.

Waylen, Georgina. 2000. "Gender and Democratic Politics: A Comparative Analysis of Consolidation in Argentina and Chile." *Journal of Latin American Studies* 32 (3): 765–793.

WEDO (Women's Environment and Development Organization). 2007. "Women Candidates and Campaign Finance." Available at www.wedo.org.

Welch, Susan, and Albert K. Karnig. 1979. "Correlates of Female Office Holding in City Politics." *Journal of Politics* 41:478–491.

WLCA (Women's Leadership Conference of the Americas). 2001. "Women and Power in the Americas: A Report Card." Inter-American Dialogue report. Available at http://www.thedialogue.org/PublicationFiles/IAD%20reportcard%20final.pdf.

World Bank. 2011. Database: GDP per Capita. Available at http://data.worldbank.org/indicator/NY.GDP.PCAP.CD.

World Values Survey. 2011. Database. Available at http://www.wvsevsdb.com/wvs/WVSData.jsp.

Wuhs, Steven T. 2006. "Democratization and the Dynamics of Candidate Selection Rule Change in Mexico, 1991–2003." *Mexican Studies/Estudios Mexicanos* 22 (1): 33–55.

———. 2008. *Savage Democracy: Institutional Change and Party Development in Mexico.* University Park: Pennsylvania State University Press.

Yáñez, Ana María. 2003. "Quotas and Democracy in Peru." Paper presented at the International IDEA workshop, The Implementation of Quotas: Latin American Experiences, Lima, February 23–24.

Young, Lisa. 2005. "Campaign Finance and Women's Representation in Canada and US." In *Funding of Political Parties and Election Campaigns in the Americas*, edited by S. Griner and D. Zobato, 133–147. San José de Costa Rica: IDEA.

Zabaleta, Marta Raquel. 2000. *Feminine Stereotypes and Roles in Theory and Practice in Argentina before and after the First Lady Eva Perón.* Lewiston, NY: Edwin Mellen Press.

Zambrano Macías, Ana María. 2004. "Intervención de Ana María Zambrano Macías (representante del Movimiento de Mujeres de Sectores Populares de Guayas." In *Reflexiones sobre mujer y política: Memorias del seminario nacional "Los cambios políticos en Ecuador: Perspectivas y retos para la mujer,"* edited by María Fernanda Cañete, 243–245. Quito, Ecuador: CEDIME.

Zernike, Kate. 2008. "She Just Might be President Someday." *New York Times*, May 18.

Zetterberg, Pär. 2008. "The Downside of Gender Quotas? Institutional Constraints on Women in Mexican State Legislatures." *Parliamentary Affairs* 61 (3): 442–460.

Zovatto G., Daniel. 2006. "Regulación de los partidos políticos en América Latina." *Diálogo Político* 23 (4): 11–39.

———. 2007. "La reforma político electoral en América Latina: Evolución, situación actual y tendencias 1978–2005." In *Gobernabilidad y reforma política en América Latina y Europa*, edited by Helen Ahrens, 295–317. Salamanca, Spain: Red Eurolatinoamericana de Gobernabilidad para el Desarrollo.

Index

Note: Page numbers followed by f indicate figures; those followed by g indicate graphs; and those followed by t indicate tables.

PDC. *See* Partido Demócrata Cristiano (PDC) (Chile)

Peñafiel, Adriana, 8, 90–91, 131, 190n7

Peñaflor (Chile): candidate selection by PS in, 64–65; gender and party composition in, 15t; municipal characteristics of, 16t

Perón, Evita, 99, 114–115, 192n16, 193n17

Perón, Isabel, 114–116, 123–125, 128, 193n18

Perón, Juan, 114–115, 123–124

Peronista Party (Argentina), 115, 193n16

Personal finances and entry into politics, 28–29

Persuaded candidates, 45

Peru: attitudes toward female political leaders in, 37g; family members in, 126–127, 132t, 134; female representation in, 5, 181n4; gender quotas in, 5, 137t, 138, 144t; hand-picking candidates in, 112–114; labor force participation and unemployment in, 27g; school enrollment in, 25g; women as governors in, 101t; women's participation in politics in, 32t; women's political representation in, 4g; women's representation by party in, 175; women's representation in legislatures in, 6g

Peru 2000 (Peru), 113

Piñera, Sebastián, 2, 39

PLN (Partido Liberación Nacional) (Costa Rica), 87–88, 165–166

Political action committees, campaign financing by, 162

Political ambition: measurement of, 47, 187n7; and political interest, 47; and self-nomination, 46–47

Political compensation, reluctance to request, 44

Political daughters, 117–121; Adriana Peñafiel as, 131–132; *dedazos* and, 118; across the globe, 121–123; importance of kinship ties for, 3, 118–121, 193n2; in Latin America, 127–128; limitations on candidacy of, 132–135, 132t

Political encouragement, 45–46, 187n5

Political instability and family ties, 121, 194n9

Political institutions and underrepresentation of women, 9

Political interest: and candidate selection, 30–33, 32t; political ambition and, 47; voting booth volunteers and, 31; voting rates and, 30–31, 185n7

Political mobilization by power monopolies, 49

Political parties: candidate selection by, 16–17; female representation in, 5, 10–12, 171–175, 181n4; included in study, 15–16, 184n20; major, 184n25

Political widowers, 125, 194n14

Political widows, 117–121; *dedazos* and, 118; Fresia Faúndez as, 129–130; across the globe, 121–123; importance of kinship ties for, 3, 118–121, 193n2; in Latin America, 123–125; limitations on candidacy of, 132–135, 132t; types of, 125

Political wives, 117–121; *dedazos* and, 118; across the globe, 121–123; importance of kinship ties for, 3, 118–121, 193n2; in Latin America, 125–127; limitations on candidacy of, 132–135, 132t; nontraditional political work by, 194n13; Reyna Enith Domínguez Wong as, 130–131

Polls: by PRD, 93; vs. primaries, 11, 158, 197n10; by UDI, 108

Positional analysis, 17

Power monopolies, 48–50; campaign financing by, 49; disadvantage to women of, 48–49; history and maintenance of, 48, 188n8; in Mexican politics, 48, 188n12; names for, 48; political mobilization by, 49; primaries and, 61–62; as recruitment pools, 48–49; and underrepresentation of women, 49–50

PPD. *See* Partido por la Democracia (PPD) (Chile)

PPF (Women's Peronista Party) (Argentina), 115, 192n16

PRD (Partido de la Revolución Democrática). *See* Partido de la Revolución Democrática (PRD) (Mexico)

PRD (Partido Revolucionario Democrático) (Panama), women in leadership in, 31

Pre-candidates, 53

Presidents, electing women as, 1–5

Press coverage: in kinship politics, 119–120; of primaries, 160

PRI. *See* Partido Revolucionario Institucional (PRI) (Mexico)

Primary elections, 56–79; abandoning the use of, 155–158; and accountability, 58; adoption in recent years of, 56–57, 188n1, 189n3; advantages of, 56–58; alternatives to, 158; as assessment of strength of group, 58; and campaign financing, 58, 62;

Magda Hinojosa is Assistant Professor in the School of Politics and Global Studies at Arizona State University. She has received awards from the Fulbright and Ford Foundations.